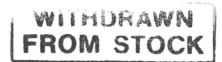
Appreciating

dance

FOURTH EDITION

A Guide to the World's Liveliest Art

Appreciating dance

FOURTH EDITION

A Guide to the World's Liveliest Art

HARRIET R. LIHS

A Dance Horizons Book
Princeton Book Company, Publishers

Design and composition by Mulberry Tree Press
Cover design by Maria M. Mann, High Tide Design

Princeton Book Company, Publishers
614 Route 130
Hightstown, NJ 08520-0831
www.DanceHorizons.com

ISBN: 978-0-87127-318-5

Library of Congress Cataloging-in-Publication Data

Lihs, Harriet R.
  Appreciating dance : a guide to the world's liveliest art / Harriet R. Lihs.
— 4th ed.

    p. : ill. ; cm.

  "A Dance Horizons book."
  Includes bibliographical references and index.
  ISBN: 978-0-87127-318-5

1. Dance—History. I. Title.

GV1601 .L54 2009
792.8

Printed in Canada

CONTENTS

PREFACE

This book is intended as an introduction to a very large subject. Of necessity the information you will find is an overview, not a comprehensive study of world dance. It is the hope of the author that this text will bring up questions about the nature of dance, its role in world cultures and its future, sparking interest and further study into some aspects of the art.

Each of the chapters in the book deals with one branch of this wide-ranging art, with the exception of the final two chapters, which survey multiple facets of current dance. People who have made a significant contribution to dance appear in italics the first time they are mentioned and are included in the index. Names of actual dances are italicized in the text as well.

The discussion questions at the end of the book summarize the material and ideas presented. Reading lists and videographies provide suggestions for additional study of the chapter subject. For this reason, you may find the same book, magazine, video or DVD in several chapter reference sections.

MIKHAIL BARYSHNIKOV

Since dance is a visual art, I encourage the use of supplementary materials, especially videotapes and DVDs, to really understand what you are reading about.

Above all, a true appreciation of dance is gained by seeing as many and varied live performances as possible, and also trying many dance forms yourself. No matter where you live, once you start looking you will find there is more live dance going on, both performances and classes, than you may have originally expected.

So take the first step, your dance adventures are just beginning!

A NOTE TO TEACHERS

If you are using this book for a one-semester dance appreciation or survey class, I have included more material than you will be able to comfortably cover. You may find that it is necessary to select people to focus your attention upon rather than all those who appear in bold print, especially in chapters four through six and chapter eight. I have intentionally included a great many notable contributors to the dance profession (with apologies to those I was not able to include) with the idea that each teacher will select a few as examples, based on their interests, the availability of videotaped examples, and time considerations. If a performance is coming to your area, this would be a fine opportunity to focus on that individual or company and use the book for background information and discussion. Those teachers who are most concerned with the current state of professional dance rather than historical development may wish to limit their use of the book to chapters one, seven and eight.

I welcome your comments on this text, and would be happy to share information on teaching-related issues. Please feel free to contact me through my publisher, Princeton Book Company. Also be aware that there is a supplementary CD available for teachers only.

ACKNOWLEDGEMENTS

I would like to thank the following people for their assistance in preparing this new edition of my textbook. First, my editors, Connie and Charles Woodford, for their encouragement and expertise. Also, Dr. Barbara Hernandez, Lou Arrington and Michelle Ozmun, fellow teachers at Lamar University, for their encouragement and comments, especially in the development of chapter eight. Thanks also go to Nan Lewin for her advice about current musical styles. Also thanks to my mother, Belle Kane, who until her death in 1999 sent me newspaper articles about dance every month for 35 years. That was the true beginning of my career as a dance historian.

This book is dedicated to my late husband, Hank Rivers.

CHAPTER ONE

ORIGINS AND DEFINITIONS

*The dance is one of many human experiences that cannot be suppressed. Like music,
the dance is a language which all human beings understand. . . . Dance, like every
other artistic expression, presupposes a heightened, increased life response.*
—*Mary Wigman*[1]

Art is the only way to run away without leaving home.
—*Twyla Tharp*[2]

What is dance? There are almost as many definitions of dance as there are people writing about dance. There is a great deal of disagreement on how broad this definition should be. Some definitions include practically all human movement, while Webster's *Dictionary* limits it to "rhythmic movement of the feet or body, ordinarily to music." Others assert that unless movement has symbolic meaning or expresses emotion, it is not dance. Still others claim that even animals can express emotions through movement, and therefore they dance.

Exploring the meaning of dance, as expressed in either choreography or the written word or both, has become a lifelong search for some individuals. The quotations in "A Sampling of Definitions of Dance" are examples of the conclusions of some 20th century writers and choreographers, and one child. While the comments highlight different aspects of dance, they have some commonalties. All of the authors believe dance to be a natural expression of the human condition and the human spirit, requiring some structured use of time, space and the body or bodies. The dancer/choreographer interprets both inner feeling and cultural realities, linking them to universal truth. In the same way a great playwright creates with words a picture of his day and age and the inner lives of specific characters, while remaining accessible to viewers from other cultures, the choreographer creates a work of art true to his own time and place but also transcending these limitations. Dance is truly a universal language.

A SAMPLING OF DEFINITIONS OF DANCE

Movement is the essence of life, dance its ultimate expression . . . The artist creates out of the world that has made him in order to remake it according to the image of his inner world.

—Walter Sorell[3]

Movement in order to have power and beauty, must spring from the organic center of the body. It must be intensely human, or it will be gymnastics, and be mechanical and empty.

—José Limón[4]

What are we looking for? To attune our inmost feelings to the mood of the time.

—Mary Wigman[5]

The dance is love, it is only love, it alone, and that is enough . . . now, I would like to no longer dance to anything but the rhythm of my soul.

—Isadora Duncan[6]

I think that dance should primarily be entertainment. It's a visual theater and an oral theater . . . beautiful people, beautifully dressed, doing beautiful and meaningful things.

—Alvin Ailey[7]

What is dance! Dance is entertainment. Experiencing the movement. Feeling the beat. Following the rhythm. Balancing the steps. Practicing on stage. That's Dance.

—Rishit Sheth,
P.S. 102 (Elementary School) Queens, NY[8]

I never think I am going to do something original. You just do what you want to do . . . our movements have to be performed in the composer's time. That's what makes ballet so exciting—the movement of bodies in time.

—George Balanchine[9]

The artist is . . . the bearer of a message, and it is his responsibility to tell it—in whatever medium it might be—intelligently, forcefully, and with his utmost artistic ability.

—Charles Weidman[10]

The dance is the mother of the arts. Music and poetry exist in time; painting in space. But the dance lives at once in time and space. The creator and the thing created, the artist and the work are still one and the same thing.

—Curt Sachs[11]

Serious and sustained reflection on a dance is inevitably hindered by a feature of all movement, namely its transitoriness . . . this would seem better regarded as a challenge to be met than as an insuperable difficulty.

—Betty Redfern[12]

Why not reclaim our distinctively human heritage as creatures who can generate their own ecstatic pleasures out of music, color, feasting, and dance?

—Barbara Erenreich[13]

Evidence of early dance, such as artifacts and cave paintings, indicates that among ancient peoples dance was one of the first arts, existing long before written language. Dance has served many purposes in human society, and its earliest purpose was probably for ritual. Dance was used to pray for favor from the gods, to portray their activities, and to connect spiritually with ancestors.

DANCING BOYS.
From a relief by Luca della Robbia, Florence. It may depict dancing processions common during religious festivals in 16th Century Europe.

Dance was also used to train warriors, heal the sick and insure fertility of the fields. It was used to solidify a sense of community within groups of people and to commemorate important victories and seasonal events for the tribe and for the passages in the lives of individuals. It was important as a storytelling medium and as a way of preserving history, using costuming, chanting and other accompaniment as enhancement.

As time went on and human communities became more complex, there were those whose skill as dancers made them highly valued as performers. Powerful leaders, who had the desire to be both honored and entertained through dance, functioned as sponsors for the training of these artists and patrons for their performances. These court entertainments were the precursors of today's theatrical dance, a product of trained professionals with a sharp line of demarcation between performer and audience. In some postmodern works, this line becomes once again flexible and interactive.

Those who created dances throughout history, called choreographers, dealt with the same raw materials that choreographers deal with today, namely, the body or groups of bodies moving through space and time. Rudolf Von Laban (1879–1958), the movement theorist who gave us both Labanotation (see chapter 7) and Effort/Shape theory, rephrased this by stating that all movement is defined by the effort used, the time taken and the shapes made in space. How these raw materials are manipulated is determined by the purpose of the dance and the style the performer or choreographer wishes to achieve. In brief, the four raw materials Laban's theory embraces are the body, time, space, and effort.

The Body

This basic building block answers the question, who is dancing? A dance may be a solo, duet, small group, or cast of hundreds. It may be a mixed group of genders and ages, trained and untrained bodies, or it may be very selective in any of these areas. What parts of the body are moving are also a consideration. Some dances concentrate on individual body parts very precisely, a technique known as isolations, while others engage in full-bodied movements.

Time

Time, for dancers, includes both the speed of the movement and the manipulation of rhythmic patterns. Like musicians, dancers divide time into repeated patterns known as measures. If the strongest emphasis (accent) is on the expected beat—the first beat of the measure—the timing of the movements will look and feel smooth. If, however, an unexpected beat or two is accented, the interesting rhythms developed are known as syncopation. These "off-beat" rhythms are derived from African drumming techniques, and form the basis of jazz music and jazz dance techniques. They are also prevalent in tap dancing, a skill that blends African rhythms and Irish step dancing (see chapter 6).

Space

The use of space includes floor patterns, direction, level and shape. *Floor patterns*, as if visualized from above, can be straight, angled or curved, and can take up a great deal of space or a very small amount. *Direction* refers to the positioning of the dancer's bodies in the performing space, described from the dancer's point of view. For example, downstage is moving toward the audience, and stage right is moving toward the dancer's the right side. *Level* refers to the height of the movements, with middle level being our normal walking level, high level elevated on the balls of the feet, toes or in the air, low level is low to the ground or in full contact with it. *Shape* refers to the use of space much like the background space in a painting or surrounding a sculpture, called *negative space* by artists. You may see in a given dance, for example, a lot of curved shapes or extended straight shapes carved out of this negative space.

Effort

Also known as *dynamics*, effort refers to the amount of force expended in a given movement. Two movements in the same direction, made with the same body part at the same speed, will look and feel completely different if one is done with light effort and the other is done with a strong effort. Choreographers must be aware of this because the use of effort can radically change the meaning of a movement from the audience's point of view.

MARTHA GRAHAM

APPRECIATING DANCE

In spite of the extended history of dance, this lively art has not always occupied a position of equality among the other arts. One reason for this has been the prevailing notion over time that dance is too closely linked to music to stand on its own as an independent art form. A second reason is the difficulty in preserving choreography. Many early dance masterpieces have been lost, or preserved by oral handing-down, an inexact method at best. Only in the 20th century have we developed accurate and complete methods of writing down movement. Also, the inventions of film and video have been a great boon in preserving dance performance.

Throughout the centuries world dance has evolved into a broad range of distinctive movement styles. These styles are constantly changing with new contributors adding to them. As society experiments with new ideas, so does this living art.

When watching dance, it is most helpful to know something about the culture and time period in which it developed and what purpose it served in that culture. Is it liturgical or recreational, theatrical or therapeutic? Often the dance itself will tell you a great deal about the culture in which it developed. For example, social dances with mixed couples are found only in cultures where men and women are free to select mates of their choice.

Theatrical dances in which women participate equally with men indicate a more liberal attitude toward women than cultures where all the women's parts are played by men. Similarly, cultures in which both men and women perform the same steps are less rigid about sex roles than cultures that specify "women's steps" and "men's steps." The more you watch dance with a critical eye, the more cultural clues you pick up from your observation. Anthropologist Alan Merriam takes this idea a step farther by stating that "dance is culture and culture is dance . . . the entity of dance is not separable from the anthropological concept of culture."[14]

As the individual dance viewer, you will add your own viewpoint to the experience. In the arts, this is known as your personal aesthetic—your likes and dislikes—which develops as a result of many experiences in your life. Whether we are aware of it or not, we all develop a personal aesthetic, and it continues to change throughout our lives. You can prove this to yourself by listening to the comments of audience members during the intermission of a live performance. Usually this reveals a broad range of aesthetic opinions, to the point where you may wonder if everyone is watching the same performance!

Here are some influences on your personal aesthetic as it pertains to watching a live performance, such as a play, a dance concert or musical offering.

1. **Your emotional state when you are attending the performance will affect your receptiveness to it.** For example, are you in a relaxed, comfortable situation when watching the performance? Was the performance an outing you planned and looked forward to, or was it forced upon you?

2. **Connecting with the performers.** If the performers are doing their job well, you will see their humanity behind the movements or lyrics. It can be helpful for them to resemble yourself and people you associate with to make this connection: age, gender, race and costuming can reinforce this sense of identification. However, you may find yourself connecting with performers from a completely different culture than your own, and leave the theater feeling you truly know

these people well; if so, you have just seen a performance done from the heart, which reaches people beyond the boundaries of language and local customs.

3. **Family.** While still an infant you may be introduced to the performing arts by parents, grandparents, older siblings and other family members. If music is played in the home, that type of music becomes an integral part of childhood experience. Family members may encourage or discourage the child from moving to the music by their own actions, for example by dancing with the child.

4. **Peers.** As children mature, they begin to select close friends, most often of a similar age and socioeconomic background. Often similar aesthetic preferences can jump-start a friendship for example several people

JODY OBERFELDER DANCE PROJECTS
in *Physically Inclined*, choreography by Oberfelder.

who all like a certain type of music or social dance begin attend these events together. On the other hand, a close friend may be the person who interests you in a new performing art, expanding your personal aesthetic. In a long-lasting friendship, both of these situations may be operative.

5. **Nationality and religion.** In spite of the availability of many international offerings on the internet, the country you live in, the region of that country, and whether you live in a rural or urban area continues to influence your aesthetic choices. So does religion, especially if the performing art in question is dealing with serious social issues. Modern and postmodern choreographers, for example, have been particularly interested in creating realistic pieces about war, alienation, racism, sexism, family violence and alternative lifestyles. (see chapters 5 and 8). For adults, the choice on whether these works are offensive or useful should be their own in a democratic society. In many countries with totalitarian governments or state-mandated religions, these choices are not available to their citizens.

Your personal aesthetic is the final judge of what you will choose to watch and truly appreciate. The more types of dance you explore and the more you learn about them, the more diverse and satisfying your personal choices will become.

SUGGESTED READING

Brown, Jean Morrison, Naomi Mindlin and Charles H. Woodford, eds. *The Vision of Modern Dance*, 2nd ed. Hightstown, NJ: Princeton Book Company, Publishers, 1998.

De Mille, Agnes. *The Book of the Dance*. New York: Golden Press, 1963.

Dils, Ann and Ann Cooper Albright, eds. *Moving History/Dancing Cultures: A Dance History Reader.* Middletown, CT: Wesleyan University Press, 2001.

Erenreich, Barbara. *Dancing in the Streets: A History of Collective Joy.* New York: Metropolitan Books, 2006.

Kaeppler, Adrienne Lois. "Dance as Myth—Myth as Dance: A Challenge to Traditional Viewpoints." *Dance as Cultural Heritage*, ed. Betty True Jones, vol. 1, 5–8. New York: Congress on Research in Dance, 1983. Dance Research Annual: 14 .

Kealiinohomoku, Joann W. "An Anthropologist Looks at Ballet as a Form of Ethnic Dance." *Journal for the Anthropological Study of Human Movement*. Vol. 1, no. 2 (Autumn 1980): 83–97.

Preston-Dunlop, Valerie, compiler. Dance Words. Chur, Switzerland: Harwood Academic Publishers, 1995. *Choreography and Dance Studies*, vol. 8.

Redfern, Betty. *Dance, Art and Aesthetics.* London: Dance Books, 1983.

Royce, Anya Peterson. *The Anthropology of Dance*. Bloomington, IN: Indiana University Press, 1977.

Sorell, Walter. *The Dance Through the Ages*. New York: Grosset and Dunlap, 1967.

Williams, Drid. *Ten Lectures on Theories of the Dance*. Metuchen, NJ: Scarecrow Press, 1991.

———, ed. *Anthropology and Human Movement: Searching for Origins.* Lanham, MD: Scarecrow Press, 2000.

CHAPTER TWO
DANCE AND RELIGION

Oh! how beautiful! . . . For you men and women strike the tambourine.
The Divine-Powers, the stars, dance for you.
—*Hymn to the Egyptian Goddess Hathor[1]*

Let them praise His name in the dance: let them sing praises unto
Him with timbrel and harp.
—*Psalms 149:3*

Here the constants of beauty, ease, proportion, vitality, technical mastery,
of the communication of ecstasy to the beholder, are within one's body-soul.
And the greatest constant of all is that we experience a rhythmic beauty,
the activity of God Himself.
—*Ted Shawn[2]*

Long ago in the mists of preliterate time, early peoples danced to please their gods and to request favors from them. Cave paintings found in France and Italy, dating back to the Paleolithic period, depict dancers in animal skins simulating a hunt. Living in close contact with and dependence on animals motivated early peoples to imitate them. With the development of agriculture, other request dances—for rain, fertility of the fields and good harvests—also developed. The evidence of stone carving, pottery making and later written languages gives us further proof of the importance of danced rituals. Dance became a way to connect with the spirit world of ancestors and gods, a means of ensuring health and good fortune and a vital part of ceremonies for major events in the community.

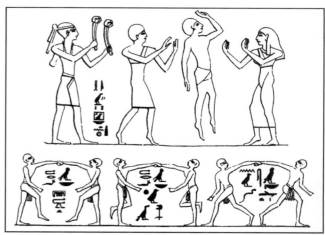

EGYPTIAN FIGURE DANCES (on a tomb carving)
may have expressed the order and harmony
of the stars as part of sacred rituals.

Although early man probably danced to express feelings and for the pure joy of movement, most dance historians agree that a belief system generated the first forms of organized dance. Today, dance remains an important part of many of the world's religions. This chapter will explore both ancient and modern forms of religious dance. It is useful to put these dances into several general categories, based on their intent.

TYPES OF RELIGIOUS DANCE

Dances of Imitation

Without question, the movements of other living things and natural phenomena were one of the earliest inspirations for dance. Even animals hunted for food were not revered as spiritually inferior to humans; often, animals or birds were considered messengers from the spirit world. Animal imitation dances, for example the Native American buffalo and eagle dances, honor such qualities as the courage of a particular animal. Other imitation dances depicted an event, such as a battle, with the belief that the depiction would make the desired outcome more likely to happen.

Medicine Dances

In many cultures, shamans or priests or priestesses perform dances to restore the health of an individual by warding off evil spirits or by pleasing a specific god or goddess. The dances may also be preventative, designed to protect an individual, family or entire community from danger or disease. The elaborate serpent rituals found in India, that are intended to prevent blindness, skin diseases and bad fortune, fall into this category. A special caste of priest/performers arrange these dances for families, and they may last several weeks.

The word *shaman*, which originally came from an ancient group of hunters in Siberia, refers to a practitioner who can will his or her spirit to leave the body and journey to upper and lower worlds, seeking the underlying causes of events. There the shaman fights, begs or cajoles the spirits to intervene for his clients by entering a trance state. These journeys are particularly effective in the areas of human health and fertility.

Commemorative Dances

These dances often involve an entire community and are used to commemorate important events in the calendar, such as winter and summer solstices. They also provide a means of preserving the history of a group, a role especially important in non-literate cultures. Some commemorative dances also celebrate milestones in the lives of individuals: birth, initiation into adulthood, marriage or death. For example, the Apache Indians perform a dance that is believed to purify girls reaching puberty as well as preparing them for womanhood. Initiation ceremonies often contain rituals to test the individual's worthiness, knowledge and endurance. Funeral ceremonies may include elaborately costumed and masked dances designed to assist the departed's voyage to the spirit world.

DRAGON DANCE, here performed at a Chinese New Year celebration in Texas, is both a commemorative dance and an imitation dance that captures the qualities of its featured creature.

Dances commemorating a special religious holiday often include a processional to a sacred site. The maypole dance, originally a pre-Christian fertility dance performed by whole communities on the first day of May, lost its religious connotations and today is performed in Europe and North America by school children as a celebration of spring.

Dances for Spiritual Connection

These dances are used as a means of reaching a more spiritual plane and establishing a connection with gods or spirits. Dances that are spontaneous expressions of gratitude toward a deity, for example, after a crisis is resolved, fall into this category. Connection may be achieved by spinning for long periods of time, as in many Native American dances and also in the Sufi Muslim whirling dervish dances. In some cultures, a trancelike state is encouraged to achieve the connection with the spirit world; dancing into a state of exhaustion, using hallucinogens or inflicting pain on oneself are means of reaching this ecstatic state. The ultimate goal is to achieve possession by the god's spirit. Other spiritual dances are designed to create a sense of beauty, order and harmony, which is pleasing to a particular god and beneficial to humans.

WORLD RELIGIOUS DANCE

Our best evidence of ancient sacred dances can be found in the examination of indigenous societies around the world who continue to perform dance rituals today. Some very old dance forms became so widespread that they appear in several belief systems as well as in social dance. Processionals to a sacred spot and circle dances, which were performed by both ancient Egyptians and ancient Hebrews, are considered the oldest dance formations. They both also appeared in ancient Greece and ancient Russia. Some of these old dance forms have lost their original religious significance; for example, the maypole dances of Europe and the British Isles are relics of ancient tree-worshiping rituals, but are now purely recreational. In Hawaii, some dances that were once connected with religion have become entertainment for tourists, but other ritual dances, for example, those to the volcano goddess Pele, have retained their sacred context.

Following is a sampling of the rich diversity of sacred dance, both ancient and modern, found in cultures throughout the world:

MAY DAY IN CALIFORNIA.
Children in the "Pageant of America," Berkeley.

Africa

The earliest evidence of sacred dance in Africa comes from stone carvings on Egyptian tombs, depicting complex funeral rituals that included dancers and acrobats. Egyptian pharaohs and their families were considered gods, and elaborate preparations were made for their preservation and resurrection after death. Royal families had troupes of dancers and musicians who were used on sacred and secular occasions. Also, bands of female singing dancers were attached to temples for the honor of specific gods, including Osiris, his sister-wife Isis and the goddess Hathor.

One elaborate Egyptian dance ritual, the *Astronomic* (thought to be the first of the circle dances), was described by Plato, although he never actually observed it. Performed by priests around a central altar representing the sun, the dancers made signs of the zodiac with their hands while turning rhythmically from east to west, representing the courses of the planets. After each turn, the dancers froze in place to represent the immobility of planet earth.[3]

In West Africa, tribes including the Ashanti, Congolese, Dahomean, Ibo, Koromantyn and Yoruba have religious practices that are primarily carried out through song and dance. The followers of Osun, the river goddess associated with curing the sick and with blessing women with children, wear white and dance with calmness and dignity. Proper dancing to the proper drums is a way of pleasing the goddess, and it is an honor if one of the dancers is possessed by her spirit. The ceremonies culminate in a processional to the river, where Osun is offered her favorite foods and spices.

The Egúngún ceremonies, celebrated by the Yoruba people of Nigeria, West Africa, are designed to open direct channels of communication with ancestors through dance. Each ancestor, depicted by a village man wearing long skirts and head coverings sometimes decorated with monkey skulls, spins and stamps in a way that portrays his personality while he lived on earth. These festivals honoring various gods vary greatly from village to village, with some localities having has many as ten festivals a year, each lasting a week or more.[4]

The ultimate spiritual experience in these West African religions is possession—becoming the vehicle through which a god speaks and makes his wishes known. *Vodu* is the Dahomean word for "deity;" thus, the practices of African-derived cults that were brought to the West Indies, forming the belief system for a large part of the population, became known loosely as Voodoo, for the Haitian French Vaudou, or Vodun (the standardized form today).[5]

While the religion of Islam, which spread across northern Africa beginning in the 800s A.D., prohibited dance and other contact between men and women, an all-male Muslim sect known as the Order of Whirling Dervishes incorporated dance into worship. These Dervishes believe that by whirling continuously for long periods of time, they will achieve a higher spiritual plane of existence and directly experience the presence of Allah. Founded in 1273 A.D., they are followers of the 13th century Persian poet and spiritual leader Rumi, and dedicated to lives of love and service.

Australian Aboriginal Dance

In aboriginal Australian culture, initiation rituals of various kinds are of great importance. These include, for men, coming to sexual maturity and becoming accredited as hunters and warriors. For women, significant landmarks in life's journey include menarche, marriage, childbirth and menopause. These rituals were designed to change the way the initiates felt about themselves. For example, Denise Carmody describes a warrior's ritual:

> *those to be initiated would come forward, accompanied by their guardians . . . to receive new names emblematic of their new spiritual status . . . A ceremonial combat would ensue to inscribe the ability to fight well on behalf of the tribe in the newly matured hunters and warriors. The bullroarer [a noisemaking device] played a significant role in this ceremony, helping to dramatize the fighting.[6]*

In another ritual, older women dance to assist the spirit of a deceased man in its return to its original totemic site. The women dress in elaborate white and ochre body paint and feathered headdresses. Other dances, performed by men, reenact the creation stories known as *dreamtime* in aboriginal mythology, emphasizing the exploits of their particular clan's creator heroes.

Greece and Ancient Rome

For the ancient Greeks, dance was personified as Terpsichore, one of the nine goddesses—known as Muses—whose purpose was to inspire creativity in humankind. To this day, dance is often referred to as the Terpsichorean art.

Dancing figures are found on the earliest Greek pottery and frequently cited in Greek literature and poetry, indicating that dance was an important part of virtually all Greek religious ceremonies and celebrations. Notable among these were the revels of Dionysus, a nature god identified with vegetation, fertility and sexual ecstasy. Processions of noisy, enthusiastic dancers and singers led by the priests of Dionysus figured prominently in the great spring festival in Athens. During the 6th century B.C., these processions were gradually transformed into choral and dramatic competitions.[7] It was typical in this Classical Greek period to combine music, theater and dance into a total performance that depicted the antics of the gods and their interactions with humans.

Conquering Romans adopted many of the Greeks' religious practices, including dance-worship, changing the names of the gods but keeping their characteristics. For example, Dionysus became Bacchus, lover of wine, women and dance, with frenzied women (maenads) and satyrs—half-man and half-goat—as his votaries. Throughout the Roman Empire, numerous "mystery religions" existed that included some kind of dance in their initiation ceremonies. Much dance in ancient Rome, however, was secular, including the bawdy dances performed at public games, which were condemned by moralists of the time.

India

The influence of Indian dance has been felt throughout Southeast Asia, as far away as China and Japan and even to the islands of the South Pacific. Archaeologists have found a wealth of evidence, including a copper figurine of a female dancer dating between 2300 and 1700 B.C., indicating that sacred dance was a part of the lives of India's earliest civilizations.[8] Among the Hindu deities, Shiva, the god of both creation and destruction, is represented posed on one leg as the Lord of the Dance; the act of creation itself is described as a dance. As Shiva sends pulsating waves of energy outward, matter is depicted dancing around him as an aureole of fire. The deity Vishnu is also associated with dance, appearing in human form. The avatar Krishna is often depicted carrying a flute and performing circle and serpentine dances with village maidens.[9] These dances symbolize the marriage of heaven and earth.

SHIVA NATARAJA, the Hindu Lord of the Dance, poised on one leg above a child, depicts creation and destruction—energy in many forms.

Since the 2nd century B.C., temple rituals that included song and dance were conducted by devadasi, young females who were educated to the service of a particular god. Concern with the exploitation of young girls resulted in the institution of the devadasi being outlawed in the early years of the 20th century, jeopardizing the preservation of India's classical dance traditions. Fortunately, influential Brahmin (upper-caste) families and some Westerners (including Ruth St. Denis and Anna Pavlova) took interest in establishing schools for the preservation of classical Indian dance as a respected living art form. Today, several forms of dance, notably *Bharata Natyam* and *Kathakali*, are still used to relate the stories of the gods. Both are highly rhythmic forms requiring years of training, using hand movements ("mudras") and facial expressions to tell stories, while the feet beat out accompaniment with the assistance of ankle bells.

JYOTI DUGAR, A YOUNG BHARATA NATYAM DANCER, continues the tradition of female Hindu dance begun in early Hindu temple rituals.

Bharata Natyam is still primarily performed by women. One theme often found in Bharata Natyam is comparing one's relation to god as to that of a lover, and describing the bliss of union with god in terms of union with a beloved. Kathakali dance-drama, performed by men only, uses elaborate costuming and makeup, spoken word and hand gestures. Stories of heroes, deities and demons from the Mahabharata and other Hindu writings are depicted, sometimes with comic effect. The popular entertainment is an invaluable tool for the transmission of culture in a country with hundreds of spoken languages, where much of the population cannot read.

Jewish Dance

There are abundant references to dancing in the Old Testament, particularly on occasions of welcoming and celebration. King David "danced before the Lord with all his might" (2 Samuel 6:14) as a way of honoring God, and the chapter in the Bible, Exodus, tells us of Miriam and other women dancing joyously after the crossing of the Red Sea. However, not all the Old Testament references to dance are positive. The dances before the Golden Calf, for example, illustrate a concern—the attraction among the early Hebrews to neighboring religions and their rituals.

As evidence of its importance to the ancient Hebrews, biblical Hebrew has twelve different verbs to describe the act of dancing. Ritual processions, whirling and hopping dances, harvest dances and wedding dances are described in the Old Testament and in the Talmud, a book of rabbinical writings from the 3rd to 6th centuries. Marilyn Daniels states, "The Jewish prophets danced in their communion with God. They danced before conveying the word of the Lord to the people, the symbolism of movement being more soul-stirring than words."[10] Although mixed dancing was common in neighboring cultures, men and women were customarily separated in Hebraic dances; this was part of the effort to make a distinction between the new monotheistic religion and surrounding pagan ceremonies.

In 18th century Eastern Europe, a group of rabbis known as the Hasidim changed the character of Judaism by proposing that joy, prayer and an ecstatic connection with God through physical action were as important, if not more so, than simply living life as an observant Jew. The Hasidic Jews "choose to actively engage in practice that not only facilitates our ability to hear celestial music, but inspires us to dance with it as well."[11] Today in Israel, many folkloric dance groups reenact Old Testament stories. In America, dance is a part of many Jewish celebrations, particularly weddings and bar/bat-mitzvahs (coming-of-age celebrations). Among the most orthodox groups, however, men and women remain strictly separated when they dance and, in some cases, only the men are permitted to dance.

Native American

Rituals of Native Americans vary from tribe to tribe. Historically the most marked differences were between nomadic hunting tribes and settled agricultural tribes. Virtually all hunting tribes had dances honoring respected totem animals, animals upon which they depended or which could teach them necessary skills. Examples of these dances are the wolf ceremonies of the Inuit peoples in Alaska and the Eagle dances of the plains Indians. Agricultural tribes, on the other hand, often danced in imitation of sowing and gathering crops.

MEN'S FANCY DANCE by the Alabama-Coushatta Tribe of Texas. Native American dance continues at annual festivals and powwows held throughout North America.

The Hopi, a Pueblo people who raise corn in the arid land of Arizona, continue to hold elaborate rituals, performed from January through July, that feature masked dancers called kachinas. When dancing, the dancer becomes the kachina, or spirit, representing the most significant forces in Hopi life: fertility, healing and sustenance. From January to March, the dances take place in underground kivas, representing the place where the world originated. Later in the season, they are moved outdoors, and the kachinas are accompanied by unmasked clown dancers. The kachinas then depart from the tribe, returning to their mountain homes with prayers and thanks from the Hopi people.

Carmody describes the sacred *Sun Dance* of the Plains Indians (Oglala Dakota), which was performed in conjunction with the buffalo hunt:

> The tribe would construct a circle of trees to represent the fullness of the people and the bounty of nature. The essence of the ceremony was for men to dance for several days gazing at the sun. They were offering themselves, their energy and pain, for the welfare of the people. To increase their pain, and so the merit of their offering, they would tie leather thongs to the trees and then affix them to their own breasts. As they danced, the thongs would pull through their flesh and tear it. Because everything else in the world already belonged to the Great Spirit, the offering of human flesh was especially significant.[12]

This dance, along with others, fell into disuse and forced into seclusion when it was outlawed by the United States Bureau of Indian Affairs in order to force assimilation. Repression of Indian dancing was government policy between 1881 and 1934, with some easing only after 1925.

South and Central America

Spanish conquerors of the Incas in the Andes mountains reported elaborate dance rituals in the complex Inca civilization. The major public ceremonials were agricultural rites, which followed a fixed cycle, but special ceremonials were held in times of crisis or when an Inca emperor was crowned or buried. God images, mummy bundles of deceased Incas, and other religious gear were brought into the public plaza, and dances and recitations were interspersed with offerings to the gods.[13]

The Indians of Central America also had a culture rich in complex ceremonies—eighteen in all in the Mayan calendar—marking various religious, political and natural events. They held the belief that dance was meritorious, advancing a person's status in the eyes of the gods. One spectacular form that has survived to the present day is the *Volador* dance, believed to be five thousand years old, in which the participants climb a hundred-foot-high pole, then lean off a platform and circle the pole thirteen times suspended on ropes. Originally, this dance was associated with an elaborate ritual depicting the descent of the gods from heaven to earth.

Forest peoples that have been hunter-gatherers for millennia still survive in parts of South America and still practice ancient dance rituals. The Yanomamo people of the Brazilian rainforests have a ritual dance performed before the hunt to ensure good luck. In this dance, the hunters enter the village center in pairs. Then each costumed and decorated hunter performs his own unique and energetic dance step, while chanting and brandishing his weapons to the cheers of the villagers.[14]

In Brazil, one can find ceremonies that are a blend of African slave rites and Catholic rituals from the Portuguese colonists. In the port town of Cachoeira, for example, the Boa Morte, or Good Death ceremony, includes worship of orixas, the deities of Yoruba tribe in West Africa. The ritual, known as Candomble, invoked the deities through dance and trances, disguised as the Virgin Mary and Catholic saints during the colonial years, when attending weekly mass on the plantations was mandatory for slaves. Today Catholic priests still supervise the ceremony, and women dress in elaborate colonial-style dresses. The three-day festival includes a parade and a great deal of samba dancing.[15]

South Pacific

In the Polynesian island cultures, such as Hawaii and the Cook Islands, dance was flourishing when US and British colonists arrived in the 18th and 19th centuries, along with Christian clergy eager to convert the natives. Many of the new arrivals took exception to the local dance forms, which often included nudity and rapid hip undulations. Dances for the men that involved juggling burning torches were designed to please Pele, the goddess of the volcano, an important and powerful force in island life. The Hawaiian hula was originally accompanied by fierce chanting in the Hawaiian language, beating drums and rattling gourds, before Europeans introduced stringed instruments. Even grass skirts were a 19th century import to Hawaii by Micronesian laborers. As the years went by and these cultures became "hapa haole" or half-white, the religious dances lost much of their sacred aspects and became social dances which connected Polynesians to their native roots.

Tibet and Nepal

Tantric Buddhist monks in Tibet have for centuries held elaborately masked and costumed rituals which included much dance. One ancient legend claims that the origin of these dances was to divert and entertain evil spirits, so that they would not interfere with the Tibetans' work, such as bridge-building. For a festival commemorating the New Year, monks form a circle and spin as an act of cleansing and preparation.

Another festival, known as Mani-rimdu, requires weeks of preparation by of the monks and includes a full day of dancing that depicts the lives of gods and kings, a joyous diversion from the hard life of the Sherpa mountain people.[16] These religious practices are fast disappearing under the rule of the Chinese. As a result of religious persecution, many Tibetan Buddhist monks, including the Dalai Lama, now reside in India and Nepal.

CHRISTIANITY AND THE DANCE DILEMMA

Over the centuries much has been written about dance by Christian ministers and scholars, some of them highly in favor of it as a form of worship and others vehemently opposed. For example, in 1879, the Reverend J. B. Gross of Pennsylvania wrote a treatise that cited examples of religious dance in early civilizations and in both the Old and New Testaments. He claimed that the "Christians' Sacred Gospel Emphatically and Benignly sanction and sanctify its [dances'] Judicious Observance." In the treatise Gross also states, "Grace of Manners and Innocent Joys are thy Charming Gifts, Gentle Muse, and not in the Rhythmism of Motion, but only in a Bad Heart, or a Vicious Tongue, is the Guilt of Sin."[17] Others point out that in Aramaic, the language spoken by Jesus, the word for "rejoicing" and "dance" are one and the same.

On the other hand, in America alone between 1685 and 1963, no fewer than 157 anti-dance books and treatises were written by Christian leaders. Their objections were primarily directed not to dance as religious expression, but toward "mixed" dancing performed for recreation. In *An Arrow Against Mixt Dancing* (1685), Increase Mather, a minister in Boston, states that men and women dancing together is "A practice in use, only amongst the Heathen, but never known among the people of God, except in times of degeneracy."[18] Other treatises claimed that meetings between the Devil and witches were characterized by dancing, which, therefore, made it a Satanic practice.

In the early development of the Christian religion, strong objections to dancing did not occur immediately. Dating from the first few centuries A.D., there are many references to dance in Christian worship. For example, the Gnostic "Hymn of Jesus," from the Apocryphal 2nd century Acts of John, is a sacred dance wherein the new disciple is united with the Master. It contains the following verse:

Grace danceth. I would pipe: dance ye all.
The whole world on high hath part in our dancing. AMEN
Who so danceth not, knoweth not what cometh to pass.
I would be united and I would unite. AMEN[19]

In the late Roman (or early Byzantine) Empire, dance and theater were proscribed by the Church Fathers as immoral, although there were orators who refuted the claim. Dance survived in court festivities and, despite rhetorical attacks against it, remained popular until the collapse of the Empire in the mid-15th century among the Byzantine population at large as an indispensable element of holiday and, especially, wedding celebrations.[20]

The Eastern Orthodox Church has preserved the spirit of rejoicing and dance in its ceremonies. Processions and spontaneous gestures are still very much a part of the Eastern Orthodox liturgy. With no chairs or pews in their churches, people stand and move naturally throughout the service. Had Constantinople, the center of the Eastern Orthodox Church located in what is now Turkey, become the chief center of Christian law in Europe instead of Rome, the church's attitude toward dance might have been much more welcoming.

During the early Middle Ages, a growing tension between the idea of the body and the idea of the soul developed in the Church centered in Rome. This derived from the movement toward otherworldliness, which required the denial of bodily desires in order to live a pure life in preparation for the Second Coming. With the philosophy of life on earth becoming a prelude to life after death came the honoring of a life of celibacy. Dancing, associated with love and the freeing of the emotions, seemed to run counter to the idea of control of bodily lusts. In the 5th century, St. Augustine encouraged the interpretation of the literal call "to dance," as found in Psalms 149 and 150, to mean singing—only. The Latin word "chorus" was thereafter used to translate the original Hebrew word meaning "to dance in a circling group."[21]

Under the pontificate of Gregory the Great, both dance and drama were excluded from the Catholic liturgy. In the later Middle Ages (1200 to 1500), church councils continued to condemn "unseemly dancing," specifically dancing of men and women together. However, at the same time a form of liturgical dance began developing within the churches. Paintings of the period frequently showed angels dancing in heaven. Many churches built during this period included symmetrical labyrinths laid out on the floor in multicolored stones: dance processions followed the leader through these labyrinths, which signified the journey through Satan's realm with a final triumphant arrival in Jerusalem or in heaven.[22] Dance was also found in the religious dramas and festivals held in village squares in front of, but not within, the church buildings.

During the Renaissance in Europe, dance returned to the sanctuary for a brief time. Up until Elizabethan times in England, a double-file Morris (see chapter 3) was danced inside churches at Pentecost, just as it was on the Feasts of Corpus Christi in Seville and Toledo in Spain. A similar dance, *Los Seises* (The Sixes), can still be seen in churches in Seville. Preadolescent boys perform this processional dance by singing and playing castanets while dancing very restrained rising and lowering of the heels and changing floor patterns.[23]

In England, ritual dancing within the church was prohibited in 1604. Then, in 1747, a Christian sect popularly called the "Shaking Quakers" appeared. This group believed in dancing for the adoration of God. Known as the *Shakers* in America, they settled in the eastern and mid-western states at a time when religious dance in this country was virtually nonexistent. Accompanied by singing and shouting, early Shaker dance was individualistic and ecstatic. As the sect itself became more organized, the dances also became codified. Large groups performed together but always with men and women separated. So strict was this sect that no sexual practices, even marriage, were permitted, yet dance became the pivotal point of their worship. Indeed the ability to dance was considered a gift from God, as the Shaker song "Simple Gifts" reveals:

> *When true simplicity is gained,*
> *To bow and bend we shan't be ashamed.*
> *To turn, turn will be our delight,*
> *'til by turning, turning we come round right.*

As Christianity spread into non-European countries with established traditions of dance in worship, dance was incorporated into Christian services. This use of movement in Christian worship can be seen in church services in Nigeria and other African countries, which in turn strongly influenced the incorporation of dance into African-based churches in North America, Brazil and the Caribbean. French and Spanish slaveholders in the West Indies, Mexico and South America were more liberal than North Americans about allowing native Africans to retain their own culture. Thus, more African religious dance was retained in these areas. When the white ruling class in Haiti was overthrown in 1803, planters and their slaves flocked to Louisiana, bringing the Afro-Caribbean dance traditions with them. Hence, much dance became incorporated into Christian worship and celebrations such as Mardi Gras and Christmas.

RELIGIOUS DANCE TODAY

As in the past, wars, colonization and displacement continue to cause the loss of many traditional religious dances. Others have changed form or have blended into the practices of newer religions. Governments that repress religion or promote a state religion to the detriment of all others have had a damaging effect on all the sacred arts. In recent years, international conferences on sacred dance have served to encourage the preservation of these dances. Additionally, some previously reluctant governments have shown new interest in preserving indigenous culture as a way of bolstering tourism.

In America, the incorporation of dance into worship is on the upswing. Dance is found in some Christian churches through the use of Shaker songs and movements, in churches that

PRAISE DANCER D'SYRE JOSEPH

incorporate praise dance into their worship services and in more liberal Jewish synagogues. New waves of immigrants whose cultures promote dance in worship have also had considerable influence. These include West Indians in New York, Cubans in Florida and new families throughout America from India and Indonesia. In part, this was the result of the American modern dance movement, with many dedicated choreographers seeking to return spirituality to dance. Early in this movement, *Ruth St. Denis* and *Ted Shawn* began presenting theatricalized versions of sacred dances from India and the Far East. Later, *Doris Humphrey* created *The Shakers*, and *Martha Graham*, *Paul Taylor* and *Erick Hawkins* produced choreography with American religious themes. In 1960 choreographer *Alvin Ailey* depicted the use of dance in black churches in his masterpiece *Revelations*, a work set to gospel music that still serves as inspiration for church-based movement choirs. This movement, know as praise dancing, has spread from black congregations into some primarily white churches in all parts of the US. Former Ailey dancer *Ulysses Dove* (1947–1996) choreographed a work called *Dancing on the Front Porch of Heaven* (1992) and *Ronald K. Brown* (b. 1966), following in the Ailey tradition of fusing dance styles, created *Grace* (2001), using modern dance and West African idioms to evoke the grace that suffuses life's journey.

Ballet has also responded to spirituality. As an example, Jackson, Mississippi, is home to the Ballet Magnificat!, a ballet company treating Christian themes. Founded in 1986, Ballet Magnificat! now has two touring companies and have presented programs in all parts of the US. They also offer summer intensives and teachers workshops.

Worship dance is also found in the group called Dances of Universal Peace. Formed in the 1960s in San Francisco, and originally called Sufi Dances of Universal Peace, this group embraces worship dance from all religions, sung in a wide range of languages including Arabic, Aramaic, English, Hawaiian, Hebrew and Sanscrit. The movements are simple and often folk-dance based.

The Sacred Dance Guild, founded in 1958, is an international, multicultural, non-profit group that promotes dance as prayer and as a means of spiritual growth and connection to the Divine. The organization sponsors trips to sacred sites for members, and an International Dance Festival, that so far has been held at American colleges except for one year when it took place in Canada. In June of 2008 it was held at Connecticut College.

But the in the 21st century, our earth, with its population of more than six billion and a steady stream of natural and man-made disasters, has seen many roadblocks to the growth and spread of religious dance. In her definitive book on religious dance, *Dancing in the Streets: A History of Collective Joy*, Barbara Erenreich states: "In today's world, other people have become an obstacle to our individual pursuits. They impede our progress on urban streets and highways; they compete for parking spots and jobs . . . they may even be criminals or terrorists[24]. . . There is no powerful faction in our divided world committed to upholding the glories of the feast and dance. The Protestant fundamentalism of the United States and the Islamic radicalism of Middle and Far East are both profoundly hostile to the ecstatic undertaking.[25] Perhaps the problem with civilization is simply a matter of scale; ecstatic rituals and festivities seem to have evolved to bind people in groups of a few hundred at a time—a group size at which it is possible for each participant hear the same (unamplified) music and see all the other participants at once. . . But there is no obvious reason why festivities and ecstatic rituals cannot survive within large-scale societies."[26]

CHARLES MOORE
in *Awassa Astrige* (Ostrich Dance)

SUGGESTED READING

Barzel, Ann. "Pilgrimage to Jerusalem: International Seminar on the Bible in Dance." *Dance Magazine*, December 1979: 80–87.

Berk, Fred. Machol Ha'am: *Dance of the Jewish People*. Susan Reimer, ed. N.p.: American Zionist Youth Foundation, 1978.

Blackmer, Joan Dexter. *Acrobats of the Gods: Dance and Transformation*. Toronto: Inner City Books, 1980.

Daniels, Marilyn. *The Dance in Christianity: A History of Religious Dance Through the Ages*. New York: Paulist Press, 1981.

De Mille, Agnes. *Book of the Dance*. New York: Golden Press, 1963.

Ellfeldt, Lois. *Dance: From Magic to Art*. Dubuque, Iowa: William C. Brown, 1976.

Erenreich, Barbara. *Dancing in the Streets: A History of Collective Joy*. New York: Metropolitan Books, 2006.

Ginn, Victoria. *The Spirited Earth: Dance, Myth and Ritual from South Asia to the South Pacific*. New York: Rizzoli International Publications, 1990.

Heth, Charlotte, ed. *Native American Dance: Ceremonies and Social Traditions*. Washington, D. C.: Smithsonian, 1992.

Kothari, Sunil. *Bharata Natyam*. New Delhi, India: Marg Publications, 1995.

Kraus, Richard, Sarah Hilsendager and Brenda Dixon. *History of the Dance in Art and Education*, 3rd ed. Englewood Cliffs, NJ: Prentice-Hall, 1991.

Ingber, Judith Brin. "Jewish Dance," *Jewish Folklore and Ethnology Review*. Columbus, OH: vol.20, #1, 2000.

Manor, Giora. "And Miriam Danced." *Ballett-International*, vol. 9, no. 9 (September 1986): 26–31.

Metz, Mark. *Conscious Dancer: Movement for a Better World*. (A quarterly magazine promoting spirituality in movement). First issue fall 2007. P.O. Box 2072, Berkeley, CA, 94702-9923.

Ortegel, Sister Adelaide. *A Dancing People*. West Lafayette, IN: Center for Contemporary Celebration, 1976.

Sachs, Curt. *World History of the Dance*. New York: W. W. Norton and Co., 1937.

Vitebsky, Piers. "What is a Shaman?" *Natural History Magazine*. March 1997, pp. 34–5.

Wagner, Ann. *Adversaries of Dance: From the Puritans to the Present*. Urbana, IL: University of Illinois Press, 1997.

Wosien, Maria-Gabriele. *Sacred Dance: Encounter with the Gods*. New York: Avon Publishers, 1974.

VIDEOGRAPHY

Circles and Cycles: Kathak Dance. Insight Media, 1989.

Dances of India—Learning Bharata Natyam. 2000. Chebrolu, Padma.

The Cosmic Dance of Shiva. 1990.

Dance of the Spirits: Mask Styles and Performance. (African Ceremonies) 1988.

Dance Black America. Dance Horizons, 1990.

Dancing vol. 5, "Lord of the Dance," Kultur.

Dervishes, Lovers of God. Insight Media, 1984.

Echoes from Tibet. Insight Media, 1980.

Ethnic Dances Around the World. Insight Media, 1983.

Four by Ailey, including *Revelations* with Judith Jamison, Kultur 1986.

Kecak Ubud Dance (Bali). Insight Media 1998.

Pow Wow Trail: Grass Dance and Men's Traditional. Insight Media, 2005.

Public Vodun Ceremonies in Haiti. Insight Media, 1991.

Sacred Choreographies of Cuba and Haiti. Insight Media, 2005.

Seven Years in Tibet. Jean-Jaques Annaud, producer/director Brad Pitt, 1997.

INTERNET SOURCES

www.balletmagnificat.org

www.dancesofuniversalpeace.org

www.whirlingdervishes.org

www.sacreddanceguild.org

www.artslynx.org/dance

CHAPTER THREE

SOCIAL DANCE

Salsa . . . has opened my mind to a new way of knowing—knowing myself, knowing my body, knowing beautiful and intense connections with other human beings . . . Sometimes when I get in "the zone" I catch a glimpse of the meaning of life. Its not just "fun," it can be a very profound experience.
—*Maria, "A Time to Dance"*

As an artist and musician, I find that an improvised social dance is the most difficult and gratifying of all other disciplines I have been exposed to and involved with. It is creation in motion. How could that not be art?
—*Natalia, A Time to Dance"*

Almost anywhere you go in the world, you will find dance used as a way of socializing and celebrating special occasions. Some of these dances embody centuries of tradition, while others appear as the latest trend; either way, they have a lot to tell you about the time, place and culture you are visiting.

Many names are applied to the world's recreational dances in literature. The term "ethnic dance" is sometimes applied to group dances that grew from tribal rituals, especially in non-Western countries. The term "folk dance" is often applied to dances of European origin, while dances appearing in our own culture are called "social dance." These distinctions have become irrelevant, since many dances have traveled from one part of the world to another, and many of these dances are blends from more than one culture. In this text, I use these terms interchangeably, as all of them apply to participatory dances that have a chiefly recreational purpose.

FRED ASTAIRE and GINGER ROGERS in "Flying Down to Rio." Movie musicals made couple dancing even more popular.

During the Industrial Revolution, which resulted in the moving about and changing of occupations of many rural people, traditional dances began to disappear in Europe. Fortunately, several dance ethnologists—people who do research on and reconstruct traditional dances—began collecting and notating songs and dances of various cultures. The work of the Englishman *Cecil Sharp*(1859–1924) in the last decade of the 19th century stimulated a resurgence of folk dancing in the British Isles. Sharp then came to America to explore dancing in New England and the southern mountain states. The result was the formation of the *Country Dance Society of America*, which has preserved many of our culture's traditional social dances.[1]

Social dances are sometimes categorized by type, based on their original uses. In this text, I have divided them into four categories: courtship dances, work dances, war dances and communal dances.

TYPES OF SOCIAL DANCE

Courtship Dances

Courtship dances appear in many forms with reels, double circle dances and couple dances being the most common in Western culture. Couple dancing is a European invention that does not exist in many cultures. For example, Native American and Asian cultures, in which arranged marriages prevailed for most of history and rules of behavior between the sexes are strict, do not have a tradition of couple dances; those that are found today in Japan, Indonesia and India are imports from the West.

Courtship dances sometimes follow a pattern of display or flirtation between the sexes. This appears in an unusual way in the annual courtship dance of the nomadic Wodaabe people in Nigeria. In this culture, men favor having several wives, with marriages arranged through family negotiations. However, marriages resulting from mutual attraction also exist. Once a year, a ceremony is held in which eligible men in heavy makeup and elaborate dress dance for the women. The women do not dance with them, as this would be considered immodest; however, a woman unhappy in her marriage may choose from the "dance line" and select a new husband. In this case the dance supplies an acceptable escape route for a woman who wishes to be a "love wife" instead of a "given wife."[2]

In Hungary, a dance known as the *Maidens' Round* has ancient origins. Young women dance in a closed circle, while men watch from the outside, "spoiling the round" occasionally when one or another drags his girl out of the chain. Eventually, the men join the dance and it transforms into a couple dance.[3]

The European emphasis on couple dances evolved during the time of the Crusades (which began in the late 11th century), along with the chivalrous code of social behavior by a gentleman toward the lady of his choice. Couple dances spread throughout Europe and the British Isles during the late Middle Ages as royal and ducal families made marriage alliances and conquests. Consequently, it is difficult to determine the country of origin for many early couple dances. By the 15th century, dancing masters were writing manuals of steps and etiquette and giving daily dancing lessons in the European courts. Italian dancing masters were held in especially high esteem. The following is an

THE WALTZ.
From a lithograph by Jacques Louis David,
it suggests the popularity of this dance in
19th century Europe and America.

excerpt from the writings of *Guglielmo Ebreo* of Pesaro, a noted Italian dancing master of the late 15th century; he directs his comments to the genteel female dancer:

> *Her glance should not be proud or wayward, gazing here or there as men do. Let her for the most part keep her eyes, with decency, on the ground . . . And then at the end of the dance, when her partner leaves her, let her, facing him squarely with a sweet regard, make a decent and respectful curtsey in answer to his.[4]*

Spain's couple dances in the *flamenco* style, infused with smoldering sensuality and strong rhythmic foot patterns, retain a characteristic flavor different from the rest of Europe. Flamenco is a mixture of Andalusian dance from southern Spain, Moorish and Gypsy influences, gradually fused together over a period of several centuries. The Gypsies (called "gitano" in Spain) originated in northern India and migrated into Egypt, Romania, Hungary, Germany, France, Spain and the British Isles, and can even be found today in Canada. The Gypsies' language, music and dance suggest their heritage in northern India, but show adaptation to their country of current residence as well. Flamenco-style dance was spread to the New World by Spanish settlers. Its influence can be found in Mexican, Argentinean, Cuban and Central American dances, such as the *tango* and *cha-cha*, and in the Latin dances popular in the United States.

Today traditional flamenco can be found in bars and night clubs in Spain and the above-mentioned countries. Drinks are served and the dancers appear on a small stage, usually sitting in a half-circle. They perform solos and couple dances accompanied by shouting, clapping, male or female vocalists, guitars, finger-snapping and castanets—hand-held wooden percussion instruments that evolved from the Indian metal finger cymbals. The sounds of intricate footwork in hard-soled shoes also provide an aural accompaniment. Unlike the couple dances from other parts of Europe, men and women look each other directly in the eyes with their spines arched backward, seldom touching. This creates a somewhat competitive aura, with the women displaying pride rather than shyness.

Nuevo flamenco, or new flamenco, influenced by both traditional and new music, enlivened the flamenco scene starting in the 1980s. The women's ruffled skirts have been replaced by black pants, creating a unisex look for men and women. Dances retain their lively footwork and may be performed in large groups as well as solos and couple dances. Flamenco dance remains very much alive in the new millennium, with classes and performances happening internationally, and Internet information available for both.

In the 1830s, the *waltzes* and *polkas* of the Austro-Hungarian Empire took Europe by storm and eventually found their way to America. Waltzes and polkas also became popular in Mexico, a result of German colonization there. These dances were considered particularly risqué, owing to the rapid whirling and dipping motions and the closed position of the dancers in which the man's hand encircles the woman's waist. Some ministers considered them the road to immorality and preached against them. Nevertheless, efforts to ban these dances failed, and both dances became entrenched in both the Old and New Worlds. Ironically, the waltz is the traditional dance most performed at weddings today.

Work Dances

Many folk dances imitate the movements of men and women in their daily work, which bonds groups of people based on occupation. The earliest of these were animal imitation dances, especially popular in hunting cultures. Reenactments of hunts can be found in the *Deer Dance* of Mexico's Yaqui Indians and in the traditional hunters' dances of Russia, among many others.

Coastal areas around the world have developed seamen's and fishermen's dances. For example, in Veracruz on Mexico's Gulf Coast, the annual Carnivale features a *Fishermen's Dance*, including net-pulling movements for groups of men. Similarly, woodsmen's chopping and sawing movements are featured in some dances from Romania and the Czech Republic. In Russia, France and India there are dances imitating the sowing, mowing, stacking and threshing of wheat. Natives of Taiwan also have ancient hand-holding line dances as part of a harvest ritual. Some Portuguese, Greek and Italian dances imitate the gathering of grapes and the making of wine.

The work of women is also represented in dance. For example, in Slavic wedding dances, rocking the cradle, baking bread, feeding guests, weaving linen, sowing and harvesting are performed by bridesmaids, mothers and sometimes the bride herself. The dances are performed rhythmically in unison, making the work more like a game. These dances express pride in work while psychologically preparing the bride for her new life.

War Dances

Weapons dances are characterized by displays of group or individual strength and agility. Many had the original purpose of keeping soldiers fit and prepared to fight, and of displaying their prowess as warriors. These motivational war dances form the basis for many all-male group recreational dances today, such as the stepping dances popular in African-American fraternities. Their influence can also be seen in modern-day pep rallies.

The Chinese were using coordinated group movements with weapons as early as the first millennium B.C. These gradually evolved into the Chinese martial arts. War dances were prevalent among Native Americans, South American Indians and in Africa. In these cultures, being a bad dancer was a sign of disgrace for a man, and it was considered cowardly not to participate. The *capoeira*, a Brazilian form of dance and acrobatics done to instrumental music, is actually a martial art in the guise of dance.

It is also surprising to find out how many European recreational folk dances were originally war dances. An example is the energetic *Morris Dance* of the British Isles, which is performed by men in a double-file formation, wearing elaborate costumes adorned with ribbons and bells. Many villages in England have local variations of this dance, in which groups of male performing teams compete with each other at festivals. The Morris Dance bears a resemblance to a Spanish dance known as the *moresque* and may originally have been an enactment of the wars between Christians and Moors. Because soldiers travel extensively, it is possible that this dance originated in North Africa and was brought home during the time of the Crusades.[5]

The *sword* dances of Scotland, danced over two swords crossed on the ground, emphasize agility and fast footwork. Likewise the Irish step dances, distinguished by complete stillness in the upper body and the rapid-fire of intricate footwork. *Reels* and *jigs* are performed in soft leather shoes laced much like ballet slippers, while hornpipes, treble-jigs and step-dances are performed in hard-soled shoes. Some of these dances mimic the advancing and retreating of two opposing armies.

In Hungary and Bulgaria many men's group dances, known as recruitment dances, were originally used for the purpose of attracting new soldiers. The *Gunner's Dance* from Thrace, performed by men in hobnailed boots, consists of fierce stomping that sounds like artillery shots.

Stepping, a recreational dance form performed by many black fraternities and sororities in friendly competitions, is a remnant of war dances from Africa. Many of these dances contain elaborate patterns using canes or batons, as substitutes for the original spears used in tribal Africa.

Communal Dances

Communal dances abound in cultures where cooperation is valued above competitiveness. Some communal dances require complete conformity to the group. For example, the dances of Bulgaria are performed in lines and circles of tightly linked dancers executing synchronized steps. English and Irish country dances also emphasize inter-weaving group patterns and fast footwork that require cooperative practice. Other dances allow room for self-expression, such as the village dances

YAMI CANOE-LAUNCHING CEREMONY
a good example of a work dance. Photographed in Taiwan.

of Nigeria. Although the dance is done in a group surrounded by spectators singing and clapping, each dancer has an opportunity to come forward and perform his or her specialty solo.

Communal dances are an important way of transmitting culture to the next generation. In the Cook Islands of Polynesia, school children learn how to perform indigenous dances and songs. The movements are practiced in large mixed groups: however, there is a distinct girls' and boys' style for the movements. The *hora*, a mixed-group circle dance considered the national dance of Israel, actually appeared much earlier in many other nations, including Greece, Romania and the former Yugoslavia. This dance allows for exuberant displays that must be done in unison because of the linked formation.

In cultures where the sexes are kept more rigidly separated, communal dances may be practiced only in single-sex venues. This is true in Islamic Morocco (North Africa), where women dance together to celebrate special occasions in the privacy of their homes, and men dance in nightclubs where paid female entertainers are the only women present. In both cases, the sensuous, rhythmic movements are designed for release and self-expression rather than for courtship purposes.

AMERICA: THE DANCE CROSSROADS

A look at social dance in America today illustrates the influence of numerous immigrant groups producing a distinctly American mix. Dances from all over the world are literally at our feet, owing to the wide diversity of cultural influences here.

Early settlers in the American colonies from England, Scotland and Ireland brought group dances that emphasized intricate footwork in repeatable patterns, such as *reels, contra-dances, jigs, square* and *round dances*. French settlers contributed the *cotillon*, a type of square dance, and the *quadrille*, a dance done in double-couple formation. Other European couple dances—waltz, *polka, schottische*—were added later.

At the same time, Africans on plantations in the South were creating rhythmic songs using hand-clapping and foot-stamping to replace the drums outlawed by slave owners. On some plantations the slaves, using the instruments available to them—fiddle, banjo, tambourine—held their own dances on Saturday nights. The most popular dance form was the *challenge dance*, in which individuals took turns entering the center of the clapping circle and performing their own specialty steps. This dance form is a direct descendant of Nigerian village get-togethers. One dance, the *Cakewalk*, became a competition; the couple who performed the best high-kicking strut won a cake as a prize.

This dance, later popularized by the minstrel shows for white audiences (see chapter 6), became the dance craze of the 1890s.

In the early decades of the 20th century, couple dances were popularized by the glamorous *Vernon* (1887–1918) and *Irene* (1893–1969) *Castle*, the inventors of the upbeat and elegant *Castle Walk*. Further impetus was given by the movie industry, especially the musicals featuring *Fred Astaire* (1899–1987) and *Ginger Rogers* (1911–1995). Dance studios began opening across the country. During the 1940s, the most popular dance was the *fox trot*, a moderate-tempo dance first introduced early in the century and ideally suited to the rhythms of the Big Bands (those of Tommy Dorsey, Benny Goodman, Duke Ellington, Glenn Miller and many more). By the end of the 1950s ballroom-style dance lessons were even given on television by *Kathryn* (1907–1999) and *Arthur* (1895–1991) *Murray*.

In African-American communities, the dance style incorporated much more torso, head and arm movement, along with a more relaxed stance that had the torso pitched slightly forward. The new ragtime music coming out of New Orleans suited this dance style perfectly. By the 1920s, African-Americans were creating their own energetic dances in places like the Cotton Club and the Apollo Ballroom in Harlem. Dances like the *Charleston, Big Apple, Suzy-Q,* and *Black Bottom* became part of the "Harlem Renaissance." Notable was the *Lindy Hop* (named after Charles Lindbergh, the pilot hero of the 1920s), and the *jitterbug*. With its wild partnering stunts and lively tempo, the Lindy Hop became the favorite of young African-American couples and the subject of numerous dance competitions.

By the 1950s, young people were blending black and white styles of music and dance, mainstreaming African-American rhythm and blues and transforming it into the songs and dances of rock 'n' roll. Elvis Presley, who copied his dance style from black neighbors in Mississippi, was in the forefront of changing the way white teenagers (and eventually adults) danced. Jerry Lee Lewis, the Big Bopper (J.P. Richardson) and numerous other performers, both black and white, also contributed to this phenomenon.

Latin dances from our neighbors to the south began filtering into our culture before the turn of the century, enriching American social dance. By the 1930s, they were the rage on the dance floor. Their popularity was enhanced by Hollywood movies that featured Latin dances, notably "Flying Down to Rio" (1933), the first movie to feature the dancing of Fred Astaire and Ginger Rogers. Brazil has contributed the lively *samba*, a mixture of Latin and African rhythms, and the *maxixe*. The Argentine tango establishes an electric attraction and connection between partners. From Cuba and the Caribbean we have acquired the *rumba, tango, conga, beguine, cha-cha* and *merengue*. Mexican dance styles vary according to regional differences, and many dances have found their way into our western states.

The dances of the 1960s broke new ground because, although they were partner dances, it was no longer necessary to do what your partner was doing. Not since the Charleston had individuals in a couple dance been so free to improvise. In dances such as the *twist*, popularized by Chubby Checker, partners never touched each other; they simply faced each other and "did their own thing." This facilitated the changing of partners, mirroring a trend in cultural mores.

The advent of discothèques (originally an import from France) in the early 1970s opened up new possibilities: partner dancing when you have a partner, solo and line dancing when you don't. *Breakdancing* and *hip-hop*, introduced to the streets of New York's South Bronx in the late 1970s by black and Hispanic youths, eliminated partners completely, making dance a form of skilled display, strength and originality. By the 1980s hip-hop had spread into the mainstream, and by the 1990s, hip-hop culture was world-wide. Words describing these movements include *B-boying, popping, locking, hitting, ticking* and *boogaloo.*

Another partnered social dance form known as "slam dancing" originated among punk-rock fans in England and became popular in the United States in the 1980s. Slam dancing has led to the violent dancing known as "moshing" found at clubs and heavy-metal concerts. More recently, reggae, new Latin dances and Latin-African blends have been added to the mix. The 1990s saw the entry of the *macarena* into the social dance repertory, with full acceptance demonstrated by its being danced at both Republican and Democratic national political conventions, although its popularity was short-lived.

While young people experiment with new social dance forms, enclaves of settlers of various nationalities continue to preserve and perform the dances of their homelands. The town of Solvang in southern California has an annual Danish Days Celebration with folk dances from the old country, while in nearby Santa Barbara dances from Mexico abound. In Chicago and western Massachusetts, Polish dances appear at family

CINCO DE MAYO IN TEXAS.
Mexican-Americans maintaining their traditional culture, celebrating the Fifth of May, 1862, victory of the Mexican militia over the French army at the Battle of Puebla.

celebrations, while the Irish festival in Boston draws thousands. At Duquesne University in Pittsburgh, authentic Bulgarian, Russian and Slavic dances are performed by the student dance company known as Tamburitzans. Other college dance programs offer classes in flamenco, Afro-Caribbean, traditional Chinese and country-western dance. Preserving the dances and other arts of our country's first people, Native American intertribal powwows are held in all parts of the country. *Hulas* and the accompanying chants, both traditional and modern, from the state of Hawaii are taught in several other states, even outdoors in Manhattan's Central Park in the summertime, and some of these students will wind up at hula competitions, the major one being in Honolulu.

Many of the dances in America reflect the blending of two or more cultures. For example, *zydeco* music and dances from southwestern Louisiana are a blend of the cultures of French-Canadian settlers (Acadians) and African-Americans, many of whom arrived via the Caribbean Islands. Our dance heritage is indeed so diverse that it would be laughable to expect a person from another country to understand the American culture by watching only one or two dance forms. Yet, sometimes we Americans limit our own viewing in exactly this way. For those who celebrate diversity, folk life festivals that exhibit dances from all over the world have become popular in every region of our country and emphasize our multicultural heritage

THE UKRAINIAN HOPAK, demonstrated by the Tamburitzans of Duquesne University, Pittsburgh, Pennsylvania.

The new millennium has evoked a different outlook on American social dance. Instead of a set pattern of steps, couples learn movements and mix them up in ever-changing rotations. In the salsa, for example, creativity abounds, and new steps are constantly being invented, spreading quickly through the ever-growing salsa community. This new outlook on dance looks freestyle but requires practice and cooperation with one's partner. But above all, it is following the true nature of social dance, which is simply enjoying yourself and the company you are with. Meanwhile, the new style of hip-hop music and dance movement got slower, heavier, and more aggressive. Some more specific styles of the new school dances are *krumping, harlem shake, snap dancing, blood walk, clown walk, booty popping, chicken noodle soup,* and *tone wop*. The new hip-hop, known as b-boying, is now being taught in dance studios throughout the US, at least those in medium-sized to large cities. At the same time some clubs and dance halls continue to feature the music and movements of earlier social dances—everything from the Big Band era to country line dances.

A BRETONNE GAVOTTE.
A French community dances together in the gavotte, a 17th century French folk dance.

SOCIAL DANCES OF EUROPE AND AMERICA

Twelfth and Thirteenth Centuries

Estampie ∞ a man with one or two women
Fandango ∞ Spanish/Moorish
Farandole ∞ gypsy/Spanish traveling line dance holding hands
Round (branle) ∞ circle dance moving alternately right and left
Morris dances ∞ English war dances
Maypole dances ∞ fertility dances
Sword dances ∞ British and Irish step dances

Fourteenth Century

German saltarello (allemande) ∞ a partnered processional

Fifteenth Century

French basse dance ∞ gliding and interweaving
Haute dances ∞ faster tempo, jumps; includes Piva, Alta, Quadernaria
Hornpipe ∞ lively English step dance

Sixteenth Century

Allemande ✐ German partner dance

Pavane ✐ stately Spanish dance

Galliard ✐ boisterous jumping dance

Sir Roger de Coverly ✐ English country reel

La Volta ✐ haute dance, in which the man throws his partner in the air

Courante ✐ lively linked line dance

Measures ✐ cross-rhythmic slower dances

Seventeenth Century

Bourrée ✐ French folk/court basse dance

Contradance ✐ British or American circular group dance

Flamenco ✐ rhythmic partnered, solo and group dances, gypsy/Spanish

Gavotte ✐ lively French folk dance

Jig (gigue) ✐ lively Irish dance, mostly done with the feet, with the upper body quite stationary

Loure ✐ French folk/court dance

Minuet ✐ French partnered court dance, moderate tempo

Passepied ✐ French folk/court dance Polonaise—stately Polish court dance

Rigaudon ✐ French folk/court dance

Mill Field, Turkeyloney ✐ English country dances

Eighteenth Century

Minuet variations ✐ solo minuet

Cotillon ✐ Ballroom dance for four or more couples, with many figures

Quadrille ✐ French dance for four

Tarantella, furlana ✐ Italian courtship dances

Nineteenth Century

Cakewalk ✐ African-American strutting dance

Gallop ✐ rapid 2/4 time travelling dance

Habanera ✐ Cuban couple dance

Mazurka ✐ Polish couple dance

Polka ✐ lively German and Polish dance in 2/4 time

Schottische ✐ British Isles couple dance

Square dances ✐ Irish folk and American country

Waltz ✐ partnered dance in 3/4 time, originally German

Twentieth Century

Latin rhythms 🙾 the rumba, samba, mambo, cha-cha, conga and tango of the 1930s

Ragtime, Charleston, black bottom, varsity drag 🙾 American dances of the 1920s

Twenty-first Century

Cumbia and vallenato 🙾 partner dances from Columbia

Lambada 🙾 partner dance with no touching

Freestyle 🙾 dance mixes

New Style hip-hop 🙾 slower and stronger than the original

Salsa 🙾 mix of any Latin rhythms

SUGGESTED READING

Aldrich, Elizabeth. *From the Ballroom to Hell: Grace and Folly in Nineteenth-Century Dance*. Evanston, IL: Northwestern University Press, 1991.

Asante, Kariamu Welsh, ed. *African Dance*. Eritrea: Africa World Press, 1996.

Beats of the Heart: Popular Music of the World. London: Pluto Press, 1985.

Buckman, Peter. *Let's Dance: Social, Ballroom and Folk Dancing*. New York: Paddington Press, 1978.

Collier, Simon. *Tango! The Dance, The Song, The Story.* London: Thames and Hudson, 1995.

De Mille, Agnes. *The Book of the Dance*. New York: Golden Press, 1963.

Dils, Ann, and Ann Cooper Albright. *Moving History/Dancing Cultures*. Middletown, CT: Wesleyan University Press, 2001.

Dodworth, Allen. *Dancing and Its Relations to Education and Social Life*. New York: Harper and Bros., 1888.

Duke, Jerry. *Recreational Dance: Ballroom, Cajun, Country-Western*. Boston, MA: American Press, 1996.

Ebreo, Guglielmo of Pesaro. *De Pratica Seu Arte Tripudii/On the Practice or Art of Dancing*. ed., trans., and introduced by Barbara Sparti. Oxford, England: Clarendon Press, 1993.

Greco, Jose. *The Gypsy in My Soul*. Garden City, NY: Doubleday and Co., 1971.

Halsey, Jan. "Five Centuries of Social Dance: Dance Through Time" with Carol Téten, *Dance Teacher Now*, vol. 5, no. 4 (Summer 1983): 25–27.

Hazzard-Gordon, Katrina. *Jookin': The Rise of Social Dance Formations in African-American Culture*. Philadelphia: Temple University Press, 1990.

Katzarova-Kukudova, Raina and Kiril Djenev. *Bulgarian Folk Dances*. trans. Nevena Geliazkova and Marguerite Alexieva. Cambridge, MA: Slavica Publishers, Inc., 1976.

Kirsten, Lincoln. *Dance: A Short History of Classic Theatrical Dancing* (1935). Reprint, New York: Dance Horizons, 1969.

Lawson, Joan. *European Folk Dance*. New York: Pittman Publishing Co., 1953.

Malnig, Julie. *Dancing Till Dawn: A Century of Exhibition Ballroom Dance.* Westport, CT: Greenwood Press, 1992.

Martin, Carol. *Dance Marathons: Performing American Culture in the 1920s and 1930s.* Jackson: University Press of Mississippi, 1994.

Martin, György. *Hungarian Folk Dances.* Budapest: Corina Press, 1974.

Rushing, Shirley and Patrick McMillan. *Ballroom Dance, American Style.* Dubuque, IA: Eddie Bowers Publishing, 1997.

Tanner, Tango. "Hula on an Island, but Hawaii It's Not." *The New York Times*, Oct. 31, 2004, p. 34.

Teten, Carol. *Dance Teacher Now*, SU. 1983:27.

Wakefield, Eleanor. *Folk Dancing in America.* New York: J. Lowell Pratt and Company, 1966.

Wood, Melusine. *Historical Dances (Twelfth to Nineteenth Century): Their Manner of Performance and Their Place in the Social Life of the Time* (1952). London: Dance Books, 1982.

VIDEOGRAPHY

Il Ballarino: The Art of Renaissance Dance. Dance Horizons 1991.

Ballroom Dancing (International Championships). narr. Juliet Prowse. 1996.

Ballroom Dancing beginner–advanced instruction). Kultur, 1993.

Burn the Floor: 44 Ballroom and Latin Dances. Universal Studios 2000

Breakin' (Breakdancing). chor. Jaime Rogers, MGM, 1984.

Brigadoon. Gene Kelly and Cyd Charisse, 1952.

Dance Black America (includes The Chuck Davis Dance Company's African dance; The Charles Moore Dance Theatre's Shango by Katharine Dunham and The Alvin Ailey Company). Dance Horizons, 1990.

Dancing, Vol III: "Sex and Social Dance," and Vol. VII: "Dancing in One World." Kultur, 1992.

Dancetime! 500 Years of Social Dance, Vols. I and II. Carol Téten, Dancetime Publications, 1997

Dirty Dancing. (Latin dances) Patrick Swayze. Vestron, 1987.

Dirty Dancing: Havana Nights. Salsa. Miramax Films 2004.

Fiddler on the Roof. Russian-Jewish dance, chor. Jerome Robbins. MGM/UA, 1971.

Flamenco at 5:10. Susanna and Antonio Robledo Teach Class. Direct Cinema, 1969.

Hey Let's Twist. First twist musical, 1961.

How to Dance Through Time, Vols. I and II. prod. Carol Téten. Dancetime Publications, 1999.

Introduction to Baroque Dance Vols. I and II. Down East Dance, 2000.

Israeli Folk Dance Festival: Night on the Sea of Galilee. Irotex, Ltd., Horon, Israel.

Jailhouse Rock. Elvis Presley, 1957.

José Greco in Performance, Flamenco. Kultur, 1990.

Latcho Drom, "Safe Journey" (Gypsy dance). CPF Video, France, 1994.

Mad About Mambo. chor. Kim Blank, Gramercy Pictures, 2000.

Millenium Part 1, "Romance" (Wodaabe dance), narr. Adrian Malone Biniman Productions, 1992.

Riverdance: Live in New York City (Irish step dance). Columbia Tristar, 1997.

Saturday Night Fever. John Travolta as a disco dancer. Paramount, 1977.

Shall We Dance (Film drama about Western social dance in Japan), Miramax, 1997.

The Spirit moves: Black Social Dance on Film 1900–1986. Dancetime Publications, 3 DVDs, 2008.

The Story of Vernon and Irene Castle. Fred Astaire and Ginger Rogers, RKO Radio Pictures, 1939.

Strictly Ballroom (Australian ballroom dance competition). Miramax, 1992.

Tamburitzans in Concert. Duquesne University (Pittsburgh), "Tradition" programs 1 and 2; "Moments in Time" 1 and 2; "Celebrate!" 1 and 2.

A Taste of Salsa, Vols. I and II. Big City Swing, 2000.

INTERNET SOURCES

www.addicted2salsa.com

www.andalucia.com/flamenco/nuevoflamenco.htm

www.artslynx.org/dance/ (African)

Country Dance and Song Society, www.adta.org info@adta.org

www.flamenco.org

www.flamenco-world.com/flamenco.htm

CHAPTER FOUR

BUGAKU AND BALLET

From the Royal Courts to Theatrical Dance

Although the Art of Dance has always been recognized as one
of the most honorable and necessary methods to train the body,
and furthermore as the primary and most natural basis for all sorts of Exercises,
including that of bearing arms, consequently it is one of the most advantageous
and useful to our Nobility, as well as to others who have the honor of
approaching Us, not only in time of War for our Armies,
but even in Peacetime while we enjoy the diversion of our court Ballets.
—*Charter of the Royal Academy of Dance, France, 1661*[1]

Court dances, like other court arts from painting to architecture, tend to be
conservative in the literal sense; they conserve attitudes about life that were
deemed essential to the society in the past. . . . Courts and court dances are
excessive, and ultimately it is the people who pay the bills.
—*Gerald Jonas*[2]

She danced with such abounding vitality, with such ecstasy of the spirit;
she surrendered herself so completely to the mood of the dance,
that she became a being transformed.
—*Cyril Beaumont describing Anna Pavlova*[3]

COURT DANCE

Dance created for the entertainment of the aristocracy, to please powerful kings and emperors, is almost as old as sacred dance. Indeed, in cultures where the rulers are both religious and secular leaders or even considered gods themselves, it is difficult to separate religious dance and court dance. An early example of this is ancient Egypt, where even the pharaoh took part in elaborate dance rituals, and the royal houses owned troupes of dancers and other entertainers. In later dynasties a class of independent professional performers developed. A record from the time of

LOUIS XIV AS APOLLO
in *Ballet de la Nuit.* Louis XIV's
support and advancement of ballet
is documented.

King Senwosret (1900–1887 B.C.) shows that he employed twelve full-time dancers, mostly foreigners, to entertain on feast days. Most of these ceremonies were dedicated to Hathor, the goddess of beauty, music and dancing.[4]

The linking of dance to the courts of nobility has been inevitable in history for two reasons. One is that the ruling classes sought ways of defining and describing their power. Dance and spectacle provided vivid displays of power in a way that copied the hierarchical organization of the court itself. Dance can be used by leaders to hold a people together. This worked well for Asante chiefs in what is now Ghana, where being a good dancer was once a requisite for becoming chief. It worked equally well for Louis XIV of France, an able dancer who also demanded from his courtiers high-quality dancing.

The second reason is that dance, like all arts, seeks patrons. The noble courts were once the most logical refuge for artists who wished to produce and survive. However, court patronage may be fickle and subject to personal whims and political changes. For example, in Rome of 200 B.C., dancing was considered an important social skill for sons and daughters of the nobility; however, about fifty years later, Consul Scipio Africanus decided dancing was not appropriate for upper-class Romans and closed the dancing schools.[5]

As cultures change, some of the court-born arts migrate and find audiences within the general public. This pattern can be traced in the history of ballet, which began as a court spectacle performed by courtiers and evolved into a theatrical art performed by highly trained professionals.

An examination of court dances that still exist in their original state in various parts of the world shows some interesting similarities. All have a sense of spectacle, including costuming that is radically different from the everyday wear of the participants, and music created especially for court occasions. The dance often begins with a stately processional as an entrance and introduction of the participants. The arrangement of the participants is based on their relation to the ruler, and the movements demand a sense of decorum and deference toward the chief, who is either observer or participant. Predictability is favored over surprises, conformity over innovation. Considerable practice is often involved for the dancers, with talented dancers gaining a privilege and advantage in court. An observer of Burmese court dance in 1937 describes it this way:

Trainees in the former (refined) type were taught not to hold the body rigid, but to move in an effortless manner as if there were no bones in the body. Their posture had to be grand and their faces mask-like. The poses struck by the dancers delighted the Burmese, who felt that the elegant deportment personified the dignity of the court.[6]

In Cambodia, despite four years of vicious genocide by Pol Pot in the 1970s, one can find court dance in its original form since the monarchy has been restored. Here there are both men and women performers, both narrative and abstract performances. The women, beautifully costumed and meticulously trained, move as a unified group, in perfect syncronicity and slow motion. The result is serene, soothing and exquisite. Stories of ancient mythology are reenacted, including marriages between Cambodian royalty and gods.

This description could also apply to the following examples of court dance:

Chinese and Japanese Court Dance

The court dances of China, now performed as theatrical events for the general public, can be traced back to the sacred rituals of antiquity. The Duke of Chou (1115–1104 B.C.) is credited with formulating music and dances to accompany various religious rites. Other members of China's royalty patronized this art form and participated as performers. During the Han dynasty, the emperor Wu set up an Office of Music. By the time of the Tang dynasty in the 700s A.D., these songs and dances had become highly developed dance-dramas, and a music and dance troupe was formed within the court. The stable political situation during the Tang dynasty allowed the art of dance to develop and an Imperial Academy to be established. The stately and lavish *Ten Movement Music* dance incorporated dance forms of the peoples of China, Korea, Sinkiang, India, Persia and Central Asia into one colossal dance. Poetry, songs, a dramatic plot and background music were included. This was the beginning of Chinese Opera. The operas had elaborate costuming and an array of archetypal characters, including the court jester, young heroes and heroines well versed in martial arts, mother and father roles and males with heavily painted faces—the "heavies" in the stories. Many different styles of opera developed in China; in the 18th century, under the patronage of Ch'ing dynasty emperor Ch'ien-lung, Peking opera became the dominant style. Originally, all roles were played by men, but today in public performances in Taiwan there are women performers as well.[7]

During the Tang dynasty, Chinese opera was also introduced from China and Korea into Japan, and formed the basis of the oldest form of court dance still being performed for ceremonies of state: the *bugaku* dance of Japan. This dance form and the accompanying court music, *gagaku*, have remained constant for twelve hundred years. It also contains elements of ancient Shinto rituals, because the Japanese imperial family claims descent from the Shinto sun goddess.[8]

Bugaku is performed by men only in the Japanese Imperial Palace theater, on a platform covered in green brocade. The movement of the two, four or eight dancers follows simple floor patterns with many pauses and repetitions. Usually the dancers, facing all four directions, perform identical movements in identical costumes. The lavish costumes, which cover the entire body, include long flowing robes of

PEKING OPERA PERFORMING IN TAIWAN.
Every costume part is significant and every gesture is highly stylized.

blue or crimson, ceremonial swords, lances, shields and trains. For strong characters, painted full-face masks are used because "to contort (the dancers') faces would violate the rules of etiquette."[9] The distinguishing characteristic to the Western observer is the extremely slow pace of the movement, erect posture, emphasis on clarity and control and symmetrical floor patterns. The total experience of bugaku is a sense of serenity; indeed, time seems to stand still.

Bugaku exemplifies the spirit of maintaining age-old traditions in Japan, a country that is also a front-runner in modern technology and commerce. New dances in the traditional bugaku style continue to be created for important ceremonies and national events, such as the marriage of a crown prince. For centuries, these dances were performed only for members of the aristocracy, heads of state and official guests. Since the end of World War II, performances have also been opened to the public in a theater located on the palace grounds.

Bugaku has also influenced a much newer Japanese theatrical dance form known as *kabuki*. Like bugaku, kabuki is all-male and performed in heavy makeup or masks and elaborate costumes. Kabuki blends music, acting and dance in highly stylized performances. However, the themes of kabuki dramas may be quite contemporary. Kabuki originated in the 19th century as a storytelling medium for general Japanese audiences; therefore, its range of expression has fewer limitations than the court-designated bugaku.[10]

THE EARLY DEVELOPMENT OF BALLET

Ballet is a theatrical dance form that grew out of European Renaissance court dances.

These dances became popular in 15th century Italy, then spread north owing to the influence of Italian nobility, who brought their dancing masters with them wherever they relocated. While many of these dances had origins in village celebrations, the dancing masters added a refined style suitable to the status and dress of the noble classes. These dances became so important for training in the social graces that many nobles took daily dance classes. It was common practice for the nobles to keep their dance manuals at their bedside along with their copy of the Bible.

Ballet might have remained simply a form of court social dance had it not been for the influence of two rulers. The first was *Catherine de Medici* (1519–1589), an Italian noblewoman who became the queen of France in the mid-16th century. Catherine brought her dancing master *Balthasar de Beaujoyeux* (originally Baldassare da Belgiojoso; d. 1587) from Italy and entrusted him with the production of lavish court entertainments. In 1581 he designed the *Ballet Comique de la Reine* (literally, the Queen's comic ballet), which is considered by historians to be the first true ballet. It contained many elements not found in ballets today. The dances, performed by the court nobles, were linked together by song, poetry and prose, which provided a story line based on Greco-Roman mythology. Sets were wheeled into the ballroom on carts, and there were intermissions for refreshments. This elaborate work lasted well into the night.

The French tradition of court ballets was reinforced a century later by the great warrior-king *Louis XIV*. Determined to consolidate his power over the lesser nobility, Louis built the lavish palace of Versailles. Nobles invited to the palace were expected to participate in ballets: indeed, being an exemplary dancer was one of the best ways for a nobleman to gain favor with the king. The ladies were also encouraged to dance, although they often wore masks when performing. Louis loved theatrical spectacle and was himself an avid dancer. He acquired the nickname "The Sun King" from his role as Apollo in *Ballet de la Nuit* (1653). The dance historian Jack Anderson wrote of Louis XIV:

> *Art and life were virtually one and the same for the king. . . . In its formality, ballet must have seemed the apotheosis of the social structure. . . . Court life had become a matter of perpetual artifice, and personality had become a matter of sustained impersonation.*[11]

Louis's most important contribution to dance did not occur until he retired from active performing. In 1661 he established the Académie Royale de la Danse, a training facility that was the first attempt to professionalize ballet. Under the direction of Louis' ballet master *Pierre Beauchamps* (1636–1705), the French ballet terminology and rules for technique developed. Beauchamps' five positions of the feet and the use of the turned-out leg, described in his own system of notation, became the basis for ballet education still used in ballet classes worldwide.

Another innovation during the reign of Louis XIV was moving ballet performances out of the palace and into a new Italian-style theater. For the first time, instead of being viewed from all four sides in a ballroom, the dances were now seen from the front only, on a raised stage framed by a proscenium arch. This encouraged the further development of turned-out leg positions, which enabled the dancer to move from side to side smoothly while facing the audience. It also separated the dancers from the audience, serving to professionalize their efforts. In this new theater, the French public got its first view of ballet, formerly confined only to the court, and they quickly developed a taste for it.

EIGHTEENTH CENTURY BALLET

During the 18th century, rulers of other European countries established royally-subsidized theaters and opera houses; England, Italy, Russia, Austria and Scandinavia followed France's example as the cultural leader. In some courts, however, ballet was not an independent art but an adjunct to operatic productions. Many of the ballets of this Baroque period had little content or continuity, while the dances themselves followed a certain formulaic pattern regardless of the subject matter. Stories were told through pantomime, a system of hand gestures, rather than through the dance itself. Heavy masks, wigs and corsets continued to limit movement, and the women's panniered skirts were even more cumbersome than in the previous century.

One choreographer, *Jean-Georges Noverre* (1727–1810), designed reforms to add greater authenticity and expressiveness to ballet. His suggestions made him so unpopular at the Paris Opera that his tenure as ballet master was cut short. He held posts in England, Vienna and Stuttgart, developing a reputation as a passionate and temperamental taskmaster.

Noverre's precepts were delineated in his *Letters on Dancing and Ballet*, published in 1760. Through this book he influenced choreographers of later periods; in the 20th century, his ideas were put into practice by many artists. His precepts are summarized here:

1. Balletic movement should not only be technically brilliant, but should move the audience emotionally through its dramatic expressiveness.

2. The plots of ballets should be unified in design, with logical and understandable stories that contribute to the central theme, and with all solos or other dance sequences that do not relate to the plot eliminated.

3. The scenery, the music, and the plot should all be unified: a reform of costumes was necessary, making them appropriate to the theme of the dance; and music should be specially written so as to be suitable for the dance as well.

4. Pantomime, which had become increasingly conventionalized and meaningless, needed to be made simpler and more understandable.[12]

The 18th century also saw the beginning of rivalries among leading female dancers. Women were beginning to emerge as stars, although the men continued to dominate the stage as directors and choreographers. Two women in particular, *Marie Camargo* (1710–1770) and *Marie Sallé* (1707–1756), developed camps of avid followers for quite different reasons. Camargo was a fine technician who longed for the freedom of movement allowed male dancers. Accordingly, she raised her skirt hems to the ankle, permitting more aerial work and beats of the legs. This caused a sensation and also made her a leader in fashion among highborn women. Sallé, on the other hand, was interested in more natural movement suited to the characters in the ballets. An expressive artist, she often created her own choreography. For her role in *Pygmalion* (London, 1734), she chose to wear a simple Grecian-style drape and even wore her hair loose and unadorned. With these reforms, she predated Noverre and probably influenced him.

MARIE SALLÉ,
the 18th century ballerina
known for her natural
movement and expression.

The great French philosopher and writer Voltaire expressed the contrast between Camargo and Sallé:

> *"Ah! Camargo, how brilliant you are!*
> *But, great gods, how ravishing is also Sallé!*
> *How frivolous are your steps and how gentle are hers.*
> *The one is inimitable and the other so new.*
> *Only nymphs can leap as you do. But the graces dance like her."*[13]

THE ROMANTIC PERIOD

The French Revolution caused a revolution in ballet as well. Ballet in France survived only because the subject matter of this former court entertainment changed radically to suit a new general-public audience. Instead of glorifying royalty, plots in this new period glorified the ordinary citizen and the qualities of innocence, playfulness, loyalty and courage that were evident in their clashes with more powerful people. Rustic comedy ballets such as *La Fille Mal Gardée* (*The Badly Guarded Daughter*, 1789) became popular.

Some realistic works about the French and American Revolutions appeared, as did others that criticized authorities such as the Catholic Church. In many of the more tragic ballets a strong element of the supernatural was present; often justice or the consummation of love, not achieved in life, came as a reward after death. Around the 1820s, ballerinas, cast as supernatural beings, began to rise onto the tips of their toes to enhance the illusion of skimming weightlessly as wilis, ghosts or

FANNY ELSSLER in the ballet *La Chatte Metamorphosée en femme*. Elssler was known for her robust, sensuous dancing.

sylphs—a technique known as dancing *sur les pointes* or on pointe. In the 1860s the dancer's shoes were reinforced to facilitate this skill, allowing for many more movements *en pointe*. To further the illusion of otherworldliness, the heavy fabrics of the previous century's court dresses were replaced by lightweight, diaphanous skirt fabrics, still known as the Romantic ballet skirt.

During this period the ballerina became the central figure of most plots, and audiences rallied around their favorites.

Once again, in the competition between two ballerinas, *Marie Taglioni* (1804–1884) and *Fanny Elssler* (1810–1884), two contrasting styles of dance were presented to the public, each having its fans and champions. Taglioni, shy and round-shouldered, excelled in ballets that emphasized her delicacy and lightness. The most famous was *La Sylphide*, created for her in 1832 by her father, *Filippo Taglioni* (1777–1871). In contrast, the Viennese-born Elssler was a great beauty who was famed for her elevation and passionate dancing. She excelled in choreographed folk dances (called character dances) such as the *Cachucha* and the *Tarantella*. The French poet-journalist Théophile Gautier, who has provided us with detailed descriptions of the ballet of this period, equally appreciated both the otherworldly purity of Taglioni and the earthy sensuousness of Elssler. He says of the rivals:

> Mlle. Taglioni is a Christian dancer . . . she flies like a spirit in the midst of the transparent clouds of white muslin . . . she resembles a happy angel who scarcely bends the petals of celestial flowers with the tips of her pink toes. Fanny [Elssler] is a rather pagan dancer; she reminds one of the muse Terpsichore, tambourine in hand . . . when she bends freely from her hips, throwing back her swooning, voluptuous arms.[14]

In 1837 Taglioni traveled to Russia, where she was received enthusiastically; during her stay she gave more than two hundred performances. The adventurous Fanny Elssler, on the other hand, brought her art to the New World in 1840. Hungry as Americans were for European culture at that time, Elssler's tour caused great excitement. Her coach was pulled through city streets by her admirers and, at one point, the US Congress de-convened in order to attend an Elssler performance. Several American dancers joined her troupe during her two-year visit and received training that furthered their own careers and the growth of the art in America.

It is interesting to note that in Denmark during this same period, ballet was developing along different lines under the aegis of *August Bournonville* (1805–1879), the director of the Royal Danish Ballet. Bournonville studied and performed at the Paris Opera, then returned to his native Copenhagen to serve as its opera ballet director for forty-seven years. He created *La Sylphide, Napoli,* and *Flower Festival in Genzano* for his protégé *Lucile Grahn* (1819–1907).[15] His company developed a more open, less ornamented style than the French, with the male dancer participating more as an equal than just a support designed to lift the ballerina. The Royal Danish Ballet continues to flourish today and is the repository for a number of delightful Bournonville ballets still in their repertory.

MARIE TAGLIONI and SIGNOR GUERRA
in *l'Ombra.*

Jules Perrot (1810–1892) choreographed many ballets in both France and Russia. These ballets, such as *The Bandit's Daughter* (1846), were based on realistic plots. He was also co-choreographer, with *Jean Coralli* (1779–1854), of *Giselle* (1841), the tragic ballet that he created for his favorite pupil, *Carlotta Grisi* (1819–1899). The role of Giselle, a peasant girl who fatally falls in love with a prince, established her career as a consummate actress as well as dancer, and still remains a coveted role for ballerinas.

Perrot created one plotless ballet, *Pas De Quatre* (1845), in which the four best-known ballerinas danced together, each performing a solo in her individual style. To bring Marie Taglioni, the Italian ballerina *Fanny Cerrito* (1817–1909), Lucile Grahn, and Carlotta Grisi together on the same stage in London required a marvel of tact on the part of Perrot. Although an immediate success, *Pas de Quatre* was danced only four times by the original cast; it has since been restaged by many ballet companies.

Musical extravaganzas began to appear in America, with rudimentary ballet sequences included for the *corps de ballet* and as many European guest stars as possible. Most successful of these was *The Black Crook*, a melodrama that opened in New York in 1866 and featured a succession of European ballerinas and a corps de ballet of American dancers. *The Black Crook* continued to run in New York in one form or another for the next forty years.

THE CLASSICAL PERIOD

During the second half of the 19th century, there was a gradual shift of the center of ballet activity from France to Russia. Once again, an important reason for the shift was royal patronage, this time offered by the opulent court of the Romanov family in Imperial Russia. In their desire to westernize their court Romanov rulers, known as czars or tsars (or czarinas or tsarinas) beginning with Peter the Great (1672–1725), began inviting artists from Western Europe to Russia. Many artists—musicians, poets, jewelers and painters as well as dancers, dance instructors and choreographers—gravitated to this court, which strove to be both lavish and culturally admirable.

A young Frenchman, *Marius Petipa* (1818–1910), arrived in Russia in 1847 to dance at the Imperial Theater. His father, Jean, had already taught at the Imperial School, and his fellow-Frenchmen Jules Perrot and *Arthur Saint-Léon* were already working in the Imperial Theater. Petipa became a ballet master there in 1862, and chief ballet master in 1869. He officially retired in 1903 from the Imperial Theaters in St. Petersburg (its Bolshoi and Maryinsky theaters). Petipa created seventy-seven works, including revisions of older classics and divertissements, and composed thirty-seven opera dances. Called the classical period, this was truly a golden age for ballet in Russia, in which ballet technique took a giant step forward. Aerial work, pointe work, turns and leg beats (*batterie*) increased in scope. The development of the short skirt, or "tutu," which enabled the audience to see more easily the advances in technique for female dancers, is associated with this period.

While many of Petipa's ballets retained the story lines of the Romantic era, he was careful not to offend his imperial patrons with royal villains, such as those found in *Giselle*; evil witches or sorcerers filled the villain roles in his stories. Many of his ballets culminated in a lavish court scene for the final act, in which, if there was a happy ending, the protagonists were blessed by the king and queen. His ballets, including *Don Quixote* (1869) and *La Bayadère* (1877), continue to be performed today by major American and European companies.

Americans are especially familiar with the three most widely performed ballets associated with Petipa with scores by Peter Ilyich Tchaikovsky. Petipa choreographed *The Sleeping Beauty* (1890) alone. *The Nutcracker* (1892) was his idea, but owing to illness he turned much of the choreography over to his Russian assistant, *Lev Ivanov* (1834–1901). *Swan Lake* (1895) was co-choreographed by Petipa and Ivanov, who did Acts 2 and 4, the lakeside scenes.

SWAN LAKE pas de deux with Patricia McBride and Conrad Ludlow.

Initially, *The Nutcracker* was not well received in Russia; critics said the story was not serious enough for a full-length ballet. However, its charming Christmas-fantasy theme, numerous children's roles and beautiful musical score have made it the most frequently produced ballet in America and a holiday tradition. The ballet was first brought to America by the Russian ballerina *Alexandra Fedorova*, sister of Mikhail Fokine (see the following paragraph). She staged a one-act version of the original Petipa/Ivanov choreography for the Ballet Russes de Monte Carlo, which premiered in New York in 1940. George Balanchine's popular full-length version did not appear until 1954. (See next section on dance in the early 20th century.)

EARLY 20TH CENTURY BALLET

The Diaghilev Era

Early in the 20th century, ballet began to change radically. While the classics from the 19th century continued to be performed, many new ballets with new motivations were developed that were radical departures from Petipa. New social orders, world wars and the demise of more and more royal families plus the influence of the new modern dance movement (discussed in the next chapter) resulted in new styles and subject matter in the ballet world. Perhaps the most influential pioneer of these departures was a man who was himself not a dancer or a choreographer, but a farsighted arts patron and entrepreneur, the Russian *Serge Diaghilev* (1872–1929). Diaghilev was a young member of the Russian nobility with a strong interest in all the arts. This interest motivated him to present a season of Russian ballet in Paris in 1909, using young Russian composers, visual artists and choreographers and leading dancers from the Imperial Ballet. This first season consisted mostly of the works of *Mikhail Fokine* (1880–1942), which were so well received that, in 1911, Diaghilev decided to move his Ballets Russes (Russian Ballet) company permanently to the Europe. He signed a financially attractive contract with the principality of Monaco, and moved his company to the principality's capital city, Monte Carlo, rather than return to the revolutionary turmoil developing in Russia.

Fokine welcomed Diaghilev's encouragement for his innovative ideas, as he was not able to put many of them into practice in Russia. He had begun choreographing while he was still a dancer at the Maryinsky Theater in St. Petersburg, and felt that the Russian choreographers in charge of the Imperial Ballet had stagnated. He developed some basic principles to reform ballet, which were surprisingly similar to the reforms of Noverre two centuries earlier. He felt that ballet's purpose was to reveal emotions rather than show off physical prowess, and that the movements should reflect the period and location of the action. He wanted all of the elements of the ballet, including the work of the corps de ballet, to coalesce into a total theatrical event. Finally, he wanted to eliminate the use of mime to tell the story, so that the movement itself reveals the drama. All of these concepts added freshness to his work and served to revitalize ballet choreography.

Fokine set many ballets for Diaghilev's star performer *Vaslav Nijinsky* (1889–1950), whose spectacular leaps and dramatic presence drew large audiences in Europe. Fokine's ballets for Nijinsky included *Prince Igor, Les Sylphides* and *Cléopâtre* (1909), *Carnaval, Schéhérazade* and *Firebird* (all 1910), *Petrouchka* and *Le Spectre de la Rose* (1911), *Daphnis and Chloe* (1912) and *Le Coq d'Or* (1914). All of these were sufficiently exotic and colorful to thrill the audiences in Paris and other Western cities . . .

MIKHAIL (or MICHEL, as he was known in other parts of the world) FOKINE as the Golden Slave in *Schéhérezade*, Diaghilev's Ballet Russes.

But in 1912 Diaghilev replaced Fokine as choreographer with Vaslav Nijinsky, and the Parisian audience's mood of acceptance took a sharp turn. Known as a stunning classical dancer, Nijinsky took a completely different tack in his own choreography. In *Afternoon of a Faun* (1912), set to the music of Debussy, Nijinsky contradicted the classical positions by making all steps and gestures parallel instead of turned out to evoke the flatness of Greek vase paintings. The sensuality of the central figure, very understated by modern standards, was shocking to the audiences of the period. A year later, he made an even more forceful statement in *Rite of Spring* (1913), set to a complex score by Igor Stravinsky. The unusual theme of the ballet was an ancient fertility ritual set in prehistoric Russia, in which the chosen virgin is forced to dance herself to death. This work so shocked and antagonized the conservative audience on opening night that it caused a riot in the theater. [16]

His work was a precursor of modern dance long before that name was even invented. Nijinsky produced only two more ballets, *Jeux* (1913) a love-triangle performed in tennis attire, and *Till Eulenspiegel* (1916), created for the American tour. In 1916 the company made its first tour to the US A falling-out with Diaghilev over his marriage to Romola Nijinska ended his career. Left with no opportunities to perform or choreograph, and deteriorating mental health, Nijinsky spent most of his remaining years in a sanitorium.

Nijinsky was replaced by *Leonide Massine* (1895–1979), who was recruited by Diaghilev at the age of 19. Massine was a dynamic performer and the creator of the innovative works including *Parade* (1917), costumed by Pablo Picasso. Nijinsky's sister *Bronislava Nijinska* also choreographed for Diaghilev.

In 1923 a young choreographer named *George Balanchine* (1904–1983) left the Soviet Union and was invited to audition for Diaghilev's Ballets Russes in Paris. He was hired as ballet master. For Diaghilev, Balanchine created ten new works, including *Apollo* (1928) and *Prodigal Son* (1929), later produced in America (and still in the repertory of the New York City Ballet). After Diaghilev's death in 1929, Balanchine worked in Europe on a variety of projects, including a short-lived company of his own in Paris in 1933.

In the early 1930s, a young American entrepreneur *Lincoln Kirstein* (1907–1996) persuaded Balanchine to come to America to create an American ballet company. They began with a school, the School of American Ballet, which opened January 1, 1934, and remains a major school today. The following year, Balanchine initiated a performing group called American Ballet, later to become Ballet Caravan, Ballet Society and finally New York City Ballet. Today, New York City Ballet is one of the largest and most prestigious ballet companies in the world, celebrating the 60th anniversary of its first performance in 2008, and Balanchine ballets have become a global phenomenon and cultural institution.

The American public was first exposed to good ballet by *Anna Pavlova* (1881–1931), a Russian ballerina whose company toured America and the world extensively until her death. Pavlova had left Russia at Diaghilev's invitation in 1911, danced for him briefly, then formed her own company of mostly English dancers and began her worldwide touring. For many Americans in small towns and cities, the name Pavlova became synonymous with ballet. A consummate actress, she is most often remembered for a poignant solo created for her by Michael Fokine, *The Dying Swan* (1907), which consisted of simple traveling movements on pointe combined with the subtle use of her arms and hands as wings. So expressive was her performance that audiences were reduced to tears by the end.

The Diaghilev company made one tour of America in 1916. Although they performed only in the largest American cities, their influence was dramatic in the young country. In fact, Diaghilev's sudden death in 1929 caused many ballet fans to believe that the art of ballet outside of Russia was finished. Such was not to be the case.

The Ballet Russe Wars

Diaghilev's death caused a dispersal of his talented company members through Europe, the British Isles and the Americas, where many became founders of their own ballet companies or teachers of Russian ballet technique in their new homelands. It also prompted various splinter companies to become rivals for the Ballets Russes legacy.

The Russian Colonel *Wassily de Basil* and his partner, Frenchman René Blum, organized the Ballet Russes de Monte Carlo in 1932, but changed the name to the Ballet Russe de Monte Carlo the following year. They were given rights to perform in the Monte Carlo Opera Theater, and even brought Diaghilev's sets and costumes out of storage. George Balanchine was hired as director of choreography for the first season. He made the daring move of hiring three young Russian girls living in Paris—two of them only thirteen years old—to be his stars. They were nicknamed his "baby ballerinas." Most of its repertory consisted of revivals of the Diaghilev-era works with a few new additions. The following year he was replaced by Leonide Massine, who choreographed many new ballets and was still an active and charismatic performer. Bronislava Nijinska and Mikhail Fokine also came to Monte Carlo as guest choreographers, and Nijinsky's *Afternoon of a Faun* was added to the repertory.

In 1934 the Ballet Russe de Monte Carlo toured America successfully, sponsored by the Russian-American entrepreneur, Sol Hurok. Massine and de Basil, however, were at odds on many issues. By 1938 Massine was ready to form his own company, taking with him many stars, including George Zoritch, Alicia Markova, Alexandra Danilova and Marc Platt, the first American in the company. In the ensuing legal tangle, Massine won the right to call his company the Ballet Russe de Monte Carlo, but lost the rights to his own choreography created while working for de Basil. Massine chose Serge Denham to manage the new company. De Basil countered by calling his company the Original Ballet Russe, but was left without an artistic director. For the 1938 season, Sol Hurok chose to sponsor Massine's company on another American tour. Since Hurok booked virtually every major theater in the US, an American tour was impossible for the de Basil company. Instead, they toured Australia for seven months, stimulating a surge of interest in ballet in that country, and the opening of several ballet schools.

Both companies found themselves in London the summer of 1939, but plans for returning to Monte Carlo and Paris came to an abrupt end due to the aggressive actions of Adolph Hitler and the advancing Nazi army. With seventeen nationalities represented among the dancers, both companies were desperate to get away from the war. Ironically, both companies found themselves on the same ship to America, where Massine's company immediately started a whistle-stop tour of the US, and de Basil's company launched a tour of the unchartered dance territory of Latin America. After four years in Latin America, enduring wartime shortages, the dancers were exhausted; but instead of resting they came to America and began extensive touring. Critics did not receive them well, comparing them unfavorably to the resident New York company, Ballet Theatre—later renamed American Ballet Theatre. This plucky group, with many American principal dancers in its ranks, listed 21 ballets in its initial season, including six world premieres and five American premieres. It continues to thrive as a world-class company today, performing both the classics and contemporary ballets.

De Basil's company struggled on for several years, but the death of de Basil in 1951 brought the final curtain down. Massine's company fared better, with several dancers making solo appearances in Hollywood films, and the entire company appearing on Broadway in "Song of Norway" (1944). They also formed a Ballet Russe School in New York in 1954. But in 1960 Serge Denham fired Massine and made himself artistic director of the company. A series of poor artistic decisions followed, and the company gave its last performance in April of 1962 at the Brooklyn Academy of Music.

Thus, two companies called Ballet Russe who never performed in Russia, went down in history as pioneers of Russian ballet on four continents—Europe, North America, South America and Australia.

FURTHER DEVELOPMENTS IN AMERICA AND EUROPE

The first ballet company to be permanently located in America was formed in 1933 by the Diaghilev star *Adolph Bolm* (1884–1951). Bolm started it under the aegis of the San Francisco Opera as the San Francisco Opera Ballet: eventually it became the San Francisco Ballet. Bolm was also instrumental in establishing a ballet company in Chicago.

Ballet in England was launched by *Marie Rambert* (1888–1982). A Polish-born dancer, Rambert was hired by Diaghilev to teach Dalcroze eurhythmics (see page 64) to his dancers. Rambert moved to London and opened a school there in 1920. She formed the Ballet Club in 1930, which later became Ballet Rambert. In addition to her own choreography, Rambert nurtured the work of Antony Tudor, Frederick Ashton and *Norman Morrice* (b. 1931). Morrice later became co-director of the company, and in 1966 Rambert and Morrice changed the company profile to contemporary dance, requiring its members to be proficient in both ballet and modern dance. The company changed its name to Rambert Dance Company in 1987 to emphasize its commitment to contemporary choreography.

In Russia, where classical traditions are so strong, two major ballet companies and schools have survived both the Russian Revolution and the fall of the Soviet Union. The Bolshoi Ballet in Moscow has a style that emphasizes strong flexible backs, vigorous high leaps and very dramatic presentations. The Kirov in St. Petersburg, on the other hand, produces dancers known for their musicality, lyrical style and purity of line. The Kirov has also groomed most of the new Russian choreographers. These companies still favor the production of full-length classical ballets, but visits by George Balanchine in the 1960s stimulated interest in programs of new, shorter works.

Under the Soviet system, dancers in Russia were guaranteed steady work, medical coverage, salary increases and retirement benefits. The Bolshoi and Kirov continue to provide live-in schooling for talented children from the age of seven. However, since the demise of the Soviet system, the Russian dancers' lives have come to resemble those of western dancers—much more uncertainty combined with more exposure to new artistic ideas and options. Russia also has many smaller companies, many of which have begun considerable touring in Europe and the United States.

With the establishment of Britain's Royal Ballet, England joined Denmark and Sweden as a nation with a royal family acting as patrons for the art. Under the direction of *Ninette de Valois*, a British dancer who trained under Diaghilev, the company known as Saddler's Wells Ballet in London eventually became the Royal Ballet of England. In 1948, many of her dancers appeared in "The Red Shoes" (1948), choreographed by Robert Helpmann (see biography below) and starring the beautiful Scottish ballerina *Moira Shearer* (1926–2006). The film was about obsession with ballet, and featured a didactic director who was modeled after Diaghilev.

Other European countries that no longer had royal families, including France, Germany and Russia, also followed this tradition by supporting ballet with public funds. Although Americans admired and copied European ballet, they did not copy the tradition of state-supported ballet companies.

During the second half of the 20th century, ballet began a process of changing even more profoundly. This process continues into the present, as ballet blends and intertwines with modern dance, jazz and ethnic forms. The story of this development of ballet continues in chapter 7.

OTHER BALLET NOTABLES, 18TH THROUGH EARLY 20TH CENTURY

Alicia Alonso (b. 1921) danced with Ballet Caravan and American Ballet Theatre. In 1948 she founded the Ballet Alicia Alonso in her native Cuba with her then husband *Fernando Alonso* (b. 1914). Under the Castro regime it became the Ballet Nacional de Cuba, a company that emphasizes the classics. In 1941, Alonso underwent the first of several eye operations for detached retinas, none of which fully improved her vision. After the last one in 1943, she was forced to lie in bed for a year without moving her head; her husband visited her daily and they rehearsed principal roles by humming the scores and moving their hands. When she was released from the hospital, she went on to serve as prima ballerina, general director, and artistic director of the National Ballet of Cuba into the 1990s. Today, the company is coming out of its cultural isolation and participating in collaborative artistic ventures. The school in Havana continues to produce outstanding dancers that have joined prestigious companies around the world.

Frederick Ashton (1904–1988), a British choreographer who began his career with Ballet Rambert, making his first work for Rambert's troupe in 1926. Joining Ninette de Valois' Royal Ballet in 1935, he remained with the Royal Ballet for the rest of his career and is considered the creator of British ballet classicism. Ashton became artistic director of the Royal Ballet in 1965. His choreography emphasizes emotional content rather than technical virtuosity. His works include *Façade* (1931), *A Wedding Bouquet* (1937), *Les Patineurs* (The Skaters) (1937). *Cinderella* (1948), *Romeo and Juliet* (1955), *Ondine* (1958), a joyous resetting of *La Fille Mal Gardée* (1960), *Marguerite and Armand* (1963) and *The Dream* (1964). He also set works for the New York City Ballet and the Royal Danish Ballet and choreographed the popular ballet films "The Tales of Hoffman" (1951) and "Tales of Beatrix Potter" (1971). Stars were born through his sensitive choreography, especially Margot Fonteyn.

Carlo Blasis (1797–1878). A talented dancer from an Italian family of dancers, while still quite young (1820) Blasis wrote *Elementary Treatise Upon the Theory and Practice of the Art of Dancing*. This was followed by the *Code of Terpsichore* in 1828, which encapsulated his philosophy and methods for training dancers. Blasis and his wife became teachers at the Imperial Academy of Dance in Milan in 1837, where he was made director. During his directorate Milan became the leading ballet academy in Europe, and sent master teachers far afield to spread the Italian technique. Blasis himself taught in Russia from 1861 to 1864.

Enrico Cecchetti (1850–1928), an outstanding ballet teacher whose training methods are still in use today. Born into a family of Italian dancers, Cecchetti went to St. Petersburg to study. He became a principal dancer then ballet master for the Imperial Ballet, and later for the Diaghilev Ballets Russes. Anna Pavlova, Nijinsky and Nijinska, Tamara Karsavina, Serge Lifar, Massine and Vaganova were among his pupils. He then opened a school in London, where his principals, based on a thorough understanding of each ballet exercise to develop balance, strength, elevation and flexibility were codified by two of his students in a manual. The Cecchetti Society was established in England in 1922 to further his training methods. Margaret Craske, one of his British students, moved to New York and opened a school, and in 1939 the Cecchetti Council of America was formed. Today the Cecchetti System is taught all over the world.

The *Christensen* brothers, *Lew* (1909–1984), *Harold* (1904–1989) and *William* (1902–2001), born in Utah, founded the San Francisco Ballet School in the 1930s. Lew, who studied with Balanchine and danced in his company, became a soloist for Ballet Caravan, where he choreographed several pieces with American themes such as *Pocahontas* (1936) and *Filling Station* (1938). In 1951 he became artistic director of the San Francisco Ballet and remained at that post for many years. William formed the first ballet curriculum at the University of Utah, and incorporated the professional company known as Ballet West in 1957.

Birgit Cullberg (1908–1999), a Swedish choreographer, rose to prominence in the 1950s, a time when female ballet choreographers were not often taken seriously. Her outstanding works include *Miss Julie* and *Medea* (both 1950), *Moon Reindeer* (1957) and *Lady from the Sea* (1960). In addition to mounting ballets for the Royal Swedish Ballet, many of her works were set for other companies, including American Ballet Theatre.

Alexandra Danilova (1903–1997). A ballerina trained in the St. Petersburg school (now Kirov), Danilova left Russia with George Balanchine and danced for Diaghilev during his company's later years. Danilova became the leading ballerina of the Ballet Russe de Monte Carlo under the artistic direction of Léonide Massine. After retirement as a dancer, she continued to teach and coach in New York. In 1979 Danilova appeared in the film "The Turning Point," playing herself.

Jean Dauberval (1742–1806), French dance and choreographer, was a pupil of Noverre's, one of the few to put his teacher's reforms into practice. He choreographed *La Fille Mal Gardée* which premiered in Bordeaux in 1786, making it the oldest ballet still performed today. Dauberval also served as ballet master in Madrid.

Ninette de Valois (1898–2001), Irish-born, danced with Diaghilev's company for two seasons, was invited to form a London-based company in 1935, first known as the Vic-Wells Ballet, then Sadler's Wells Ballet and finally, in 1957, the Royal Ballet. De Valois, who created more than thirty ballets of her own, attracted gifted choreographers like Frederick Ashton, Kenneth MacMillan (see their biographies in this chapter) and *John Cranko* 1927–1973) to the company. Several stars of de Valois' company also appeared in the British film "The Red Shoes," a movie that brought ballet to many new audiences, proving a film about ballet could be commercially successful. Today the Royal Ballet is internationally recognized, and continues to mount full-evening classics as well as newer experimental works.

Charles Didelot (1767–1837), French choreographer, was the first western European to be invited to the Russian court to revitalize ballet. His reforms set the basis for the St. Petersburg style. Arriving in 1815, he choreographed twenty ballets for the tsars and dramatically improved ballet training in Russia. Didelot's ballets frequently used flying wires and platforms for special effects, in addition to the new pointe work.

Margot Fonteyn (1919–1991). Ballerina of the Royal Ballet, Fonteyn began dancing in the 1940s. The New York critic Clive Barnes said of her, "She was British ballet almost before there was British ballet . . . an example, a statement, and a personal miracle."[16] Frederick Ashton created *Ondine* for her in 1958, but she is best remembered in the role of Aurora, the princess in *The Sleeping Beauty*. A successful partnership with Rudolf Nureyev in the 1960s rejuvenated her performing career. She retired in 1979 after a 45-year performing career and tumultuous, tabloid-headline life, and lived in Panama with her husband, the diplomat Roberto Arias. During the last three years of her life, she reconstructed a full-length classic for the Houston Ballet, *Sleeping Beauty*, and also coached their dancers in *Swan Lake*.

Frederick Franklin (b.1914), a native of Liverpool, he danced in his early years with Bronislava Nijinska, Alexandra Danilova, Josephine Baker in Paris, and the Markova-Dolin Ballet in London. Between 1937 and 1968, he served as a principal dancer and ballet master for the Ballet Russe de

Monte Carlo School in New York. He also held the post of artistic director of the National Ballet in Washington during the entire life of that company, 1963 to 1974. In later life he staged many of the ballets from this company in the US and England, thanks to his nearly photographic memory for choreography, and performed mime roles for American Ballet Theater in classics such as *Swan Lake* and *Romeo and Juliet*.

Yuri Grigorovitch (b. 1927). A Kirov-trained dancer, Grigorovich became director of the Bolshoi Ballet in 1967. He produced the epic *Spartacus* (1968) for the company, followed by several other lavish full-length ballets. Grigorovich resigned from the Bolshoi in 1995 to form his own company, Grigorovitch Ballet of Russia.

Robert Helpmann (1909–1986), an Australian dancer and choreographer who moved to England and became noted for character roles in the Sadler's Wells Ballet. He was the choreographer for the film "The Red Shoes" which was not a hit in England but was widely shown in the United States, stimulating many young girls to train in ballet. The Helpmann Academy, a partnership of visual and performing arts in South Australia, was named after him.

David Howard (b. 1930s). A soloist with the Royal Ballet of England before joining the National Ballet of Canada, he returned to Europe to dance in a series of variety entertainments. After retiring from performing, Howard was named the director of the Harkness School in New York in 1966. He became an internationally known coach, guest teacher, and festival adjudicator and served as president of the National Association for Regional Ballet in the 1970s. In 1986 he opened his eminent ballet school in New York, the David Howard Dance Center.

Nora Kaye (1920–1987), American dancer, was a well-known interpreter of Antony Tudor's work. In 1942 Tudor created the role of Hagar in his ballet *Pillar of Fire* for her. The wife of choreographer and producer Herbert Ross, she shared several producing and directing projects with him.

Mary Ann Lee (1823–1899) was an American ballerina who trained in the US with European teachers. When Fanny Elssler arrived in America for her two-year tour, Lee attempted to rival her popularity.

Catherine Littlefield (1905–1951). Founder of the Philadelphia Ballet, Littlefield is credited with presenting the first full-length *Sleeping Beauty* in America. Hers was also the first American ballet company to appear in France and England.

Eugene Loring (c.1911–1982) trained at Balanchine's School of American Ballet during the Great Depression, and joined his company, then called Ballet Caravan in 1936. Three years later he created *Billy the Kid*, a cowboy ballet. This dramatic story-ballet became Ballet Caravan's greatest success, and later was adopted into the repertory of American Ballet Theater. Loring also choreographed

Broadway musicals, including "Carmen Jones," "Silk Stockings," and "Funny Face." In the 1950s he moved to Hollywood to direct the American School of Dance.

Kenneth MacMillan (1929–1992) began mounting works for England's Royal Ballet under Ninette de Valois in 1952, and created full-length ballets such as *Romeo and Juliet* (1965) as well as shorter, psychologically probing modern works like his shocking final ballet, *The Judas Tree* (1992). MacMillan became artistic director of the company, succeeding Frederick Ashton.

Augusta Maywood (1825–1876), the first internationally known American ballerina, studied with Paul Hazard in Philadelphia, making her debut in 1837 at the age of twelve. Two years later she appeared at the Paris Opera, receiving enthusiastic reviews for her robust style and elevated leaps. She became a celebrated ballerina in Milan and Vienna during the last years of the Romantic period. In 1859 she and her second husband opened a ballet school in Vienna, where she continued to choreograph.

Natalia Makarova (b. 1940). A Russian ballerina who defected to the West in 1970, Makarova was noted for her sensitivity to dramatic roles and exquisite lyrical technique. She performed extensively with American Ballet Theatre and mounted several classics, including Petipa's *La Bayadère*, on Western companies.

Alicia Markova (1910–2004). Née Alice Marks, Markova was the first British-born ballerina. As a teenager, she danced in Diaghilev's company and then, with her partner *Anton Dolin* (1904–1983), formed the Markova-Dolin Ballet in London (1935–1937). The company disbanded when Markova signed a contract with Leonide Massine's Ballet Russe de Monte Carlo as prima ballerina. Later she appeared as a guest with the Royal Danish Ballet and the Royal Ballet of England and served briefly as artistic director of the Metropolitan Opera Ballet in New York. She is especially remembered for her portrayal of *Giselle*, which earned acceptance of this ballet for 20th century audiences.

Leonide Massine (1895–1979), a graduate of the Moscow school of the Imperial Russian Ballet, was invited by Diaghilev to join his company as a dancer. His first solo part was that of Joseph in *The Legend of Joseph*, choreographed by Fokine. He choreographed for Diaghilev from 1915 to 1928, and is credited with developing the symphonic ballet as a separate form. He choreographed over fifty ballets in his lifetime, most as the artistic director of the Ballet Russe de Monte Carlo. These include the first ballet done to symphonic music, *Symphonie Fantastique*, disapproved of by the London music critics but a major hit with the London ballet audience. His *Parade*, with decor and costumes by Pablo Picasso, was not a hit in 1917, but was revived successfully in the 1973 by the Joffrey Ballet.

Mikhail Mordkin (1881–1944), one of Anna Pavlova's partners, settled in New York, forming the Mordkin Ballet which later became Ballet Theatre. This company, which grew considerably over the next two decades under the direction of Richard Pleasant and Lucia Chase, presented works of Russian, American, and British choreographers. As the American Ballet Theatre it remains a major force in the world of ballet.

Bronislava Nijinska (1891– 1972), Vaslav Nijinsky's sister, became principal choreographer for Diaghilev's Ballet Russes replacing her brother. She was a highly innovative choreographer in her own right. Her choreography was more balletic than Vaslav's and therefore more acceptable to the western audiences—for example *Les Noces*, (1923) a piece about a wedding in Russia from the points of view of both bride and groom. She was replaced by George Balanchine in 1925.

Rudolf Nureyev (1938–1993). A dancer from the Soviet Union who defected in 1961 and developed a career in the West, Nureyev danced extensively with the Royal Ballet, National Ballet of Canada and American Ballet Theatre. His elegant dancing and dynamic presence quickly made him a ballet superstar. He is best known for a long-lasting partnership with Margot Fonteyn, which greatly furthered both their careers. Later in his career, Nureyev directed the Paris Opera Ballet until his death from AIDS.

Ruth Page (1900–1991). Founder of the Chicago Opera Ballet, Page danced with Diaghilev's Ballets Russes in Monte Carlo. Her company performed classics as well as her own choreography, such as *Frankie and Johnny* (1938), which favored American themes.

Roland Petit (1924–) modernized the French ballet aesthetic in the mid-20th century. His extremely popular version of *Carmen* (1949), created for his wife Renée "Zizi" Jeanmaire, has been set for the Royal Ballet of England and other companies.

Arthur Saint-Leon (1821–1870), a versatile Frenchman who had careers as a dancer, choreographer and violinist in France and in Russia, created one of the last and best-loved comic ballets of the Romantic era, *Coppelia,* also titled *The Girl with Enamel Eyes* (1870). The ballet's lively choreography and plot, featuring a clever peasant girl who outwits an elderly alchemist, was well received at the Paris Opera. Both the leading ballerina and Saint-Léon himself died within months of the ballet's debut. Soon afterward, ballet in France went into a period of decline.

George Washington Smith (1820–1899), considered America's first male ballet star, joined Elssler's troupe during her American tour. He continued his career in pantomimes in Philadelphia, specializing in the role of Harlequin, and later performed in opera. Smith became Mary Ann Lee's favorite partner, and in 1846 the couple appeared in the first American production of *Giselle* in Boston.

Maria Tallchief (b. 1925). A preeminent Native American–born ballerina, Tallchief studied with Bronislava Nijinska in California. She danced with the Ballet Russe de Monte Carlo, studying during that time with Mia Slavenska, then joined New York City Ballet in its earliest years and became George Balanchine's third wife. After retiring from performing, she began teaching in Chicago and formed the Chicago City Ballet in the 1980s. Her sister Marjorie was also a gifted dancer.

Antony Tudor (1909–1987), a British choreographer. As a teenager, he watched Serge Diaghilev's Ballet Russes and became entranced by dance in general. Tudor began studying ballet with Marie Rambert, and his performing career began as a dancer for Marie Rambert's Ballet Club. For Rambert, he created several dramatic ballets, including *Lilac Garden* and *Dark Elegies*. In 1938 Tudor formed his own company, the London Ballet, and produced several works in a lighter vein, including *The Judgment of Paris* and *Gala Performance*. His ballets, especially those that explore psychological themes through expressive movement, found a responsive public in the United States when he became a choreographer for the new Ballet Theatre company. Tudor's works, such as *Lilac Garden, Undertow*, and *Pillar of Fire* helped to revolutionize ballet by replacing princes and princesses with ordinary people. At the Tudor birthday centennial at New York's City Center, the above-mentioned ballets were performed, along with lesser-known Tudor works—*Continuo, The Leaves are Fading*, and *Romeo and Juliet pas de deux*.

Galina Ulanova (1910–1998). The first Bolshoi Ballet ballerina to be acclaimed by the West since the Russian Revolution, Ulanova danced with the Bolshoi from 1944 to 1962. She was featured in the Bolshoi's first London tour in 1956 and its first American tour three years later. In spite of her advanced age, she won unanimous acclaim as *Giselle* and as Juliet in *Romeo and Juliet*. Arnold Haskell called Ulanova "the spiritual child of Pavlova and Duncan . . . she is the Dance."[17] She died at the age of eighty-eight.

Agrippina Vaganova (1879–1951). Considered the greatest Russian teacher of her day, Vaganova became a ballerina for the Imperial Ballet in 1915, retiring two years later to become a teacher. She is credited with formulating the training methods that made the Kirov Ballet company great. Vaganova's successful methods are outlined in her *Fundamentals of the Classic Dance*, published in 1934. The Agrippina Vaganova Choreographic Institute is still located in St. Petersburg.

Gaetan Vestris 1729–1808) and *Auguste Vestris* (1760–1842), father and son from a prestigious Florentine family of dancers and choreographers. Gaetan was involved in the choreography and production of ballets in Italy, while Auguste was a strong technician and a noted teacher, credited with launching the lyrical French style. His pupils included Fanny Elssler and Jules Perrot.

SOME BALLET TERMINOLOGY

Adagio ✎ slow, sustained movement; the opening section of a duet

Allegro ✎ fast movements, including leaps, turns and beats

Arabesque ✎ pose on one leg, the other extended backward with a straight knee

Attitude ✎ pose on one leg, the other lifted behind with bent knee

Ballet blanc ✎ "white ballet," in which female dancers appear in white dresses or tutus, as sylphs, wilis or other supernatural creatures

Barre ✎ bar used for warm-up exercises in class

Beats (batterie) ✎ hitting the legs together while in the air

Character dance ✎ folk dances used in ballets, often blended with ballet steps

Corps de ballet ✎ the chorus of female and/or male dancers, background to the principal dancers

Demi-caractère ✎ name applied to personality roles, such as the stepsisters in Cinderella, the alchemist in Coppelia or the witch in Sleeping Beauty. Often they are women's roles played by men.

Grand pas de deux ✎ a suite of dances from the Classical period consisting of a partnered adagio, the male solo, the female solo, and a lively finale danced together.

Mime, pantomime ✎ a system of storytelling gestures found in ballets of the Romantic and Classical periods

Pas ✎ literally, "step;" pas de deux is a duet, pas de trois is a trio, etc.

Pointe (en pointe) ✎ dancing on the tips of the toes, using specially designed toe shoes

Premier danseur ✎ the highest rank for a male ballet dancer

Prima ballerina, prima ballerina assoluta ✎ the highest rank for a female ballet dancer

Turnout ✎ refers to the outward rotation of the legs from the hips, used exclusively in all ballets until some Twentieth-century choreographers began to add other leg rotations.

Tutu ✎ the short, layered ballet skirt still seen in classical ballet

SUGGESTED READING

Algeranoff, Harcourt. *My Years With Pavlova*. Melbourne, Australia: Wm. Heinemann, Ltd., 1957.

Anderson, Jack. *Ballet and Modern Dance: A Concise History*, 2nd ed. Hightstown, NJ: Princeton Book Company, Publishers, 1992.

———. *The One and Only: The Ballet Russe de Monte Carlo*. New York: Dance Horizons, 1981.

Beaumont, Cyril. *Michel Fokine and His Ballets* (1935). Reprint, New York: Dance Horizons, 1981.

Bland, Alexander. *A History of Ballet and Dance in the Western World*. New York: Praeger Publishers, 1976.

———. *The Nureyev Image*, New York: Quadrangle, 1976.

Blasis, Carlo. *An Elementary Treatise Upon the Theory and Practice of the Art of Dancing*. Trans. Mary Stewart Evans. New York: Dover Publications, 1968.

Martha Bremser. ed. *International Dictionary of Ballet*. 2 vols. Detroit/London: St. James Press, 1993.

Dance Magazine, January 2007. *Cecchetti's Choices*, pp. 214–216.

Cohen, Selma Jeanne. *Dance as a Theatre Art: Source Readings in Dance History from 1581 to the Present*. New York: Dodd, Mead & Company, 1974. 2nd ed., Princeton: Princeton Book Co., 1992.

———, ed. *International Encyclopedia of Dance*. New York: Oxford University Press, 1998.

Fonteyn, Margot. *The Magic of Dance*. New York: Knopf, 1979.

Garafola, Lynn. *Diaghilev's Ballets Russes*. New York: Oxford University Press, 1989.

———, ed. *Rethinking the Sylph: New Perspectives on the Romantic Ballet*. Hanover, NH: University Press of New England/Studies in Dance History. Wesleyan University Press, 1997.

Gadan, Francis, Robert Maillard, and Selma Jeanne Cohen, eds. *Dictionary of Modern Ballet*. New York: Tudor Publishing Co., 1959.

Greskovic, Robert. *Ballet 101: A Complete Guide to Learning and Loving the Ballet*. New York: Hyperion, 1998.

Grigoriev, S.L. *The Diaghilev Ballet: 1909–1929*. Harmondsworth, Eng.: Penguin Books, 1960.

Gruen, John. *The World's Great Ballets*. New York: Harry N. Abrams, 1981.

Jonas, Gerald. *Dancing: The Pleasure, Power, and Art of Movement*. New York: Harry N. Abrams, 1992.

Joseph, Charles M. *Stravinsky and Balanchine: A Journey of Invention*. New York University Press, 2002.

Kirstein, Lincoln. Dance: *A Short History of Classic Theatrical Dancing* (1935). Reprint, New York: Dance Horizons, 1969.

Kraus, Richard, Sarah Hilsendager, and Brenda Dixon. *History of Dance in Art and Education*, 3rd ed. Englewood Cliffs, NJ: Prentice Hall, 1991.

Le Clercq, Tanaquil. *The Ballet Cook Book* New York: Stein and Day, 1966.

Lee, Carol. *Ballet in Western Culture*. Boston: Allyn and Bacon, 1999.

Martin, John. *The Story of Dance in Pictures and Text*. New York: Tudor, 1946.

McConnell, Joan. *Ballet as Body Language*. New York: Harper and Row, 1977.

McDonagh, Don. *How to Enjoy Ballet*. Garden City, NY: Doubleday, 1978.

Migel, Parmenia. *The Ballerinas: From the Court of Louis XIV to Pavlova*. New York: Macmillan, 1972.

Mondadori, Arnoldo, ed. *The Simon and Schuster Book of the Ballet*. New York: Simon and Schuster, 1979.

Montague, Sarah. *The Ballerina*. New York: Universe Books, 1980.

Noverre, Jean-Georges. *Letters on Dancing and Ballets*. Trans. by Cyril W. Beaumont. London: Beaumont, 1930; reprint, Brooklyn, NY: Dance Horizons, 1975.

Pagels, Jurgen. *Character Dance*. Bloomington: Indiana University Press, 1984.

Petipa, Marius. *Russian Ballet Master: The Memoirs of Marius Petipa*. Trans. Helen Whittaker, ed. Lillian Moore. London: Adam and Charles Black, 1958; reprint. London: Dance Books Ltd.

Perlmutter, Natalie. *Shadowplay: The Life of Anthony Tudor*. Viking Press, 1991.

Singer, Noel. *Burmese Dance and Theater*. Kuala Lumpur: Oxford University Press, 1995.

Sorell, Walter. *The Dance Through the Ages*. New York: Grosset and Dunlap, 1967.

———. *The Dancer's Image: Points and Counterpoints*. New York: Columbia University Press, 1971.

Souritz, Elizabeth. "Carlo Blasis in Russia (1861–1964)". *Studies in Dance History* vol. 4, no. 2 (Fall 1993).

———. *Soviet Choreographers in the 1920s*. Durham and London: Duke University Press, 1990.

Tallchief, Maria. *Maria Tallchief: America's Prima Ballerina*. New York: Henry Holt, 1997.

Vuillier, Gaston. *A History of Dancing*. New York: D. Appleton and Co., 1898.

Wiley, Roland John. *The Life and Ballets of Lev Ivanov: Choreographer of "The Nutcracker" and "Swan Lake."* Oxford: Clarendon Press, 1997.

VIDEOGRAPHY

Il Ballarino: The Art of Renaissance Dance. Dance Horizons, 1991.

Ballets Russes. Dayna Goldfine and Dan Geller, Zeitgeist Films, 2005.

The Children of Theater Street. Documentary on the Kirov Ballet School. Kultur, 1978.

Carmen, chor. Roland Petit. Barishnikov and Jeanmaire, Kultur, 1990.

Cinderella, The Royal Ballet, chor. Frederick Ashton, with Robert Helpmann, Anthony Dowell, Antoinette Sibley, 1969, Kultur, 2007.

Coppelia, Fernando Bujones and the Ballet of San Juan. Kultur, 1980.

Le Corsaire, chor. Petipa, American Ballet Theatre. Kultur, 1988.

Dance of the French Baroque Theater. Insight Media, 2005.

Dancing, Volume IV, "Dancing at Court" (Japanese, Asante, and Javanese court and ballet dance). Kultur, 1992.

Don Quixote, chor. Petipa and Gorsky. Barishnikov, American Ballet Theatre. Kultur, 1999.

The Dream (after A Midsummer Night's Dream), chor. Frederick Ashton, American Ballet Theatre, Kultur, 2007.

Gaîté Parisienne, Danilova, Massine, 1954. Video Artists International, 2006.

Giselle, Nureyev, Seymour, Royal Ballet. 1979. Northridge, 1995.

Jean-Georges Noverre's Medea (1780). Dance Horizons, 2000.

Khmer Court Dance (Cambodian dance). Khmer Studies Institute and CSU, 1997.

l'Enfant et les Sortileges, Nederlands Dans Theater. Kultur, 1986.

La Fille mal Gardée. Australian Ballet. Kultur, 2000.

Medea, Jean-Georges Noverre's (1780). Dance Horizons, 2000.

Napoli, chor. Bournonville. Royal Danish Ballet. (cassette or videodisc).

The Nutcracker, chor. Balanchine, New York City Ballet. Warner Home Video, 1992.

The Nutcracker, chor. Baryshnikov. Gelsey Kirkland, American Ballet Theatre. MGM/UA, 1976.

Parts of the Suite, The: Baroque Music and Dance. Insight Media, VHS, 2003.

Pavlova. narr. Leslie Caron. Kultur, 1983.

Pointe by Point. Lecture/demonstration, Barbara Fewster. Kultur, 1988.

A Portrait of Giselle. (Interviews with nine Giselles), narr. Anton Dolin. Kultur, 1987.

The Red Shoes. Robert Helpmann, Leonide Massine, Moira Shearer. Paramount, 1948.

Reflections of a Dancer. Alexandra Danilova. Direct Cinema, 1981.

The Magic of the Kirov Ballet. Galina Ulanova and Maya Plisetskaya. Kultur, 1988.

The Sleeping Beauty, chor. Petipa. Kirov Ballet. Kultur, 1996.

Swan Lake, chor. Petipa and Ivanov. Kirov Ballet. Kultur, 1996.

OTHER RESOURCES

Baroque Dance Summer Workshops, Department of Dance, Stanford University, Palo Alto, CA.

Cecchetti Council of America, 23393 Meadows, Flat Rock, MI 48134. 734-379-6710
email: info@cecchetti.org

CHAPTER FIVE

MODERN DANCE

New Voices, New Ideas

The dancer is the divine normal. . . . The dancer's world is the heart of man.
—*Martha Graham*, A Dancer's World (film)

Nowhere does one experience the reality of art so greatly as in the dance. Here the constants of beauty, ease, proportion, vitality, technical mastery, of the communication of ecstasy to the beholder, are within one's body—soul—they are as much you as your blood and your breath.
—*Ted Shawn*[1]

As dancers and choreographers explore new ways of moving and create more meaningful ways to communicate with the audience, modern dance changes, incorporates and adapts to these new ideas. The difference between the pioneers and the dancers of today is that today's dancers have a strong, proven foundation from which to work.
—*James Penrod and Janice Plastino*[2]

Very early in the 20th century a new movement in dance began to take shape. The impetus for this movement was the desire to return to the expressive motivations for dance. Thus, the modern dance movement, as it was then called, was both old and new in that it was a return to one of the oldest and most basic impulses for dancing: using movement to reveal the dancer's personal vision. It was also a revolt against the predominant theatrical dance form of its time—ballet—which emphasized formal design and patterned movement.

Arts historian Dennis Sporre describes the efforts of the early modern dancers:

DORIS HUMPHREY in *Passacaglia*, choreography by Humphrey, ca. 1939.

The basic principle of modern dance probably could be stated as an emphasis on natural and spontaneous or uninhibited movement . . . the earliest modern dancers found stylized ballet movement incompatible with their need to communicate in twentieth-century terms.[3]

Each person who has contributed to this art form holds a unique perception of the world and expresses his perception through movement in highly individual ways. These artists have not functioned in a vacuum, however, but have been influenced by events and social issues in the larger world around them and have often felt compelled to comment about this outer world in their work. Thus, each generation of modern dancers has a flavor of its own, and a place of its own in history.

FORERUNNERS AND PIONEERS

The first glimmerings of modern dance began in America and Germany. Both of these branches were influenced by two 19th century European movement theorists: *François Delsarte* (1811–1871) and *Émile Jaques-Dalcroze* (1865–1950), who were forerunners in new methods of understanding human movement.

Delsarte, a French 19th century music teacher, developed a system of categorizing movement and a series of exercises to develop freedom and relaxation, which were widely adopted by modern dancers. Dalcroze, a Swiss professor of music, created a system for improving expressiveness and musicality known as "eurhythmics," also called music visualization. One of his pupils, Marie Rambert, taught members of Diaghilev's company and particularly influenced Nijinsky (see chapter 4). The Dalcroze method was also important to Mary Wigman, Kurt Jooss and Ruth St. Denis. Germany subsequently produced Rudolf von Laban (see biography below) who devised systems of analyzing and notating dance and all movement. He transmitted his concepts to German modern dancers and they were disseminated especially to England and America.

Mary Wigman (1886–1973), one of Rudolf von Laban's students, developed a reputation in Germany for her many dramatic solo and ensemble dances. Her works often dealt with the struggle between conflicting powers. She sometimes used masks and performed some of her dances in silence or to music created after the choreography, both innovative techniques for the time. Wigman toured the United States between 1930 and 1933.

America's modern dance movement owes its birth primarily to three individuals: *Isadora Duncan* (1877–1927), *Ruth St. Denis* (1879–1968) and *Ted Shawn* (1891–1972). Isadora Duncan's personal revolution began at the turn of the 20th century. Born in California, she was inspired more by nature than by standardized dance technique. Isadora gave a new dignity and meaning to dance by linking it to the pre-theatrical reasons for dancing: expression of spiritual feelings and deeply felt emotional states. She literally stripped dance of all ornamentation, including ballet technique, tutus, corsets and all shoes. "I am an enemy to the ballet, which I consider a false and preposterous art" she stated.[4] For freedom of movement, she replaced the costume of pink tights, long skirts and ballet or toe shoes, choosing a simple Greek tunic and bare feet. For music, she chose the finest symphonies and classical works at her disposal. Not satisfied with the roles she was getting in America, she moved to Europe in 1900, performing chiefly as a soloist with a simple blue curtain as a backdrop. During this period she had two children from two different fathers, both of whom she refused to marry—a scandalous deviation from the norms of the day. She lost both these children tragically in a drowning accident in Paris in 1913.

While critics in America continued to label her style and costuming as vulgar, others saw it as a free-flowing expression of her inner spirituality. Agnes De Mille describes it: "Her achievement was a point of view. She cleared away the accumulated debris of six hundred years of artificiality." Using her idealized vision of ancient Greece as a springboard, she expressed new ideas about individual will and connection to nature through her dances. She was able to move from performing in the private homes and small salons of America and Europe to international recognition as a concert artist. During her two-year tour of post-revolutionary Russia, her work became highly pro-Bolshevik, a political leaning that was not appreciated in America. Despite her early death at the age of 50, when a long, dramatic scarf she was wearing wound around the moving wheels of a convertible, Duncan left disciples and pupils all over Europe and the United States, chief among them, six former students known as the "Isadorables." As a result, reconstructions of Duncan technique and repertory are still being performed.

Ruth St. Denis and her husband, Ted Shawn, brought a world of exotic dance forms to American audiences, including dances from India, Japan, Egypt and Spain. Audiences were captivated by St. Denis's ability to impersonate oriental goddesses and priestesses. Ted Shawn, who was already touring with his small company from Los Angeles, met her in New York and became her dance partner. They were married in 1914, and together founded the Denishawn School and Company in Los Angeles in 1915. Unlike Duncan, their performing included ethnic dance

RUTH ST. DENIS and TED SHAWN
in *A Dance Pageant of Egypt, Greece and India,*
with the first Denishawn Company, 1916.

forms and large casts of dancers, elaborate costumes and sets. The company also appeared in some early Hollywood epic films. Denishawn toured extensively, including a fifteen-month tour of the Orient in 1925–1926. Wherever they toured, Shawn and St. Denis learned indigenous dance forms which they adapted to their own performing needs.

Denishawn training nurtured the talents of Martha Graham (1894–1991), Doris Humphrey (1895–1958), and Charles Weidman (1901–1975). All three left Denishawn in the 1920s, seeking independent opportunities for personal growth and expression.

Although their partnership ended in the early 1930s, Shawn and St. Denis continued to actively develop their individual specialties. She became a spokesperson for liturgical dance and a choreographer for movement choirs, which served as the impetus for the sacred dance movement

TED SHAWN in *Japanese Spear Dance*, 1919

in America. He continued as a teacher, author and the founder of the first men's company of dancers in America in 1933. In this last area, he did a great service to dance by improving the image of the male dancer as a complete artist, not a mere adjunct to the female.

After closing the Denishawn House in New York City, Shawn acquired a farm in Becket, Massachusetts, named Jacob's Pillow, which become the home of the Jacob's Pillow dance school and eventually the Jacob's Pillow Dance Festival. This summer gathering of dance students, teachers and international dance companies for performances and classes continues today. It was the school at Jacob's Pillow, with its inclusive approach to the study of dance in all its aspects that had the most profound effect on the next generation of modern dancers. At this "University of the Dance," students explored all types of movement, opening their minds to possibilities beyond the present cultural norms.

While films and reconstructions of the pioneer generation seem innocuous today, this intrepid group created a whole new direction for dance. As summed up by dance writer and critic Deborah Jowitt:

> *"At a time when dancing was "show business" and dancers morally suspect, Duncan and St. Denis insisted on the ability of dancing to deal with lofty ideas and emotions. This, along with the freedom of the body to be expressive in ways not prescribed by the [ballet] academy, was their bequest to contemporary dance."*

FIRST GENERATION

Martha Graham left Denishawn in 1923 with her mentor and accompanist, Louis Horst, and gave her first independent concert in 1926. A year later she opened a school, where she developed a technique supportive of her powerful performing style. Graham devised a system of muscular tension and relaxation for the torso known as "contraction and release." Her technique also included seated exercises to develop flexibility in the hips and spine, standing exercises to strengthen the legs and many series of controlled falls to the ground.

Graham had a wide range of choreographic interests: religious dance, including both pre-Christian and Christian themes, such as *Primitive Mysteries* (1931), based on Native American ritual; pieces concerned with the American pioneer experience, such as her solo *Frontier* (1935) and the most renowned of her group works, *Appalachian Spring* (1944); and psychological explorations such as *Letter to the World* (1940) about Emily Dickinson. She had a strong affinity for Greek tragedies and biblical stories, especially those with strong female central protagonists. For example, *Night Journey* (1947) is a retelling of the story of Oedipus from his mother Jocasta's point of view. The daughter of a psychiatrist, Graham's works often analyzed the psyche in a strikingly dramatic way. Other, lighter pieces, such as *Acrobats of God* (1960), were simply abstract and movement-driven.

Graham was a dedicated artist who gave her last performance at the age of seventy-six, and choreographed a body of 181 works over sixty years. She was honored with the Kennedy Center Award in 1979 and performed for eight US presidents. However, she did not encourage the creative work of her own company members. During its entire existence under Graham's direction, the Martha Graham Company performed Graham choreography exclusively. As a result, many talented Graham dancers left to form their own companies in order to explore their own movement ideas. Because of a dispute in ownership of Graham's works after her death, her company was temporarily forced to stop performing in 2001. The Martha Graham School of Contemporary Dance, however, won a court decision that allowed it to continue to teach her unique technique. In the new millennium, some of her earlier pieces which had been dropped from the repertory before her death in 1991 were revived. These included early works from the nineteen-thirties in 2003, and *Circe* in 2004, originally choreographed in 1963 with Ms. Graham playing the goddess role.

MARTHA GRAHAM in *Primitive Mysteries*

Doris Humphrey began experimenting with music visualizations while still dancing with the Denishawn company. Fascinated by the process of choreography, she developed a technique based on the body's natural reaction to gravity known as "fall and recovery." A keen analyst of movement, she authored the first training manual for modern choreographers, *The Art of Making Dances*, which was published in 1959 and remains inspirational to choreographers.

Humphrey's early works, such as *Water Study* (1928) and *Air for the G String* (1929) had a Duncanesque lyricism. Her later, full-length works dealt with human relationships and social vision. A major contribution to modern dance repertory was her full-length trilogy *New Dance* (1935), *Theatre Piece* (1936) and *With My Red Fires* (1936).

Humphrey met *Charles Weidman* at the Denishawn School in California in the early 1920s. In 1928 they broke their association with Ruth St. Denis and Ted Shawn to form the Humphrey-Weidman School and Dance Company. Weidman's choreography specialized in character studies that were either dramatic or humorous. His comments on American life through dance and mime were both profound and strongly appealing to audiences. His works include *Lynchtown* (1936), based on a personal experience of a lynch mob; *On My Mother's Side* (1940), a series of portraits of family members; and *Flickers* (1941), a commentary on silent movies.

Arthritis forced Humphrey to retire from performing early, but she continued teaching and became the artistic director of the José Limón Dance Company (see Second Generation, below). After Humphrey's untimely death, Weidman struggled with severe depression for several years. He then opened a studio in New York and continued to choreograph and teach until his death. It was during this period that Weidman produced several works of great lyrical strength for his students, including Bach's *Christmas Oratorio* and *St. Matthew's Passion*.

Not all first-generation choreographers came out of Denishawn. On the West Coast, *Lester Horton* (1906–1953) developed a system of technique that emphasized a strong, fluid torso and ease of movement. He choreographed seventeen works for his dance group, also creating costumes and decor for most of the pieces, before his untimely death at the age of forty-seven. The historian Walter Sorell called him "a unique, spectacular personality possessed of a rage to create."[5] His *Rite of*

DORIS HUMPHREY, first generation choreographer, giving advice to the second generation, José Limón.

Spring, choreographed in 1937 and staged at the Hollywood Bowl, caused almost as much of a furor as the original by Nijinsky (see chapter 4). Other works dealt with social problems like bigotry and war. Many Horton students, such as *Alvin Ailey, Carmen de Lavallade, Joyce Trisler* and *James Truitte*, became influential as the second generation of modern dance.

OTHER NOTABLE FIRST GENERATION MODERN DANCE CHOREOGRAPHERS AND PERFORMERS

Maud Allan (1873–1956). Born in Toronto, originally a pianist, Allan trained in Vienna as a dancer and made her debut there. She developed a reputation in Europe as a solo dancer largely from a vision of Salome, which she performed nightly for a year in London (1908). Like Isadora Duncan, she favored symphonic music and classical Greek costuming. In the height of her success, between 1910 and 1918, she was as well-known as Isadora Duncan.

Loïe Fuller (1862–1928). An essentially untrained American dancer, Fuller established a successful career touring in Europe, becoming the rage of Paris. She experimented with unusual lighting and costuming effects, like lighting huge panels of fabric from beneath to create swirling effects like a butterfly or fire or water. These effects were widely imitated, and for ten years after her death, a troupe of Loïe Fuller girls continued to tour Europe.

Hanya Holm (1893–1992), a student of Mary Wigman in Germany, was designated in 1931 to open a Wigman school in New York City. Holm became a noted choreographer and teacher in her adopted country. After her own company of American dancers disbanded in 1944, she became the first modern dancer to make a major success at choreographing Broadway musicals.

Kurt Jooss (1901–1979), a student of Rudolf von Laban, choreographed many works as founder of Ballets Jooss (Germany), including *The Green Table* in 1932, an antiwar piece that was revived in the 1980s by the Joffrey Ballet. A number of his pupils fled to South America during World War II and established modern dance companies in Chile, Peru, Argentina and Venezuela. Jooss himself fled to England, where he established an important school in Devon.

Harald Kreutzberg, a dramatic concert dancer trained by Mary Wigman, also toured in the United States with partners Yvonne Georgi and (later) Ruth Page.

Rudolf von Laban (1879–1958) was born in Austria-Hungary to a military father. He followed his artistic bent at the Ecoles des Beaux Arts in Paris after military school, studying dance, drama and stage design; then became interested in the concept of movement choirs, which he considered an extension of natural movement. Between 1910 and 1930 he opened schools in Germany, which incorporated his ideas about space patterns and harmonies as well as his signature movement choirs. When Hitler branded his ideas as "too universal," he moved to

England, where he spent the rest of his life. His two systems, Labanotation (dance writing) and Laban Movement Analysis are still in use today.

Daniel Nagrin (b. 1917). Beginning by working with his partner and wife, Helen Tamiris, Nagrin became known for his use of jazz and for solo works such as *Strange Hero* (1948) and *Indeterminate Figure* (1957). After Tamiris's death, he continued to choreograph and teach for many decades. Nagrin's books include *How to Dance Forever: Surviving Against the Odds* (1988), *The Six Questions: Acting Technique for Dance Performance* (1997) and *Choreography and the Specific Image* (2001).

Helen Tamiris (1905–1966). The daughter of Polish immigrants, ballet-trained Tamiris began her concert career in 1927, choosing a new direction for dance through use of everyday movement as a basis, social consciousness and Negro spirituals as accompaniment. She choreographed a number of solo concerts as well as works with her partner and husband Daniel Nagrin. During the Great Depression(1929–1939), Tamiris taught movement to actors, then went on to choreograph in the theater. She choreographed the Broadway revival of "Up in Central Park" as well as the movie version in 1948. Her greatest Broadway successes were "Show Boat" and "Annie Get Your Gun," both in 1946. Her concert works include *How Long Brethren,* composed in the 1930s to the music of a Negro protest song. She was one of the first modern dancers to employ jazz movements and rhythms in her choreography.

SECOND GENERATION

Three of the most prominent second-generation choreographers, Erick Hawkins (1909–1994), Merce Cunningham (1919–2009) and Paul Taylor (b. 1930), began their performing careers in Martha Graham's company. Each of them left to form his own company and to pursue his own choreographic muse, thus leaving their individual stamp on the development of modern dance.

Erick Hawkins (who danced first with George Balanchine's American Ballet) the first man in Graham's company and her husband for a brief time, began choreographing for his own company in 1951 and continued until his death. Hawkins had a strong interest in historical and literary American themes and American composers. His work *Plains Daybreak* (1983) explored the spiritual connection between Southwest Indians and animals. *God's Angry Man,* originally titled *John Brown* (1947), revived in 1965 and 1985, a work about the abolitionist John Brown, incorporated a spoken text, making it the precursor of the performance art pieces popular with postmodern choreographers. *Killer of Enemies* (1991) is a narrated Navajo tale about a young hero, with masked performers and a commissioned score by Alan Hovhanness. Hawkins used only 20th century original musical scores, many by his second wife, the composer Lucia Dlugoszewski. He believed that dance accompaniment should always be performed live. Frequently, his musicians were situated onstage, making them an integral part of the total performance.

Performing the Hawkins technique took strength, control and prolonged study. Toward the end of his life he struggled to gain acceptance from a wider, rather than an elite, audience. After his death, Lucia Dlugoszewski made an unusual career move by choreographing several works. The first was a 50-minute solo for a young dancer, Pascal Benichou, titled *Taking Time to be Vulnerable*, a catharsis for her mourning for Hawkins.

Unlike the storyteller Hawkins, *Merce Cunningham* is more interested in movement for its own sake. He strives to incorporate into his technique both the modern dancers' emphasis on torso and spine and the ballet dancers' use of arms and legs. Cunningham believes that dance and its musical accompaniment co-exist in the same time and place, but that neither should be dependent upon the other. Some of his works are performed in silence, while others were the result of a lifelong collaboration with the innovative composer and theorist John Cage. The abstract artist Robert Rauschenberg designed the costumes, lights and sets for many of his early pieces. Often the choreographer did not know what atmosphere he was creating until the opening performance because it was the first time the dance, music, sets, costumes and lights were united.

Cunningham also explored "chance dance," a semi-improvisational form of choreography in which set movements were rearranged for each performance in terms of the sequence, location and dancers involved. This technique, which defied expected traditions and sometimes bewildered audiences, he stated, perfectly suited his dislike of repeating something he had already done. Always in the vanguard, he continues to choreograph into the new millennium, exploring

the possibilities of choreographic invention using computers. In 2007 Cunningham choreographed *Xover* (pronounced "Crossover), a piece which incorporated the last stage designs by Rauschenberg completed before his death. (Rauschenberg had been working with Cunningham since the 1960s.) The ideas of Cunningham, Cage and Rauschenberg were, of all the second generation, most influential in the experiments of the postmodern generation (see chapter 8).

Paul Taylor's introduction to modern dance came during his college years when a friend invited him to perform with her in a concert. After graduation, he moved to New York where he quickly rose to soloist in Martha Graham's company. He was not afraid to explore ballet traditions as well, even performing several Balanchine ballet roles with the New York City Ballet. He

PAUL TAYLOR in *Arden Court*

has a love of 18ᵗʰ century music, which he had used in more abstract pieces such as *Aureole* (1962) and *Airs* (1978), both by the music of Handel (1685–1759).

Taylor's greatest genius, however, is in portraying human experience and its contrasts by juxtaposing light and dark, humor and tragedy, for dramatic effect. An example is *Company B* (1991), a work choreographed to the music of the Andrews Sisters (a famous singing trio of the 1940s and l950s) and set during World War II. In this work, young Americans romp and romance in the foreground, while the war goes on inescapably in the background. Other Taylor works that have stood the test of time are *Big Bertha* (1970), *Esplanande* (1975), *Cloven Kingdom* (1976) and *Speaking in Tongues* (1988), a critique of the evangelist Jimmy Swaggert's hypocritical preaching. Taylor's choreographic and musical interests are so varied, and his work such a mixture of everyday gestures and technical virtuosity, that he has aptly described himself as "an American mongrel." Each new piece shows new growth, making his work refreshingly unpredictable. When he first presented *Esplanade* in 1975, critics argued whether all that crawling, rolling and frantic running should even be considered dance. In 2003, it was revived at the Juilliard Theater and now is considered a modern dance classic. Commenting on his work *Black Tuesday* (2001), set to escapist lyrics from the Depression era, Taylor states: "Basically I am an outsider . . . I've always felt different. I've never been able to go along with a lot in this country."[6] In spite of this perception, ballet companies continue to clamor for his choreographic works.

Taylor continues to choreograph into the new millennium, with works that have become increasingly literal. *Promethean Fire*, which debuted in 2002, is broadly seen as a response to 9/11. In 2006 he produced an explicit anti-war piece, *Banquet of Vultures*, with a central death figure who clearly references Kurt Jooss' *The Green Table*, created in 1932 during the rise of Hitler.

Alvin Ailey (1931–1989) and *Bella Lewitzky* (1916–2004), students of Lester Horton, each developed strong choreographic styles and formed long-lasting performing groups. Born in Rogers, Texas, Ailey moved to Los Angeles as a boy, where he began serious dance study. He formed his first company in New York in the 1950s, soon to become the Alvin Ailey American Dance Theatre. *Cry* (1971), a solo, was created "in honor of my mother and all black women." *Revelations* (1960), set to black spirituals and reflecting Ailey's experiences, which he called "blood memories" of growing up in Texas, remains the Ailey company's signature piece. He also explored more balletic themes and jazz works. By the early 1960s, the company was touring Southeast Asia, Australia and Brazil, the first African-American company to tour under a US State Department program.

Ailey's choreography encompasses modern, jazz and ethnic dance styles. The solo *Cry* memorializes the struggles of black women, while *Night Creatures* (1975) is a playful piece set to Duke Ellington music. Another work, *Memoria* (1979), is a tribute to the life of the choreographer *Joyce Trisler*. Although he created 79 ballets in his lifetime, Ailey maintained that his company was not exclusively a repository for his own work; its ever-evolving repertoire now encompasses 200 works by more than 80 choreographers. Since his death, his company continues to perform Ailey repertory and the work of other choreographers, under the direction of one of his outstanding soloists, *Judith Jamison* (see chapter 8).

Bella Lewitzky remained in Los Angeles, choreographing and teaching. Three notable pieces were *On the Brink of Time* (1969), *Kineisonata* (1970) and *Greening* (1976). *Spaces Between* (1975) explored the special world of the proscenium area. In 1991, she and her company sued the National Endowment for the Arts over their required anti-obscenity pledge; a federal judge ruled in her favor by finding the pledge unconstitutional and Congress promptly reduced funding for NEA. The company disbanded in 1997, but she remained a strong spokesperson for dance in public education for many years after retirement.

All of these artists paved the way for the work of the next generations of choreographers, called postmodern, contemporary or next wave. A discussion of this varied and interesting group appears in chapter 8.

OTHER SECOND GENERATION CHOREOGRAPHERS

Talley Beatty (1923–1995) a native of Chicago, joined the Katherine Dunham Company when he was 16. He appeared in three Broadway shows, then formed his own touring company. His choreography, a blend of modern and jazz, often had African-American themes. One of his most acclaimed works is *The Road of the Phoebe Snow* (1959), depicting life along a railroad line. *The Stack-Up*, which he created for the Alvin Ailey company in 1982, is still in their repertoire.

Carmen de Lavallade (b. 1931) Born in Los Angeles, she was a Lester Horton dancer who came to New York with his company and was quickly offered several Broadway and movie roles, including "House of Flowers," choreographed by producer Herbert Ross. She made her ballet debut with the Metropolitan Opera Ballet, and danced for two seasons as a guest artist with American Ballet Theatre. Coming from the same background as Alvin Ailey, she later became a soloist in his company. She was known for her leading roles in Gian-Carlo Menotti's television opera *Amahl and the Night Visitors* (1951) and John Butler's *Carmina Burana* (1959), as well as in works choreographed by her husband, Geoffrey Holder. For the Dance Theatre of Harlem, she choreographed the world premiere of *Sensemaya*. In her later years she developed a strong desire to become an actress, and received an Actor's Equity Award for her role as Titania in "Midsummer Night's Dream."

Dudley-Maslow-Bales Trio (1942–1954). This concert company, formed under the support of the New Dance Group in New York, consisted of *Jane Dudley* 1912–2001), *Sophie Maslow* (1912–2006) and *William (Bill) Bales* (1910–1990), each a gifted dancer and solo choreographer. In collaboration,

THE MOOR'S PAVANE with Betty Jones and José Limón, choreography by Limón—his most famous work, and considered a masterwork in 20th century dance.

they produced comic pieces, abstract works and works of social protest, incorporating any movement style they felt suited the subject matter.

Pauline Koner (1912–2001). A dancer-choreographer who pioneered dance for television, she spent fifteen years as a dancer in the José Limón Company, creating the role of His Friend's Wife in *The Moor's Pavane* (1949).

José Limón (1908–1972). A dynamic performer, the Mexican-born Limón studied and performed for many years with Doris Humphrey; she created for him the lead role in *Lament for Ignacio Sánchez Mejías* (1946), the story of a bullfighter. Limón began choreographing while still part of her company, and after serving in World War II, he established his own company. Many of his works, such as the great *The Moor's Pavane* (1949) (based on Shakespeare's "Othello,") *The Exiles* (1950) and *The Emperor Jones* (1956), are strikingly dramatic while others, such as *Concerto Grosso* (1945), are lyrical and abstract. Limón also became a master teacher. Even after his death in 1972, his New York–based company still performs Limón and Humphrey repertory, and Limón technique is taught extensively in the United States and Europe.

Donald McKayle (b. 1930), director, choreographer and writer for films and television, created *Games* (1951), an evocation of children's street-games played in Harlem, and *Rainbow 'Round My Shoulder* (1959). His Broadway choreography credits include "Sophisticated Ladies," "Raisin" and "Golden Boy," while film credits include "The Great White Hope" and "Bedknobs and Broomsticks."

Alwin Nikolais (1910–1993) was a student of Hanya Holm. He was also a visual artist with a strong interest in creating a total stage environment using lighting, costumes and props of his own design; on many occasions he even created the musical scores for his pieces. "Nik" often used the human body in the abstract as part of his visual design.

ALWIN NIKOLAIS DANCE THEATER in *Tensile Involvement*, choreography by Nikolais.

For example, in *Masks, Props and Mobiles* (1953) the dancers appear encased in fabric bags. With his partner *Murray Louis* (b. 1926), a more technique-oriented choreographer, he established the Louis-Nikolais Dance Theater Lab in New York. Louis, who was an invigorating teacher known for his quirky, witty personal style, maintained a focus on the body's movement potential while Nikolais explored other theatrical elements, providing a good balance for each other's work. Louis's 1994 solo *Alone* is a tribute to Nikolais. Louis continues to create works for leading modern dance and ballet companies as well as solo artists.

Eleo Pomare (1937–2008). A student of Kurt Jooss among others, Pomare established his own company which toured Europe and had its American debut in 1966. His choreography deals largely with the issues of African-Americans. His masterpiece *Blues for the Jungle* (1966) is a look at the historical oppression of blacks in Harlem, and his solo *Narcissus Rising* (1968) explores the arrogance and rage of a black-leather motorcyclist.

Anna Sokolow (1912–2000) was an early student of Martha Graham. Sokolow's interest lay in developing dance as a form of communication, emphasizing dramatic intensity, lyricism and humor. She also had a deep commitment to and understanding of 20th century music. In 1939 she was invited to teach in Mexico and became influential in the formation of a modern dance movement there. *Lament for the Death of a Bullfighter, Mexican Retalbo,* and many other notable works came out of this period. Beginning in 1953, she divided her time between Israel and the United States, creating works and teaching in both countries. Many of her works are social commentaries, such as *Dreams* (1961) about the Holocaust, and *Rooms* (1955), which explores the loneliness of city-dwellers. Others include *Songs of a Semite* (1943), *Ride the Culture Loop* (1973) and *Los Conversos* (1981).

ANNA SOKOLOW
in *Slaughter of the Innocents*, 1939.

Glen Tetley (1926–2007). Born in Ohio, Tetley became interested in dance while in medical school. He studied ballet with Antony Tudor and Jerome Robbins and modern dance with Martha Graham and Hanya Holm, forming his own chamber dance company in 1962. *Pierrot Luniere* premiered the same year, and is still thought to be one of his best works because of the masterful blending of modern dance and ballet vocabularies. In 1969 he closed the New York company and went to Europe, where his choreography became extremely popular. He co-directed the Nederlands Dance Theater for three years, and served as director of Stuttgart Ballet from 1974 to 1976.

Altogether he choreographed more than 50 ballets, including a version of *Rite of Spring* with a male sacrificial victim and a different ending from Nijinsky's original. His works have been performed by American Ballet Theatre, Dance Theatre of Harlem, Houston Ballet, National Ballet of Canada, Royal Danish Ballet, Royal Ballet of England and Ballet Rambert.

SUGGESTED READING

Ailey, Alvin and Peter Bailey *Revelations*. New York: Birch Lane Press, 1995.

Alter, Judith B. "Dancing and Mixed Media: Early Twentieth-Century Modern Dance Theory." *New Studies in Aesthetics*, vol. 17, New York, Berlin, Paris, 1996.

Anderson, Jack. *The American Dance Festival*. Durham, N.C.: Duke University Press, 1987.

———. *Ballet and Modern Dance, 2nd Edition: A Concise History*. Hightstown, NJ: Princeton Book Co., 1998.

———. *Art Without Boundaries: The World of Modern Dance*. Iowa City: University of Iowa Press, 1997.

Au, Susan. *Ballet and Modern Dance*. New York: Thames and Hudson, 1988.

Benbow-Pfalzgraf, Taryn, ed. *International Dictionary of Modern Dance*. Detroit: St. James Press, 1998.

Bremser, Martha. *Fifty Contemporary Choreographers*. London: Routledge Press, 1999.

Brown, Jean Morrison, Naomi Mindlin, and Charles H. Woodford, eds. *The Vision of Modern Dance*, 2nd ed. Hightstown, NJ: Princeton Book Co., 1998.

Cohen, Selma Jeanne. *The Modern Dance: Seven Statements of Belief.* Middletown, CT: Wesleyan University Press, 1965.

———. *Doris Humphrey: An Artist First*. Middletown, CT: Wesleyan University Press, 1972.

———. *Dance as a Theatre Art: Source Readings in Dance History from 1581 to the Present*. 2nd ed., Pennington, NJ: Princeton Book Co. 1992.

Cribb, Michael, "Glen Tetley, 1926–2007." *Dance Magazine,* January, 2007.

De Mille, Agnes. *The Book of the Dance*. New York: Golden Books, 1963.

———, *Martha: The Life and Work of Martha Graham*. New York: Random House, 1991.

Defrantz, Thomas F. *Dancing Revelations: Alvin Ailey's Embodiment of African-American Culture*. New York: Oxford University Press, 2004.

Denby, Edward. *Dance Writings*. New York: Alfred A. Knopf, 1986.

Dunning, Jennifer. *Alvin Ailey: A Life in Dance*. Reading, MA: Addison-Wesley, 1996.

Garafola, Lynn, ed. "Of, By and For the People: Dancing on the Left in the 1930s." *Studies in Dance History*, vol. 5, no. 1, Spring 1994.

Graff, Ellen. *Stepping Left: Dance and Politics in New York City, 1928–1942*. Durham, NC: Duke University Press, 1997.

Gruen, John. *The World's Great Ballets*. New York: Harry N. Abrams, 1981.

Horosko, Marian. *Martha Graham: The Evolution of Her Dance Theory and Training, 1926–1991*. Pennington, NJ: A Cappella Books, 1991.

Humphrey, Doris. *New Dance: Writings on Modern Dance*. Hightstown, NJ: Princeton Book Co., 2008.

———. *The Art of Making Dances*. New York: Grove Press, 1959. Reprint, Princeton, NJ: Princeton Book Co., 1987.

Jonas, Gerald. *Dancing: The Pleasure, Power, and Art of Movement*. New York: Harry N. Abrams, 1992.

Kostelanetz, Richard, ed. Merce *Cunningham: Dancing in Space and Time*. Pennington, NJ: A Cappella Books, 1999.

Kraus, Richard, Sarah Hilsendager and Brenda Dixon. *History of Dance in Art and Education*. 3rd ed. Englewood Cliffs, NJ: Prentice-Hall, 1991.

Kreemer, Connie. *Further Steps: Fifteen Choreographers on Modern Dance*. New York: Harper and Row, 1987.

Kriegsman, Sali Ann. *Modern Dance in America: The Bennington Years*. Boston: G.K. Hall, 1981.

Lloyd, Margaret. *The Borzoi Book of Modern Dance*. New York: Alfred A. Knopf, 1949.

Love, Paul. *Modern Dance Terminology*. Pennington, NJ: Princeton Book Co., 1997.

Manning, Susan A. *Ecstasy and the Demon: Feminism and Nationalism in the Dances of Mary Wigman*. Berkeley: University of California Press, 1993.

Maynard, Olga. *Judith Jamison: Aspects of a Dancer*. Garden City, NY: Doubleday, 1982.

Mazo, Joseph H. *Prime Movers: The Makers of Modern Dance in America*. New York: William Morrow, 1977. 2nd ed., Hightstown, NJ: Princeton Book Co., 2000.

McDonagh, Don. *The Complete Guide to Modern Dance*. Garden City, NY: Doubleday, 1976.

———. ed. *The Rise and Fall and Rise of Modern Dance*. Pennington, NJ: A Cappella Books, 1990.

Nagrin, Daniel. *How to Dance Forever: Surviving Against the Odds*. New York: William Morrow, 1988.

———. *The Six Questions: Acting Technique for Dance Performance*. Pittsburgh, PA: University of Pittsburgh Press, 1998.

Penrod, James, and Janice Gudde Plastino. *The Dancer Prepares*, 4th ed. Mountain View, CA: Mayfield Publishing, 1998.

Preston-Dunlop, Valerie. *Rudolf Laban: An Extraordinary Life*. London: Dance Books, 1998.

Reynolds, Nancy and Malcolm McCormick. *No Fixed Points: Dance in the Twentieth Century*. New Haven: Yale University Press, 2003.

Ruyter, Nancy Lee Chalfa. *Reformers and Visionaries*. New York: Dance Horizons, 1979.

Shawn, Ted. *Every Little Movement*. Reprint, New York: Dance Horizons, 1968.

Siegel, Marcia B. *At the Vanishing Point: A Critic Looks at Dance*. New York: Saturday Review Press, 1972.

———. *Days on Earth: The Dance of Doris Humphrey*. New Haven, CT: Yale University Press, 1987.

Sorell, Walter. *The Dancer's Image: Points and Counterpoints*. New York: Columbia University Press, 1971.

Sporre, Dennis J. *Perceiving the Arts*. Englewood Cliffs, NJ: Prentice Hall, 2000.

Taylor, Paul. *Private Domain*. New York: Alfred A. Knopf, 1987.

Toepfer, Karl Eric. *Empire of Ecstasy: Nudity and Movement in German Body Culture, 1910–1935*. Berkeley: University of California Press, 1997.

Warren, Larry. *Lester Horton: Modern Dance Pioneer*. Reprint, Pennington, NJ: Princeton Book Co., 1991.

———. *Anna Sokolow: The Rebellious Spirit,* new ed. Chur, Switzerland: Harwood Academic Publishers, 1998.

Wigman, Mary. *The Language of Dance*. Walter Sorell, trans. Middletown, CT: Wesleyan University Press, 1966.

———. *The Mary Wigman Book*. Walter Sorell, ed. and trans. Middletown, CT: Wesleyan University Press, 1975.

VIDEOGRAPHY

Anna Sokolow, Choreographer. Dance Horizons, 1978.

Four by Ailey. Kultur, 1986.

Cage/Cunningham. Kultur, 1991.

Charles Weidman: On His Own. Dance Horizons, 1990.

Dance of the Century, Pts. I–IV. Sonia Schoonejans, dir. Pathé TV, 1992.

Dancing, Volume VII, "The Individual and Tradition." Kultur, 1992.

The Dancing Prophet (Ruth St. Denis), 2 vols. Pyramid, 1970 and 1999.

Dance Works of Doris Humphrey, Part 1: *With My Red Fires* and *New Dance*. Dance Horizons, 1989.

Dance Works of Doris Humphrey, Part 2: *Ritmo Jondo / Day on Earth*. José Limón Dance Company, Dance Horizons, 1999.

Denishawn: The Birth of Modern Dance. Kultur, 1988.

Doris Humphrey Legacy: *The Shakers*. Dance Horizons, 1998.

Doris Humphrey Legacy: *Two Ecstatic Themes*. Dance Horizons, 1998.

Doris Humphrey Legacy: *Water Study*. Dance Horizons, 1998.

Doris Humphrey Legacy: *The Call / Breath of Fire*. Dance Horizons, 1998.

Doris Humphrey Legacy: *Air for the G String*. Dance Horizons, 1998.

Enduring Essence: Isadora Duncan. S. Arslanian, director. Images, 1990.

Erick Hawkins' America. Dance Horizons, 1992.

The Erick Hawkins Modern Dance Technique. Dance Horizons, 2000.

Hanya Holm: Portrait of a Pioneer. Dance Horizons, 1988.

Isadora, feature film with Vanessa Redgrave. Universal Pictures, 1968.

Isadora Duncan Dance: Technique and Repertory. Dance Horizons, 1994.

Isadora Duncan Masterworks: 1905–1923. Dance Horizons, 2008.

Lester Horton: Genius on the Wrong Coast. Green River Road, dist., 1993.

Martha Graham: The Dancer Revealed. Kultur, 1994.

Martha Graham in Performance: *A Dancer's World*, *Night Journey* and *Appalachian Spring*. Kultur.

Mary Wigman, 1886–1973. Dance Horizons, 1990.

The New Dance Group Gala Historical Concert, 2 disks. Dancetime Publications, 2008.

Paul Taylor, Dancemaker. Matthew Diamond, dir. Medium, Inc., 1999.

Three by Martha Graham: *Cortege of Eagles*, *Seraphic Dialog*, *Acrobats of God*. Pyramid, 1996.

The World of Alwin Nikolais, five vols. Nikolais/Louis Foundation, 1996.

OTHER SOURCES

Alvin Ailey Dance Center
www.alvinailey.org
405 West 55th Street, New York, N.Y. 10019. 212-405-9000

Cunningham Dance Foundation Inc.
www.merce.org

The Doris Humphrey Foundation for Dance at Goucher College
dhfd@goucher.edu

The Doris Humphrey Society
www.dorishumphrey.org
605 Lake Street, Oak Park, IL 60302. 708-848-2329

Isadora Duncan Foundation for Contemporary Dance, Inc.
Duncan classes and public performances.
141 W. 26th St., New York, N.Y. 10001–6800
www.isadoraduncan.org

José Limón Dance Foundation
www.limon.org
307 West 38th Street, Suite 1105, New York, N.Y. 10018. 212-777-3353.
email: info@limon.org

Martha Graham
www.marthagrahamdance.org

Paul Taylor Dance Company
551 Grand Street, New York, N.Y. 10002. 212-431-5562.
email: ao@ptdc.org

CHAPTER SIX
TAP, JAZZ, MUSICAL THEATER AND FILM DANCE

The American Originals

Gotta dance, gotta dance!
—from "Broadway Melody" sung by Gene Kelly

Do motion pictures harm children? They do if their parents are in vaudeville . . .
—vaudeville joke, ca. 1929

People ask, "How do you make a dance?" My answer is simple.
"Put yourself in motion."
—Twyla Tharp[1]

Tap and jazz dance, Broadway and Hollywood dance and hip-hop are considered truly American arts, though often they draw from older forms and other cultures. In the same way that waves of immigrant groups have contributed to all aspects of American culture, they reflect a variety of cultures hybridized and theatricalized into a spicy American blend. They are called American originals. vernacular dance, or dance of the people. The groups and individuals who have shaped these dance forms will be introduced to you in this chapter.

TAP DANCE

Early Tap Dance: Minstrel Shows

The rhythmic, precise sounds and movements of tap dance are a blend of two quite different folk dance traditions—one African, the other from the British Isles. The idea of putting metal taps on the soles of shoes to

BILL 'BOJANGLES' ROBINSON in "King for a Day."

accentuate the dancer's steps apparently came from England, where 19th century step dancers were performing lively dances in wooden clogs. When they switched to lighter leather-soled shoes, some performers attached pennies to the heels and soles to retain the rhythmic sounds of their dances. For some young dancers in America, taps were bottle caps, still used by street dancers in our cities. The nails and metal reinforcements used on work boots and military boots also made early versions of tap shoes.

In the early 19th century, lively dances of English, Scottish and Irish origin—especially *jigs, hornpipes* and *waltz clogs*—were appearing in American theatrical entertainments, most often performed by a featured soloist. By the 1830s white performers were also imitating the songs and dances of the African-Americans in theatrical entertainments known as minstrel shows. Considered the first truly original American theatrical form, these all-male shows followed a strict structure; the performers all sat onstage, getting up to present their specialty song, dance or comedy routine. White performers performed dances in the black style. *John Durang* (1768–1822), whose specialty was the Hornpipe, may have been the first to use burnt cork as makeup to perform in "blackface." Many stereotypical black characters developed from these shows, with *Thomas Dartmouth Rice* (1808–1860), known professionally as Daddy "Jim Crow" Rice, originating the limping "Jim Crow" character in a dance called the *Jump Jim Crow*. The finale of the minstrel show was an audience-participation *Cakewalk* (see chapter 3).

Despite limited opportunities even for free African-Americans before the Civil War, a handful of black dancers, singers and musicians became extremely popular entertainers. Notable among these was the freeborn northern black *Master Juba* (William Henry Lane; 1825–c. 1852), whose songs and dances, including the jig, earned him acclaim both in America and Britain in the 1840s. Juba took his name from the *giouba*, an African step-dance that was the precursor to the *Charleston* of the next century. Juba's fame was so legendary that in 1845 he toured with four white minstrels and received top billing.

After the Civil War, black touring minstrel shows became competitors of the white groups. By this time, audiences were so used to seeing entertainers in blackface that the black performers also darkened their faces with burnt cork. During this period, the easygoing style of tap dance known as *soft shoe* was developed. In this moderate-tempo dance, the movement style became more important than the tap sounds.

The Rise of Vaudeville

Vaudeville first appeared in America in the 1870s, and by 1900 had replaced minstrel shows as the most popular form of entertainment until 1932. The name vaudeville derived from the French phrase *voix de ville*, which means "voices of the town." This new theatrical form had greater audience appeal because of the greater variety of performers, including choruses of female precision line dancers, comedy acts, circus-style jugglers and acrobats and many child performers. Distinguishing itself from other variety shows suitable for men-only venues such as saloons, vaudeville was family entertainment performed in theaters. Some of the shows ran continuously from morning to night, and families could stay and watch it over and over.

At its peak in the 1920s there were 20,000 vaudeville acts in the country. A typical show had anywhere from nine to twenty acts. Touring black or white (and a few mixed) vaudeville troupes crisscrossed the country on tours known as circuits, and over two million people saw vaudeville shows every day. Vaudeville was the training ground for many performers who later became stars in Broadway revues, nightclubs and films, including *Bill "Bojangles" Robinson* (1878–1949) and *Fred Astaire* (1887–1987).

Vaudeville shows also spread the new music coming out of New Orleans: ragtime. Because of its use of both syncopation (unusual accents) and polyrhythms (multiple rhythms played simultaneously), ragtime is the first music that can truly be called jazz.[2] Although ragtime was primarily piano music at first, these rhythmic innovations, new to Western music, can be traced directly to African drumming. In addition to changing social dance, the new "Dixieland jazz" also changed the formula for theater dance. Instead of chorus lines of girls dancing with military precision, both vaudeville and Broadway shows began to incorporate a freer tap style that included a lot of improvisation on the part of solo dancers.

The development of movies with sound added, the spread of radio, and the Great Depression (of the 1930s) combined to kill vaudeville. The money crunch of the Depression encouraged people to stay home and listen to the vaudeville shows on the radio instead of buying tickets. Also theater managers found it cheaper to show short films between the vaudeville acts with popular stars, rather than hire these stars to tour with the shows. By the late 1930s, with the exception of a few big-city theaters such as Radio City Music Hall in New York (that continued to show variety acts in between full-length films) vaudeville had become a thing of the past.

In 1921 *Eubie Blake* and other artists created the first all-black hit Broadway show, "Shuffle Along," launching a decade of "colored musicals" that featured black tap dancers. The popular revue "Runnin' Wild" (1923) introduced the lively Charleston to white New York audiences. Similar white Broadway revues soon followed, notably Florenz Ziegfeld's annual "Ziegfeld Follies," showcasing American singers, dancers, comedians and lavishly costumed choruses of beautiful girls. The 1920s was also the decade of the Harlem Renaissance, when audiences flocked to nightclubs like the Cotton Club and the Apollo Ballroom in the largely African-American section of New York to hear the finest in jazz music and watch dancers do their specialties.

Tap Dance in Hollywood

Even before the advent of the "talkies" (sound added to film), dance began appearing frequently in Hollywood movies. During the 1930s and 1940s, the Hollywood film replaced vaudeville as the most popular form of entertainment in the small towns and cities of America. Vaudeville performers and routines were adapted to film. Lavish and popular Broadway revues such as the Ziegfeld Follies found even larger audiences as movies. As the Depression wore on, movie musicals featuring star tap dancers and large dancing choruses became the escapist fare for the American public. Theaters devoted to live touring shows were converted to movies. A few theaters, such as the Roxy and Radio City Music Hall, continued to offer vaudeville-style live revues between films, but by the advent of World War II the vaudeville touring circuits had virtually disappeared.

The films directed and choreographed by *Busby Berkeley* (1895–1976) used hundreds of dancers, elaborate sets and imaginative photography. However, except for the imaginative floor patterns that Berkeley filmed from overhead, the choreography for the chorus was not very interesting. Only a few choreographers, like Fred Astaire, tried to integrate the dances into the plots of these early movie musicals.

Many notable performers, each with a personal style and specialty steps, added to the tap vocabulary. Bill "Bojangles"[3] Robinson created a light, clear tap sound by keeping his weight on the balls of the feet. He was a Broadway star, already fifty-seven, by the time he made his first film, dancing with child star Shirley Temple in "The Little Colonel" (1935).

The *Nicholas Brothers, Harold* (1921–2001) and *Fayard* (1914–2006), were the best of the "flash" tappers, and were the first African-American team to get a contract with a Hollywood film company. They began as a child singing-dancing act, making their debut in Philadelphia in 1929. They were spotted by a New York agent and signed for the Lafayette Theater in Harlem. When Harold was eight and Fayard fourteen, they moved to Harlem's Cotton Club, where they stayed for two years. In the 1930s the team moved to Hollywood, and began adding high-powered stunts like back somersaults, jump-splits and split-slides to their tap routines. By the 1940s they were taking ten-foot leaps into their splits and sliding down staircases to land in a split. The Nicholas Brothers appeared in more than fifty movies in the 1930s and 1940s and toured South America, Africa and Europe extensively. In their later years they developed a nightclub act and made an appearance in a Janet Jackson music video. Harold appeared in the 1989 movie, "Tap!"

Among female tappers, *Ruby Keeler* (1910–1993) was the first to move from Broadway to become a full-fledged Hollywood star. She made her Hollywood debut in the 1933 film, "42nd Street," followed by "Footlight Parade," "Flirtation Walk" and "Dames." At the age of 61, she returned to Broadway in the 1971 revival of "No, No, Nanette." A winsome performer, her tap style was rather flat-footed compared with her successors.

The beautiful *Eleanor Powell* (1910–1982) was known for a tap style that included acrobatic flexibility, balletic beats and series of very rapid turns. Several Hollywood films were built around her unique abilities and box-office appeal, including "Born to Dance" (1936), "Rosalie" (1937), and "Broadway Melody of 1938." Many female stars such as comediennes *Lucille Ball* and *Shirley MacLaine* began their performing careers as dancers. Even serious actors like *Clark Gable* and *Joan Crawford*, who was Astaire's first film partner ("Dancing Lady," 1933), could be found tap dancing in these early years of the film industry.

During his very successful career in Hollywood, Fred Astaire's personal style consistently added an easygoing suaveness to highly rhythmic footwork and perfect musicality. Astaire's solos were always meticulously rehearsed and often contained "gimmicks," such as dancing with a coat rack as a partner, with animated shoes, up a wall and across the ceiling, or accompanied by firecrackers. With *Ginger Rogers* (1911–1995) as his partner, Astaire developed a smooth, elegant dance form that combined tap and ballroom dance. Although they made only ten movies together and Astaire had many other dance partners in films, Fred and Ginger became the epitome of ballroom-tap couples in the eyes of an adoring American public.[4] Through more than thirty years of successful dancing in films and on television specials, Astaire was most responsible for popularizing tap dance. His consummate ability won him the admiration of dancers and choreographers in all forms of dance: Baryshnikov, Nureyev, Michael Jackson, Gregory Hines and George Balanchine, who said of him "he is the most interesting, the most inventive, the most elegant dancer of our times."

Jazz Dance

The Birth of Jazz Dance

During the 1940s, tap dance continued to dominate the Hollywood musicals, but there were signs of change. A new form, not dependent on tapping sounds, was growing; this new dance eventually became jazz dance. It combined elements of tap, ballet and many ethnic forms, including African, Middle-Eastern and European as well as American social dance influences.

Jazz dance on Broadway took a giant leap forward in 1936 when George Balanchine choreographed *Slaughter on Tenth Avenue*, with the assistance of African-American rhythm tap choreographer Herbie Harper. This blend of ballet and tap created a new style of theatrical dance. Agnes De Mille's choreography for "Oklahoma!" in 1943 also demanded dancers trained in ballet; the *Dream Ballet* from this show has become a theatrical dance classic. The addition of ballet has expanded the theatrical dance vocabulary by adding movements such as leaps, multiple turns and lyrical style contrasts. These movements are now taught in jazz dance classes. De Mille also set a precedent as the first of the "dance directors" (not yet called choreographers) to assume the overall direction of a Broadway show with "Allegro" (1947).

Katherine Dunham (1909–2006) and *Pearl Primus* (1919–1994), two African-American women, brought the excitement of African and Afro-Caribbean dance to the attention of the public in the 1940s. Both of these women were outstanding performers who researched folk forms—Dunham, in Haiti; Primus, in Africa—and made them into theater pieces.

KATHERINE DUNHAM

Dunham, who formed the Katherine Dunham Dance Company in Chicago in the early 1930s, received a fellowship in 1935 to travel to the Caribbean and study African-based dances. This led to works for her company that depicted dance as religious ritual, notably *Shango* (1945). She also choreographed and danced in a Broadway revue called "Le Jazz Hot," in 1940, which featured Harlem-style social dance movement. She began touring the United States and Mexico with her own company of dancers and was received ecstatically in London. In 1945 she opened the Dunham School of Dance and Theater in New York's theater district—a unique academy that offered courses in anthropology, philosophy, sociology and island dialects as well as tap, ballet, folk, primitive dance and Dunham technique, which was based on a series of body isolations. Dunham-trained dancers still teach Dunham technique today. Her dance company can be seen in the film "Stormy Weather" (1943), also starring Bill "Bojangles" Robinson. She choreographed for George Balanchine, Agnes DeMille, Ruth Page and the Senegalese National Ballet. Some of her works, such as *Southland*, performed in 1951 in Chile, spoke out against oppression, as did her decision not to perform in segregated theaters during her touring days.

In 1949 the historian Margaret Lloyd described Pearl Primus's dancing:

> *She presents the African, Caribbean, and American Negro rhythms with excellent stagecraft, but with less showmanship than Katherine Dunham, though she is a more powerful dancer. The performance is rife with rhythmic excitements and emotional undercurrents. The pulsations of the diaphragm are something straight out of Africa; but the element of trained element of trained athleticism in her co-ordination, speed and skill, is strictly North American.[5]*

Another choreographer from this period who had a major influence on the growth of jazz dance was *Jack Cole* (1914–1974). Cole set the style for Broadway jazz, demanding a high level of technique from his dancers. He is remembered with love for his dynamic choreographic genius and with fear for his perfectionist personality and violent temper in rehearsals. Cole used ballet and ethnic moves in his choreography, especially East Indian and oriental motifs learned while he was a student at the Denishawn School, and exemplified in the hit shows "Alive and Kicking" (1950) and "Kismet" (1953). For the former he created a dance routine titled *Hindu Serenade*, which the show's star, Milton Berle, called "a jam session at the Taj Mahal."[6] Cole also borrowed themes from the Caribbean and Harlem.

Cole continued to choreograph for Broadway shows and films until 1960. He was skilled at developing stage movement for female stars such as Betty Grable and Rita Hayworth; "Let's Make Love" (1960), starring Marilyn Monroe, was his last film. One of the most important contributions Cole made to the dance world was to establish a dance studio on the lot of Columbia pictures, where he trained a whole generation of jazz dancers. His protégés during his forty-year career as a choreographer/director include *Gwen Verdon* (1925–2000), *Carol Haney* (1924–1964), *Rod Alexander* (1922–1992) (see "Other Notables" in this chapter) and *Matt Mattox* (b. 1921). His ballet/jazz style has gone into the vocabulary of later choreographers including as *Bob Fosse* (1927–1987), and *Michael Kidd* (1915–2007). So great was Cole's influence that he has been called "the father of jazz dance."

Jazz Choreographers of the 1950s–1970s

The 1950s saw a new group of choreographers make their mark. One of them was *Jerome Robbins* (1918–1998), whose Broadway credits include "Call Me Madam" (1950), "The King and I" (1951), "Peter Pan" (1954), "Gypsy" (1959) and "Fiddler on the Roof" (1964). His stunning choreography for rival street gangs in his masterpiece "West Side Story" (1957, based on Shakespeare's *Romeo and Juliet*) has earned him a permanent place in dance history. He conceived the play and directed it, as well. The movie version won seven Oscars in 1961, Robbins receiving one of them, the first Academy Award given for choreography. He also directed the film versions of "West Side Story," "Fiddler on the Roof" and "The King and I." In all of these shows, the dance sequences were well integrated into the plot and developed the central characters of the stories.

Robbins also choreographed many jazz-style pieces for ballet companies. The first of these was *Fancy Free* (1944), a ballet about three sailors on leave, which inspired the film "On the Town" (1949). This was followed by *New York Export: Opus Jazz*, first performed in 1958 by Robbins' own company Ballet: USA and revived in 1974 by the Joffrey Ballet. This piece featured the innovation of ballet dancers performing in sneakers instead of ballet shoes. "Jerome Robbins' Broadway," a musical retrospective of Robbins's extensive career as a choreographer and director, opened a successful Broadway run in 1989. His history also includes a long association with American Ballet Theatre and then George Balanchine and the New York City Ballet, almost from its inception (see chapter 8).

In the 1950s, some excellent Hollywood musicals were produced, but fewer than in the previous decade, because of the advent of television. Broadway, television and film choreographers all took advantage of the popularity of rock 'n roll, incorporating its danceable beat into their routines. Television cashed in on new dance crazes, with shows like "The Dick Clark Hour," followed a few years later by "Hullabaloo" and "Let's Go-Go." Inspired by Elvis Presley, torso and hip movements began to appear in stage dance as well as in social dance. New dances, such as the *twist* made popular by Chubby Checker, continued to evolve in the 1960s. The making of "beach blanket" movies and other films made especially for teenagers gave the current dances an additional popularity.

GENE KELLY in the classic movie musical
"Singin' in the Rain."

The versatile dancer *Gene Kelly* (1912–1996), whose career spanned several decades, distinguished himself by performing both in tap and jazz styles. His early movies were primarily tap; he appeared only once with Astaire, in a lively duet in the film Ziegfeld Follies (1945). His best-remembered dance (and movie) is a classic soft-shoe in "Singin' in the Rain" (1952). Kelly was an extremely strong dancer who did his own stunt work, which "The Pirate" (1948) showcases along with his performance in a "flash" trio with the Nicholas Brothers. His more lyrical side could be seen in films such as "An American in Paris" (1951) co-starring the French ballet dancer Leslie Caron, and "Brigadoon" (1954) with *Cyd Charisse* (1922–2008). Favoring large movements like leaps, his energetic, masculine dance style soon made Kelly a household name. A passable singer and actor with an engaging smile, Kelly truly danced his way to stardom.

During the 1960s, several Broadway musicals, notably "Hair" (1968), choreographed by Julie Arenal, depicted the rebellious "hippie" antiwar youth. "Hair" was later made into a movie, with new choreography by Twyla Tharp. It was clear that in the sixties, tap was no longer a dance requirement for Broadway and Hollywood audiences, and many choreographers were eager to jump on the jazz bandwagon. The tradition of comedic dance, minus the taps, was continued in films by new performers like Dick Van Dyke, dancing in "Mary Poppins" (1964) and "Bye Bye Birdie" (1963).

In the 1970s, jazz dance continued to flourish in Broadway musicals and films, and *Bob Fosse* rose to prominence as the most notable choreographer. Born in Chicago, Fosse began his career as a nightclub dancer. He began choreographing for Broadway in the 1950s with "Kiss Me, Kate"

BOB FOSSE as The Snake in "The Little Prince."

(1953) and "The Pajama Game" (1954), both collaborations with Jerome Robbins. During the next two decades he choreographed a series of hit shows that were also made into films, including "Damn Yankees" (1955), "Redhead" (1959) and "Sweet Charity" (1966). Many of his biggest hits were vehicles for his wife, the versatile comedienne/dancer/singer *Gwen Verdon*, who remained the foremost interpreter of his early work until her death. She started a dance lab in New York where dancers could learn Fosse's style and participate in reconstruction of his numbers.

Fosse ultimately tried his hand at directing. "Redhead" was his first endeavor in directing a Broadway musical and "Sweet Charity" the first movie. Early Fosse choreography was energetic and rhythmic, characterized by a crouched position of the body and turned-in legs. His later choreography was erotic and sensuous; always, it was clever and imaginative. During his career, Fosse garnered eight Tony awards for Broadway choreography, including "Little Me" (1962), "Chicago" (1975) and "Dancin'" (1978). In 1973 he won three awards for his choreography: an Oscar for the film "Cabaret," a Tony for the Broadway show "Pippin" and an Emmy for a Liza Minnelli television special, "Liza with a Z." In 1979 the roughly autobiographical movie "All That Jazz," which Fosse conceived, choreographed and directed, was nominated for an Oscar. Although displaying a new choreographic direction, the folk-opera "Big Deal" (1987), Fosse's last Broadway show, was not a box-office success. Fosse died of a heart attack while walking to the opening of a Broadway revival in 1987.

Continued interest in Fosse's choreography has resulted in a revival of "Chicago" (1996), re-choreographed by the former Fosse dancer *Ann Reinking* (b. 1949). This movie received six Academy Awards in 2003. It was also Ann Reinking who conceived the idea of creating a retrospective of Fosse's work, "Fosse" (1999), in the form of a Broadway revue and later a television special, with the co-direction of Gwen Verdon. To do this, dances had to be selected that could stand on their own out of the context of the original story line of their book musical.

Michael Bennett (1943–1987), who choreographed "See-Saw" in 1973, conceived the idea for "A Chorus Line," a show based on the actual life histories of a group of Broadway "gypsies" (chorus dancers). "A Chorus Line" became the longest-running Broadway show of any kind, running from 1975 to 1990, until "Cats" broke this record in 1997. "A Chorus Line" is frequently revived in regional theaters and was also made into a successful film in 1985, choreographed by Jeffrey Hornaday. A Broadway revival, staged by *Baayork Lee*, appeared in 2007, and followed the original Bennett choreography meticulously. (See the author's interview with Lee in this chapter.)

Two American jazz teachers of this period, *Gus Giordano* (1930–2008) and *Luigi* (b. 1925), had a strong impact on the international jazz dance community. Giordano moved to Chicago to stage a television series, "The Jazz Dance," in 1955. He opened a dance school in Evanston, Illinois, and became the director of the touring jazz company, Gus Giordano Jazz Dance Chicago. Many of his protégés continue to teach new generations of dancers at conventions and workshops nationally and internationally.

Luigi suffered an automobile accident as a young man that left his right side paralyzed. Determined to recover totally, he worked with ballet teacher Edith Jane and was able to return to full mobility. He then created a jazz technique with a strong ballet foundation and a flowing and highly musical style. His former students include actors Gretchen Wyler, Robert Morse and Julie Newmar. (See the author's interview with Luigi in this chapter.)

In 1990 Giordano and Luigi, along with Matt Mattox, initiated the American Jazz Dance World Congress in Chicago. Continuing to this day, the event offers classes and performances in a variety of jazz styles, bringing together teachers, students and proponents of jazz dance from all parts of the world. Luigi received the Living Legend award at the first Congress.

THE TAP REVIVAL, VIDEO DANCE AND HIP-HOP

The 1980s was an outstanding decade for dance on film, comparable in numbers and quality to the 1930s. "The Turning Point," a movie about dancers' lives, was immensely popular in 1978. Movies such as "Saturday Night Fever" (1982), starring *John Travolta*, further popularized the disco dance craze. Breakdancing appeared in a series of films that mixed trained jazz dancers and street dancers: "Breakin'" and "Fast Forward" (both 1984) included sequences of electric boogie (sequential movements traveling through the body), popping (any strongly percussive isolated movement) and shoulder and head spins. "Fame" (1980), the story of dance students at the High School of Performing Arts in New York City, was a box-office hit that inspired a television series. "Grease" (1982) and "Dirty Dancing" (1988) featured dances of earlier eras (the 1950s and 1960s, respectively). Other films, like "Staying Alive" (1983) and "White Nights" (1986) depicted the lives of professional dancers. Most of these films were thin on plot but offered the opportunity to see favorite stars in some excellent dance sequences.

Several of these movies featured former Broadway and even vaudeville tap dancers, serving to spark a revival of interest in tapping. Three films starring *Gregory Hines* (1946–2003)—"The Cotton Club" (1984), "White Nights" (1985) and "Tap" (1989)—reestablished his career as both dancer and actor. "Tap" brought to a new generation of viewers some of the old vaudeville greats, and also introduced a rising young tapper, thirteen-year-old *Savion Glover* (b. 1973). Glover later distinguished himself as the choreographer of the 1996 Broadway hit "Bring in 'da

Noise, Bring in 'da Funk," for which he invented a powerful new street-driven tap style known as "tap-rap." In 2002, he hosted the 15th annual Tap Extravaganza, a four-hour live tribute to tap, held in New York City's Town Hall. Savion continues to choreograph and perform for musicals and music videos. More recently, in 2006, he choreographed the movie "Happy Feet," in which he appeared dancing in his unique style as a penguin.

The 1970s and 1980s also saw the acceptance of women not just as precision line tap dancers but as members of the new rugged and syncopated rhythm tap groups. For the first time ever, young girls in dance schools were trained in rhythm tap and encouraged to find their own expression. While some of the early female rhythm tappers dressed as men (this happened in the first Broadway version of "Bring in Da Noise"), today's hard-hitting female tappers apply their own standards of dress and movement style to their art. Even more recently, women have made inroads as "b-girls" in the flamboyant and acrobatic art of hip-hop.

The 1980s also saw the rise of tap festivals, one of the earliest being By Word of Foot, held at the Village Gate in New York in 1980. This and later festivals were the gathering places of tap legends who got their start in vaudeville, as well as newer generations of tappers.

The all-male touring group known as *Tap Dogs*, originating in Australia but now including American men, uses rock, heavy metal and homemade percussion in their gritty new tap dance style. Stripped of the old elegance and wearing workmen's clothes, their style might be described as "urban street tap." Broadway also has offered tap-revival shows featuring older, more nostalgic forms of tap, such as "Bubblin' Brown Sugar" (1976), "Sophisticated Ladies" (1981), and "42nd Street" (2001). Other musicals, for example the smash hit "Cats" (1982–2002), choreographed by *Gillian Lynne* (b. 1926) (see biography at the end of this chapter), and "Contact" (1999), written, choreographed and directed by *Susan Stroman* (b. 1960), pushed theater dance beyond the usual jazz forms in order to express specific characters and situations.

The sinuous, feline vocabulary of "Cats" is an amalgam of ballet, modern and jazz; "Cats," which continues on the touring circuit, became the longest-running musical ever on Broadway but this title was lost to the "Phantom of the Opera" (1988), also choreographed by Gillian Lynne.

Stroman's "*Contact*" consist of three playlets containing quasi-baroque dance, ballet and new swing, respectively. Stroman first made the transition from performer to choreographer when she was given the rights to choreograph "Flora the Red Menace" off-Broadway by its composers, John Kander and Fred Ebb. She crossed into dance fusion with *Blossom Got Kissed* (1998) for the New York City Ballet in honor of its fiftieth anniversary and *But Not For Me* (2000) for the Martha Graham Company. Teaming up with writer Mel Brooks, a hit musical version of his movie "The Producers" appeared on Broadway, followed by "Young Frankenstein" in 2007.

With the advent of music videos, rock groups and pop singers began hiring choreographers and backup dancers to add street moves and visual interest to their acts. Promoted by stars such as *Michael* and *Janet Jackson* and *Madonna*, dance quickly became an integral part of music videos. The music video "Thriller" (1984), choreographed for Michael Jackson by *Michael Peters* (1948–1994), presented dance sequences in a creative way to a new viewing public, further increasing its popularity.

Music videos, with their emphasis on quick cuts and flashes, and the addition of computer-generated special effects, have changed the way dance is filmed. Fred Astaire demanded the full dancer on camera with the fewest possible camera changes. He would be amazed at the fragmented views of dancers and choreography, lightning-fast editing, and instant background and costume changes now used in music videos. Martin Scorcese, the director of Michael Jackson's video "Bad" (1987), summarizes this change by stating, "The camera itself is dancing . . . it speaks another language to a younger generation."[7] More recent music videos, while technologically creative, have deemphasized the use of interesting choreography and trained dancers.

Hip-hop had its early budding in the 1970s in New York, with early rap records like "Fatback Band's King Tim 111," widely regarded as the genre's first single. All female rap ensembles such as *The Sequence* also appeared in the 1970s. As rap and hip-hop continued to flourish, a sense of grievance among the old-school rappers and djs from the lean beginning years toward today's artists who "can drive around in Bentleys, with their jewelry and million-dollar homes"[8] also developed. Hip-hop continued to grow from a New York specialty to an international craze. By the 1990s, the pervasive and long-lasting popularity of hip-hop music and movement had created a whole subculture in the jazz dance world. Separate classes in hip-hop movement, which teach the difficult skills involved in this sometimes daredevil style, now can be found in many dance studios and dance conventions.

THE AMERICAN ORIGINALS IN THE NEW MILLENIUM

The movie-going public continues to be fascinated by the real stories behind the glamour of the dance profession. Two films in 2000 explored dancers' lives and the motivations behind the young people who seek out this demanding career. "Center Stage," choreographed by Susan Stroman, dealt with the importance of mental attitude as opposed to the "perfect body" for success as a dancer. It also contained outstanding examples of blended ballet and jazz movement. "Billy Elliot" openly explored issues of gender roles and the stigmatization of men in ballet by the general public. A successful British film in 2000, it opened as a Broadway musical in 2008.

Jazz dance continues to be influenced by developments in popular music. Disco music, punk rock, new wave, rap and reggae all have found their way into the jazz class and stage performance.

Fusion music, combining jazz with pop or rock, is also being used by choreographers. The craze for Latin rhythms continues into the new millennium with a string of energetic and sensuous dances. Latin rhythms are now an integral part of jazz dance. The proliferation of "world beat," multicultural blends of music, have opened up intriguing new choreographic possibilities.

Also in the new century, televised dance competition shows continue to grow in popularity. In 2008, "America's Best Dance Crew" challenged the popularity of "American Idol." Dance Crew favored young people, with a lot of hip-hop and acrobatic movements, but other dance forms including ballet also appeared. A lot of regional pride was engendered in the audience reactions, rather like a combination of sport and art. "Hip-hop being watered-down can happen with the media, but we do study up on our roots," states *Ben Chung*, a member of JabbaWockeeZ, a group that appears on "America's Best Dance Crew."

Both hip-hop and tap were featured on the Disney Channel's smash hit, "High School Musical" which premiered in 2007.

The international popularity of American films and music videos, the youthful vitality of jazz and tap dance, and the opportunity to make a personal statement in these dance forms are what make them so satisfying to many participants. New technology makes American culture more easily available to audiences everywhere, and interest in the "American hybrids" will continue to grow.

PROFILE: LUIGI ON JAZZ DANCE

Note: At the time of this writing, in early 2009, Luigi, (Eugene Louis Facciuto), a living jazz legend, at the age of 83 was teaching two classes a day at his studio in New York, the Luigi Jazz Center.

Harriet Lihs   Luigi, most people know about the auto accident that changed your life, but you were a professional dancer before that happened. What were the early influences that led you into dance?

Luigi   I've been dancing all my life! When I was ten years old I was competing in amateur contests and I was winning a lot of them with my singing and tap dancing. I had a very supportive brother, Tony, who worked out with me and stretched me. I had wonderful ballet teachers in Los Angeles: Adolph Bolm, Mme. Bronislava Nijinska and mostly Edith Jane. Back then there was no such thing as a "jazz" class—I took ballet and tap.

HL   Tell me about the auto accident and how you rehabilitated yourself. Is it true the doctors told you that you would never be able to walk again?

L The accident came after World War II, December of 1946. After I woke up from a month-long coma, the right side of my body and the left side of my face were paralyzed. During that time a voice in my head kept repeating "never stop moving!" I developed my own rehab, based on ballet barre exercises. It took two and a half years before I could dance again, but I was better than before because I HAD to put my body in correct

LUIGI

positions to have balance. After I started working on movie sets I did my own warm-ups and other dancers started to follow me. Gene Kelly said to me, "Luigi, you should do something with this."

HL So you began working with Hollywood choreographers and their dancers?

L That's how I got the nickname of "the Body Doctor." My technique was based on using space as your barre. I was never interested in choreographing, just teaching.

HL What are some of the Hollywood films you worked on?

L I worked on "White Christmas," "On the Town," "Annie Get Your Gun" and "Singin' in the Rain." I worked a lot with Hermes Pan, Astaire's choreographer, also Bob Alton, Gene Kelly and Michael Kidd. I coached Eugene Loring's dancers in the film "The Five Thousand Fingers of Dr. T," a Dr. Seuss movie. About the only one in Hollywood I didn't work with was Jack Cole.

HL You were doing so well in Hollywood, how did you wind up in New York?

L I first went to New York to perform on Broadway with Ethel Merman in "Happy Hunting." The choreographer, Alex Romero, knew my dancing because we worked together in L.A. After that, June Taylor invited me to teach at her school. She had the June Taylor Dancers, who were appearing on TV frequently. I taught for her for six or eight months, then went out on my own. That was in the late 1950s. At that time there were only four other jazz teachers in New York. I've been running my own studio ever since, plus teaching master classes. I've taught in many places around the world—South Africa, Italy and Germany; my technique is very popular in Japan. I am still doing some touring, along with my assistant, Francis J. Roach. I worked with Twyla Tharp, who choreographed the Broadway version of "Singing in the Rain;" the night the show closed she brought me onstage for a bow. Among my students are Ben Vereen, Ann Reinking, Bobby Morse, Susan Stroman, Alvin Ailey, Valerie Harper, Tony Roberts, Charlotte D'Amboise and many of the early New York City Ballet stars. I continue to work with Liza Minnelli and really brought her back to performing after a series of injuries. Prince Maximillian of Austria has taken my classes when he's in New York, and I've also worked with both Down Syndrome and young deaf adults.

HL Do you have a favorite quote (from someone else, or your own)?

L   Susan Stroman said: "There's a little bit of Luigi in every dancer." As for me, the worst thing that ever happened to me was the best thing that happened to me. I developed the Luigi technique and stayed with it all these years. I want others to continue my work, but only those who really understand how to teach it.

HL Anything else you would like to say about your technique?

L   I've written two books on my warm-ups that explain my technique, and there is also a DVD of my teaching. My technique relies heavily on *épaulement* [use of the shoulders]. I use *épaulement* even more than the ballet people today. It's also about learning that your body parts are instruments, put together from the heart and conducted by the soul.

Learn to feel from the inside, and never stop moving.

PROFILE: BAAYORK LEE ON BROADWAY DANCE
Choreographer, Director and Producer in Theater, Film and Opera, New York, 2008

Harriet Lihs Baayork, you are one of the busiest choreographers I know. What are you working on right now?

Baayork Lee Well, the revival of "A Chorus Line" which I choreographed, closed on Broadway last August. It never recouped fully from the stagehand's strike. So I have been working with the touring company auditioning and training new people. We just came back from five weeks in Toronto.

HL I understand that Michael Bennett designated you to be the person to reproduce the choreography of "A Chorus Line" (ACL). But what happened with the movie?

BL Yes, I had been working with Michael since his first Broadway show "A Joyful Noise." ACL opened in 1974 off-Broadway, then moved to Broadway. No one expected it would be such a smash hit. I have the entire choreography of ACL in my head, plus all the formations written down in a book called "Baayork's Bible." As for the movie, Michael Bennett left the project in the middle due to disagreements with the producers, and the they wouldn't hire any of Michael's people. The show was offered to Bob Fosse, Jerome Robbins, Tommy Tune and Mike Nichols; they all turned it down because it was Michael's project. Jeffrey Hornaday accepted it. The only thing left of Michael's choreography was the tap number.

HL You started performing on Broadway when you were a small child. How did that happen?

BL For "The King and I," casting people came to Chinatown. I was only five, I don't remember either singing or dancing at the audition. I stayed in the show almost three years. That was when I decided I wanted to be a dancer. When I left the show, Jerome Robbins helped me get a scholarship at the School of American Ballet. I started in the first division and went through all the divisions. Finally they told me I was too short for ballet—at that point I gave up going to SAB. But I had also studied Afro–Cuban with Katherine Dunham on Saturdays and ballet there with Karel Shook. Arthur Mitchell would pick me up and take me to class. So by the time I auditioned for the High School of Performing Arts I had had some very good training. The modern teachers wanted me to be a modern major but I insisted on staying in ballet.

HL Tell me about your own choreography and directing.

BL The first show I choreographed on my own was "Where's Charley?" for the Montclair, NJ Operatic Society. Then I was asked to choreograph "Animal Crackers" for the Arena Stage in Washington, DC. This led to a series of operas choreographed for the Washington Opera, starting with "The Merry Widow." I was their resident choreographer for several years. Our opera "Porgy and Bess" was sent to Australia. Years later I was to direct and choreograph a company that played in Japan, Germany, Italy and other European cities for the next twelve years. From this production, a German producer saw my work and invited me to direct and choreograph a European company of "Jesus Christ Superstar," which ran for two years.

HL What are some of the most memorable moments of your career?

BL When "A Chorus Line" broke the record for the longest running show on Broadway in 1983, there were 500 dancers on the Schubert Theater stage. Every company that ever performed in the US and around the world was there.

Directing "Porgy and Bess" at the Rome Opera and bowing on that magnificent stage was another memorable experience. Establishing two musical theater schools, one in Japan and the other in Korea, was a third. And finally, establishing myself as a producer in Japan and Korea.

HL What do you do to stay fit and relax?

BL I take Bikram Yoga classes and I love to walk in Central Park. As for relaxing, I spend so much time in hotels, it feels like a vacation just to be at home.

HL Do you have any projects left that you still would like to do?

BL Yes. I would like to form an Asian performing company in New York, giving Asian singers, dancers and actors more opportunities to perform.

HL How would you sum up your career?

BL I've had a wonderful exciting life because of my career. I've had the opportunity to work all over the world thanks to ACL helping me get my foot in the door. I hope I have made a difference in many lives in the theater. I am not done yet, it will take years of preparation for me to continue to produce something truly worthwhile.

Profile: Lou Arrington, on Tap Dance
Beaumont, Texas, January 2009

Harriet Lihs Do you think the content and style of tap performances has changed during these early years of the new millennium, including your own pieces?

Lou Arrington I think that Gregory Hines started bringing changes back in the '80s, and he mentored Savion Glover, and now that Savion has gotten older, rhythm tap has grown. In rhythm tap, there are new names for the old steps, the style is less up and bouncy, the new style is lower. In my new tap, I'm taking that new style, current jazz styles and hip-hop style and incorporating it into the footwork in my teaching and choreography. Definitely you will see it at conventions—it's spreading all over the country. Tap in general is being seen more on television lately.

HL Can you define rhythm tap, and what makes it different from the older styles?

LA Well, it's a funny name since all tap is rhythm. In the old days, the rhythms would be simpler, the hands are placed and set. This is the old Broadway or chorus line style. In the rhythm tap it is more free, you aren't trying to dance exactly like the person next to you, you do more heel work, you might not get off the floor, you can actually move faster, its noisier, like drumming on the floor, and more intricate. You will be in time with the person next to you but you aren't trying to copy someone. Savion has done rhythm tap to all kinds of music, everything from hip-hop to Bach.

HL Are there any other people that you would cite beside Savion that are in the forefront of this new style?

LA Jason Samuel Smith, Derek Grant—there are many I could add. Smith danced on one of the television competitions, so did Savion. There are some teachers that are crossovers like Charles McGowan, who was in "A Chorus Line" and Corey Finn—they do the old style but very creatively. They were the transition people, in the 1990s, not as hard-hitting as the real rhythm tappers. Today you kind of have to know all the styles because you still will see the old styles used, wherever they revive "42nd Street" or other period musicals.

HL Is tap still a male-dominated dance style, or is it changing?

LA It is changing gradually. Here in Texas, Tapestry and Austin on Tap have female performers. But the men do seem to have a little more power and speed and energy. I don't know if that is the reason, but tap was developed originally by men who mentored boys, while girls gravitated to ballet or jazz. The new companies will welcome you regardless of your sex if you know what you are doing. Lately there has been a lot of solo, duo and trio pieces where individuality is encouraged, but in the larger-group works you have to downplay individuality because it gets too messy, it clashes with precision line dancing. I also saw Austin on Tap do a modern piece in tap shoes.

HL Tell me how your style has evolved in the last five or six years. In the lecture-demonstration you did here at the university, I saw your rhythm tap dancers do a step rising on their toes with bent knees, which Savion did at age 13 in the movie "Tap."

LA My rhythms have become more luscious, more super-syncopated. I take basic steps like flap ball-change, shuffle-ball-change and changed the rhythm completely, a whole wonderland of ways of doing the step. You don't have to invent new steps, just new ways of doing them; new accents like stepping on your flat foot instead of always on the balls of you feet. So that's what I try to do in my tap classes. We don't do steps, we do rhythms. When Tap Team Two came here on tour, they made us stand in a circle and "trade eights," continuing around the circle and improvising on the spot, making tap into a musical form as well as a dance form. In a 2008 piece the whole body danced, we didn't dance from the knees down, Irish-style, we studied the way the body takes weight, the whole body is put where you make the noise. It's much more interesting to watch. There were people doing this in the 1940s, great tappers like the Nicholas Brothers and Gene Kelly, so we're really just getting tap back into its stride again. Just the music has changed. Good tapping is good tapping!

OTHER TAP AND JAZZ NOTABLES

Paula Abdul (b. 1962) began her choreographic career working with the L.A. Laker Girls, then became dance coach to Janet Jackson. She choreographed for both Janet and Michael Jackson and the film "The Doors" (1991) and the televised 1990 Academy Awards, before debuting as a singer and using her considerable talents as a tap and jazz dancer in her own music videos.

Rod Alexander (1919–1992) danced and acted in many television shows in the 1950s. He assisted Helen Tamaris in the choreography of "Great to Be Alive" on Broadway in 1950 and choreographed "Shinbone Alley" in 1957. He choreographed the 1956 film "Carousel" (except for Louise's ballet choreographed by Agnes De Mille). This was followed by the film "The Best Things in Life are Free."

Debbie Allen (b. 1950). An actress and dancer from Houston, Allen received an Emmy award in 1982 for Best Choreographer for the television series "Fame" as well as a nomination for her role in that series as Lydia Grant. She has choreographed five Academy Awards shows, and holds honorary doctorate degrees from Howard University and the North Carolina School of the Arts. Married with two children, she has also authored two children's books.

Cholly Atkins (1913–2003) and his partner *Charles "Honi" Coles* (1921–1992) formed a duo vaudeville act called Atkins and Coles. Atkins specialized in soft shoe, while Coles was known for fast-paced rhythm tap. In later life, Atkins became a choreographer for Motown Records' music videos. Coles made a performing comeback in the 1970s and also choreographed the Broadway hit "Bubblin' Brown Sugar" in 1976. His show-stopping number in Broadway's "My One and Only" earned him a Tony Award in 1983. Movie audiences saw him in supporting roles in "Dirty Dancing" and "Cotton Club." In 1991 he was awarded the National Medal for the Arts by President George H.W. Bush.

Josephine Baker (1906–1975) began her career as a vaudeville chorus girl and performed in all-black musicals on Broadway, helping to popularize dances such as the *Black Bottom* and the *Charleston*. She then moved to France, where she was highly successful in night clubs, becoming the toast of Paris. She is credited with bringing the "jazz craze" and popular American dances of the era to Paris.

Toni Basil (b. 1943) began recording pop songs in 1966, achieving a major hit with the single "Mickey" in 1986. She is credited with bringing street dance to prominence in music videos, forming a backup group known as the "Lockers." She choreographed videos and live shows for David Byrne's Talking Heads, The Monkees, and more recently, Bette Midler.

Pepsi Bethel (1918–2002) was the founder of the Pepsi Bethel Authentic Jazz Dance Theater. In 1969 his company toured eight African countries, sponsored by the US State Department. In

1981 he received a grant to make a documentary film on jazz dance that is now in the Library of Congress. Bethel has taught at the Alvin Ailey School of Dance (New York) and choreographed shows in London and Vienna.

Andy Blankenbuehler (birthdate not available), a prolific choreographer of Broadway and Off-Broadway shows, won the 2008 Tony Award for best choreography for the hit show "In the Heights." He choreographed the Broadway revival of "The Apple Tree," the West End (London) musical "Desperately Seeking Susan," "A Wonderful Life" (Papermill Playhouse, Milburn, NJ) and "Quark Victory" (Williamstown Theatre Festival, Massachusetts). He also teaches theater classes at Frank Hatchett's Broadway Dance Center.

Ray Bolger (1904–1987) distinguished himself as the Scarecrow in Hollywood's "Wizard of Oz" and was master of a slapstick dance style complete with comic pratfalls.

Brenda Bufalino (b. 1937), called the Grande Dame of Tap Dance, trained with Charles "Honi" Coles and toured Europe with him from 1975 to 1983. She is the artistic director of both the American Tap Dance Orchestra and the International Tap Dance Orchestra, groups of highly skilled tap dancers who have been instrumental in the revival of interest in tap dance since the early 1980s. Bufalino has operated the Woodpeckers Tap Center in Manhattan and been the guiding force in the creation of many tap festivals. She has received a Lifetime Achievement Award at Town Hall in New York, and the Tapestry Award in Boston. Ms. Bufalino has appeared as a soloist in Carnegie Hall, Avery Fisher Hall, the Apollo Theater and the Joyce Theater (all in New York) and the Kennedy Center in Washington D.C.

Danny Buraczeski (birthdate not available) is the director of Jazzdance, a company located in Minneapolis since 1993. He works in a wide range of musical forms and American dance forms, using styles such as the cakewalk, the blues, the Charleston and the Lindy as well as modern jazz choreography. Burazceski has also choreographed for the Boston Ballet.

Gregg Burge (1957–1998) began studying tap at the age of seven and performed in the Off-Broadway show "Bojangles" when he was 13. He attended the High School of Performing Arts and the Juilliard School in New York, and won the Astaire award for tap in 1986 and 1990. In 1987 he choreographed the music video "Bad" for Michael Jackson. He distinguished himself dancing in the movie version of "A Chorus Line" and was also featured in the PBS series "Dancing."

James Cagney (1899–1986) starred in Hollywood's "Yankee Doodle Dandy" (1942), the story of composer George M. Cohan. Cagney exemplified in his tap dancing the erect Irish style of step dancing, with arms held almost motionless at his sides.

Gower Champion (1920–1980), with his wife Marge (b. 1921), formed a highly popular dance pair in shows and on television during the 1940s and 1950s. They became the first husband-and-wife movie star dancing team. Gower also choreographed and directed successful musicals, including "Bye, Bye, Birdie" (1960), "Carnival" (1961), "Hello, Dolly!" (1964), "I Do! I Do!" (1966), and "42ⁿᵈ Street"(1980). At the age of eighty, Marge danced in the 2001 revival of "Follies."

Cyd Charisse (1922–2008). Born in Laredo, Texas, Ms. Charisse studied ballet and was accepted into the Ballet Russe Company in New York. She became a popular dance partner in Hollywood films in the 1940s and 1950s, appearing with Gene Kelly in "Singin' in the Rain" and "Brigadoon," and with Fred Astaire in "Dancing in the Dark" and "Silk Stockings."

Lou Conte (b.1942) grew up in Illinois, where he studied ballet and tap at an early age. He performed in his first Broadway show in 1964. From the mid-sixties to the early 1970s, he choreographed more than thirty musicals. He returned to Chicago, establishing the Lou Conte Dance Studio. In 1977, the Hubbard Street Dance Company was formed, a jazz-oriented group that has become immensely popular on the touring circuit, with Conte as artistic director. It is now called Hubbard Street Dance Chicago. Conte has been the recipient of several awards, and the company has become known for its Twyla Tharp repertory.

The company faced a major change in 2000, when Conte stepped down as artistic director. He was replaced by Jim Vincent (b. 1953). Vincent, who holds dual French and American citizenship, continues to encourage an eclectic mix of choreographers from within and outside the company. Since 2004 Hubbard Street Dance has done an annual performance with the Chicago Symphony Orchestra.

Agnes De Mille(1905–1993), remembered for her stunning ballet-based choreography in the Broadway shows "Oklahoma!" (1943) and "Carousel" (1945), first made a great contribution to the ballet world with *Rodeo* (1942). Choreographed for the Ballet Russe de Monte Carlo, *Rodeo's* representations of roping, riding and Western body language formed the basis of her choreography for "Oklahoma!" She was also a prolific author, producing several books on the history of dance, a biography of Martha Graham and her autobiography, *Dance to the Piper.*

Paul Draper (1909–1996), a noted, elegant tap dancer and teacher. Draper teamed up with the harmonica player Larry Adler in 1939 to form a popular touring act that lasted for nearly ten years. Draper wrote monthly articles for *Dance Magazine* during the years 1954–1963. He also wrote the book *On Tap Dancing,* published in 1978. He often tapped to classical music, which made him unique.

AGNES DE MILLE

Arthur Duncan (b. 1933 in California) first danced in junior high school and began studying tap with renowned teachers, including Nick Castle, who with Henry Mancini became his manager. In 1963, he auditioned for the television weekly "Lawrence Welk Show," becoming its first African-American performer. He sang and danced on the show until its finale in 1982. Duncan describes his style as rhythm tap. In 1989 he appeared in the movie "Tap." In his eighties, Duncan received the Living Legend Award from Oklahoma State University, a three-page spread in *Dance Magazine* and continues to offer tap clinics around the country.

Peter Gennaro (1919–2000), a popular choreographer in the 1960s, added a new style to jazz that was light, loose and flexible; he used ballet exercises to develop quick, articulate footwork in his dancers.

Frank Hatchett (birthdate not available), a New York jazz teacher, founded the Broadway Dance Center with Maurice Hines. He has taught jazz to thousands of young people and adults at the Center. His strongly rhythmic style, which he calls "Vop-ing the music," emphasizes personal interpretation. He co-authored a book on his unique dance technique in 2000.

Adrienne Hawkins is the artistic director of the Impulse Dance Company in Boston. She is a popular guest jazz dance teacher at schools and universities and has toured internationally as a solo performer.

Leticia Jay (birthdate not available) kept interest in tap alive in the 1960s with a series of televised "Tap Happenings" (1968), featuring former vaudeville tap greats such as "Honi" Coles and "Sandman" Sims.

Michael Kidd (1919–2007). In a career spanning fifty years he choreographed several Broadway shows, including "Finian's Rainbow" (1947), "Guys and Dolls" (1950), "Can-Can"(1953) and "Subways are for Sleeping"(1961), which he also directed. His energetic full-screen choreography for "Seven Brides for Seven Brothers" (1954) was a major factor in the film's success. It was followed by the films "Guys and Dolls" (1955), "L'il Abner" (1959), "Star!" (1968) and "Hello Dolly!" (1969). He earned five Tony Awards for Broadway dance, and in 1997 received an Honorary Oscar for Exceptional Contributions to the Making of Motion Pictures.

Jimmy Locust's (birthdate not available) height is only 4' 9" but his artistic output looms large. His work can be seen in films, television, videos, and commercials. He has choreographed for Debbie Allen, Quincy Jones, Paula Abdul, Janet Jackson and Michael Jackson. He choreographed for both the opening and closing of the 1996 Olympics and the musicals "Sweet Charity" and "Jesus Christ Superstar" for the Inland Theatre League of Los Angeles. In 2008 he joined the staff of New York's festival "Feelin' the Beat," where he taught hip-hop. The same year he produced "No Hate But Harmony," an anti-bullying symposium for middle school and high school students.

Gillian Lynne (b. 1926 in Bromley, England) began studying ballet on the advice of a doctor because of her restlessness in school. She joined the Sadler's Wells Ballet during World War II and became an admired dramatic ballerina. She left the ballet in 1951 and began performing in London's West End and in British films. As a choreographer and director, she has distinguished herself in both London and New York in theater and film, starting in the early 1960s. A total of 48 musicals include three highly successful collaborations with the composer/librettist team of Kander and Ebb: "Cats," "Phantom of the Opera" and "Aspects of Love." She also has thirteen film choreography credits. She has won a number of theatrical awards for her work, and is currently writing an autobiography.

Kathleen Marshall (b. 1962) is best known for her choreography for the revival of "Kiss Me, Kate"(1999) and staged the popular revivals series "Encores!"

Rob Marshall (b. 1960) both co-directed and choreographed the critically acclaimed 1999 production of "Cabaret." His other credits include "Kiss of the Spider Woman" (1992), a revival of "Damn Yankees" (1994), and "Victor/Victoria" (1995).

Matt Mattox (b.1921) is an American master teacher who introduced jazz dance technique to Europe. A student of Jack Cole, Mattox began choreographing for Broadway and television in the 1950s. He established himself as a prominent New York teacher and television choreographer. He taught in Paris for several years, subsequently moving to The Place, a dance school in London. In 1976 Mattox and his wife opened a dance school in Perpignan, France, which has become internationally known.

Ann Miller (1919–2004)) was a popular song-and-dance film star in the 1940s and 1950s. She was known for series of multiple turns and lightning-fast tapping speed. She continued her career as a television actress on shows such as "The Love Boat." Her last television appearance was in 1993 on "Home Improvement," in a segment titled "Dances with Tools."

Hermes Pan (1910–1990). Pan worked with Fred Astaire for most of the star's career, contributing dances to seventeen of Fred Astaire's films and three of his four television specials. He also choreographed many Hollywood movies without Astaire, including "My Fair Lady" (1964).

Rosie Perez (b. 1964), who started as a hip-hop dancer and choreographer, is credited with combining jazz and hip-hop into a new dance form for the Fly Girls of the television series "In Living Color." Perez has later developed a successful film acting career.

Chita Rivera (b. 1933), an accomplished dancer, singer and actress, has had an extensive career both in Broadway and film. She appeared in "Guys and Dolls" and "Can Can" but it was her role as the fiery Anita in "West Side Story" that made her a star. She appeared in the film "Sweet Charity" (1969), and as the lead in the Broadway musical "Kiss of the Spiderwoman" (1992).

Herbert Ross (1927–2008) began choreographing original and daring ballets in the 1950s for American Ballet Theatre. It was there that he met his first wife, Nora Kaye, who became his partner in a variety of projects. With her he formed the company Ballet for Two Worlds, which disbanded after a year of touring in Europe. On Broadway, Ross replaced George Balanchine as choreographer for "House of Flowers," and helped Barbara Striesand launch her career in "I Can Get it for you Wholesale" (1962). He also oversaw the choreography for "Funny Girl," starring Streisand, and its sequel, "Funny Lady" (1975). In 1967 he choreographed the dance sequences for the Hollywood film "Dr. Dolittle," followed by "The Goodbye Girl" in 1977 and "Footloose" in 1984. With Nora Kaye he produced the film "Nijinsky," starring Rudolph Nureyev, in 1980.

Donald Saddler (b. 1920 in California) joined Ballet Theatre when it was formed in 1939. In 1947 he appeared in his first Broadway show "High Button Shoes." He also danced at Radio City Music Hall and in nightclubs. He received his first Tony award for "Wonderful Town" (1953) and a second for "No, No, Nanette" (1971). At the age of eighty-one, he appeared in the 2001 revival of "Follies" on Broadway, a role he played at the Paper Mill Playhouse in 1998.

Lynn Simonson (birthdate not known) has been a master jazz teacher in New York for more than forty years. At present her jazz technique is being taught in nineteen countries worldwide. She developed the Jazz Project and New Vision teacher's workshop for the annual Jacob's Pillow Dance Festival, teaching there for more than twelve years. In 1984 she co-founded the Dance New Amsterdam in New York, which emphasizes the development of improving teaching methods in the jazz class. The focus is on anatomical training, and understanding how students vary in the way they learn "It's about clarity," she states . . . how students develop a muscle memory." She also presents workshops nationally and internationally.

Randy Skinner (b. ca. 1955) director/choreographer, choreographed the opening production number for the 2001 Tony Awards. He subsequently received Tony nominations for numerous Broadway revivals. He was chosen head choreographer for *The Gershwins' An American in Paris*, which debuted in Houston in 2008.

Subway Entertainment Crew, three cousins from the Bronx, *Travis Steele, Dante Steele* and *David Steele*, have organized a group of hip-hop artists who use moving subway cars as a performance venue four hours a day. While the use of the subway for dance is not a new idea in New York, the level of skill and daring in this new-millennium group makes it particularly successful.

Lee Becker Theodore (1933–1987) was devoted to the reconstruction of historically important social and theater dance for modern audiences. In 1975 she formed the American Dance Machine, a company devoted to jazz choreography. ADM preserved works by choreographers *Danny Daniels* (b. 1924), Agnes De Mille, Carol Haney, Michael Kidd and Bob Fosse. The company was especially noted for preserving the work of Jack Cole, recreated by former Cole dancers. In 1976 ADM produced a video of Cole dances (*Jack Cole: Interface 1976*). ADM also offered workshops in Cole technique.

Joe Tremaine (b. 1938), who studied with Luigi and Matt Mattox, opened his own school in Los Angeles in 1969. In addition, he choreographs commercials, television specials and nightclub acts. Tremaine dance conventions and competitions, which offer Tremaine technique and other dance styles, tour about fifteen cities twice a year.

Tommy Tune (b. 1939), an outstanding Houston-born tap dancer, received his first Tony award in Michael Bennett's "Seesaw" in 1973. He has choreographed and directed a number of shows, including "Best Little Whorehouse in Texas" (1977), "Cloud 9" (1981), "Nine" (1982) and "My One and Only" (1983). He received Tony awards for both directing and choreography for "The Will Rogers Follies" (1991), and appeared on Broadway in his one-man show, "Tommy Tune Tonite!" (1993).

Ben Vereen (b. 1946), a dynamic song and dance performer, attended New York's High School of Performing Arts, and while still a teenager was selected as the understudy for the lead role in "Golden Boy," starring Sammy Davis, Jr. He played the role of Judas in "Jesus Christ Superstar" on Broadway, then distinguished himself in Bob Fosse's "Pippin," receiving both the Tony and Drama Desk awards in 1972. After a long recovery from a stroke he returned to dance in "Jelly's Last Jam" (1992). He also starred in the Broadway retrospective of Fosse's work, "Fosse." In 2005 he appeared as the Wizard of Oz in Broadway's "Wicked," as well as live concerts in Carnegie Hall and Radio City Music Hall. Vereen has also appeared in many television musical specials, in the mini-series "Roots," and in acting roles on "Grey's Anatomy," "Law and Order" and "Law and Order: Criminal Intent."

Liz Williamson (1919–1996), noted jazz teacher and choreographer, received a master's degree in dance from New York University. She has taught and choreographed in Canada, Germany, Brazil and at several American universities, including Howard University and the Tuskegee Institute. She was the first artist-in-residence at Jacob's Pillow Dance Festival in 1973, where she choreographed "The Many Faces of Jazz" for 65 dancers.

Suggested Reading

Bean, Anne Marie, James V. Hatch and Brooks McNamara, eds. *Inside the Minstrel Mask: Readings in Nineteenth Century Blackface Minstrelsy*. Middletown, CT: Wesleyan University Press, 1996.

Billman, Larry. *Film Choreographers and Dance Directors*. Jefferson, NC: McFarland and Co., 1997.

Bloom, Juli. "Street Moves in the TV Room." *The New York Times,* June 8, 2008 (p. 8).

Carlson, Ginger Macchi. "Katherine Dunham." *CORD Newsletter,* Fall 2006.

Chang, Jeff. *Can't Stop, Won't Stop: A History of the Hip-Hop Generation.* New York: St. Martin's Press, 2005.

Cutcher, Jenai. "Dancing Like a Girl" (rhythm tap). *Dance Magazine,* May 2006, (pp. 48–50).

De Mille, Agnes, *The Book of the Dance.* New York: Golden Press, 1963.

———. *Dance to the Piper.* New York: Little, Brown and Co. 1952.

Draper, Paul. *On Tap Dancing.* New York: Marcel Dekker, Inc. 1978.

Emery, Lynne Fauley. *Black Dance From 1619 to Today.* 2nd, rev. ed. Princeton, NJ: Princeton Book Company, Publishers, 1988.

Engel, Lehman. *The American Musical Theater.* New York: Collier Books, 1975.

Frank, Rusty. *Tap! The Greatest Tap Dance Stars and Their Stories.* Rev. ed. New York: Da Capo Press, 1994.

Fricke, Jim and Charlie Ahearn. *Yes Yes Y'All: The Experience Music Project Oral History of Hip-Hop's First Decade."* New York: Da Capo Press, 2002.

Ganzl, Kurt. *Song and Dance.* London: Carlton Books, Ltd., 1995.

Glover, Savion and Bruce Weber. *Savion: My Life in Tap.* New York: William Morrow and Company, 2000.

Goldman, Phyllis. "Susan Stroman: Playing in the Major Leagues." *Dancer* Magazine, Nov. 2007 (pp. 66–71).

Gottfried, Martin. *All His Jazz: The Life and Death of Bob Fosse.* New York: Bantam Books, 1991.

Gottschild, Brenda Dixon. *Digging The Africanist Presence in American Performance.* Westport, CT: Greenwood Press, 2002.

Haskins, James. *Black Dance in America: A History Through Its People.* New York: HarperCollins, 1990.

Hatchett, Frank and Nancy Myers Gitlin. *Frank Hatchett's Jazz Dance.* Champaign, IL: Human Kinetics, 2000.

Hill, Constance Valis. *Brotherhood in Rhythm: The Jazz Tap Dancing of the Nicholas Brothers.* New York: Oxford University Press, 2000.

Jonas, Gerald. *Dancing: The Pleasure, Power, and Art of Movement.* New York: Harry N. Abrams, 1992.

Kriegel, Lorraine and Kim Chandler-Vaccaro. *Jazz Dance Today.* Minneapolis/St. Paul, MN: West Publishing Co., 1994.

La Rocco, Claudia A. "Breaking Battle Women Hope to Win." *The New York Times,* Aug. 6, 2006.

Lee, Baayork, and Thommie Walsh. *On the Line: The Creation of "A Chorus Line."* New York: Limelight Editions, 2006.

Lihs, Harriet. *Jazz Dance,* 3rd ed. Boston: American Press, 1993.

Loney, Glenn. *Unsung Genius: The Passion of Dancer-Choreographer Jack Cole.* New York: Franklin Watts, 1984.

Long, Robert Emmet. *Broadway, the Golden Years: Jerome Robbins and the Great Choreographer-Directors, 1940 to the Present.* New York: Continuum, 2001.

Magriel, Paul, ed. *Chronicles of the American Dance.* New York: Henry Holt and Co., 1948.

Mueller, John. *Astaire Dancing.* New York: Wings Books, 1985.

Spencer, Caitlin. "Tap's Renaissance." *Dance Spirit* Magazine, Dec. 2007 (p. 78–9).

Perron, Wendy. "Katherine Dunham: A One-Woman Revolution, in Art and Life" *Dance Magazine*, August 2000.

Reeves, Marcus. *Somebody Scream: Rap Music's Rise to Prominence*. New York: Faber and Faber, Inc. 2008.

Rogers, Ginger. *My Story*. New York: HarperCollins, 1991.

Stearns, Marshall and Jean Stearns. *Jazz Dance*. New York: Schirmer Books, 1968; new ed., New York: Da Capo Press, 1994.

Stratyner, Barbara. "Ned Wayburn and the Dance Routine: From Vaudeville to the Ziegfeld Follies." *Studies in Dance History*, No. 13, 1996.

Thomas, Tony. *That's Dancin'*. New York: Harry N. Abrams, 1984.

Viagas, Robert and Baayork Lee. *On the Line* ("A Chorus Line"). New York: William Morrow and Co., 1990.

VIDEOGRAPHY

Broadway: The American Musical, 3 DVDs, Insight Media, 2004.

Dance Black America. Dance Horizons, 1990.

Dancing. Volume IV, "The Individual and Tradition," and Volume VII, "New Worlds, New Forms." Kultur, 1992.

Dien Perry's Tap Dogs. CBS Fox Video, 1996.

Everybody Dance Now. Margaret Selby, VDI, 1992.

Every Little Step. Documents the making of the "A Chorus Line" revival. Sony, 2008.

Jazz Technique and the Dance Experience. Tremaine Conventions, Inc.

Leonard Reed's Shim Sham Shimmy. www.swingshiftontap.com (Rusty Frank) 2005.

Luigi: The Master Jazz Class. Hoctor Products, 1988.

Masters of Tap. "Honi" Coles, narr. Home Vision, Inc., 1988.

Memories of Vaudeville. American Masters Series, 1997.

Radio City Christmas Spectacular and Diamond at the Rock. MSG Entertainment, 2008

Sophisticated Ladies. Facets, 1989.

That's Dancing. MGM-UA, 1985.

That's Entertainment, I, II & III. MGM-UA, 1974, 1976, 1993.

HOLLYWOOD MOVIE MUSICALS

The following movies, listed in chronological order, with featured dance numbers are available on DVD or videocassette from stores and libraries.

1933 Dancing Lady, Fred Astaire, Joan Crawford,

Goldiggers of 1933, chor. Busby Berkeley.

Flying Down to Rio, Fred Astaire & Ginger Rogers (their first screen partnership).

1934   The Gay Divorcee, Astaire & Rogers.

Dames, Ruby Keeler, chor. Busby Berkeley.

Goldiggers of 1935, Ruby Keeler, chor. Busby Berkeley.

1935   Roberta, Astaire &Rogers.

Top Hat, Astaire &Rogers.

The Little Colonel, Bill "Bojangles" Robinson, Shirley Temple.

The Littlest Rebel, Bill "Bojangles" Robinson, Shirley Temple.

1936   The Great Ziegfeld, William Powell, Myrna Loy, Ray Bolger.

Follow the Fleet, Astaire &Rogers.

1937   Shall We Dance?, Astaire & Rogers.

Swing Time, Astaire &Rogers.

A Damsel in Distress, Fred Astaire, Joan Fontaine.

1938   Carefree, Astaire &Rogers.

The Goldwin Follies, Features the American Ballet of the Metropolitan Opera, chor. George Balanchine.

1940   Broadway Melody of 1940, Fred Astaire, Eleanor Powell.

1942   For Me and My Gal, Gene Kelly's film debut.

Yankee Doodle Dandy, James Cagney.

Holiday Inn, Fred Astaire.

1943   Stormy Weather, Bill "Bojangles" Robinson, the Nicholas Brothers, Katherine Dunham Dancers.

1944   Up in Arms, Danny Kaye.

Anchors Aweigh, Gene Kelly.

1945   Ziegfeld Follies, Fred Astaire, Gene Kelly, Cyd Charisse.

1948   Easter Parade, Fred Astaire, chor. Robert Alton.

1949   On the Town, Gene Kelly, Frank Sinatra, Ann Miller, Vera-Ellen, chor. Gene Kelly.

1950   Let's Dance, Fred Astaire, chor. Hermes Pan.

1951   An American in Paris, Gene Kelly, Leslie Caron, chor. Kelly.

1952   Royal Wedding, Fred Astaire, chor. Nick Castle.

Singin' in the Rain, Gene Kelly, Cyd Charisse, Debbie Reynolds, Donald O'Connor, chor. Kelly.

The Belle of New York, Fred Astaire and Vera Ellen, chor. Fred Astaire with Robert Alton.

1953   The Band Wagon, Fred Astaire, Cyd Charisse, chor. Michael Kidd.

1954   Kiss Me Kate, Ann Miller, Bob Fosse, chor. Hermes Pan.

       Seven Brides for Seven Brothers, Jacques d'Amboise, Matt Mattox, Russ Tamblyn, chor. Michael Kidd.

       The Pirate, Gene Kelly, the Nicholas Brothers.

1955   Kismet, chor. Jack Cole.

       It's Always Fair Weather, Gene Kelly, Cyd Charisse, chor. Kelly.

       Daddy Long Legs, Fred Astaire, Leslie Caron, chor. Roland Petit.

       Hit the Deck, Ann Miller, Debbie Reynolds, chor. Hermes Pan.

       Guys and Dolls, chor. Michael Kidd.

1956   The King and I, chor. Jerome Robbins.

       Carousel, chor. Agnes De Mille.

1957   Silk Stockings, Fred Astaire, Cyd Charisse, chor. Hermes Pan, Eugene Loring.

       The Pajama Game, chor. Bob Fosse.

1958   Damn Yankees, Gwen Verdon, chor. Bob Fosse.

1959   L'il Abner, chor. Michael Kidd, Dee Dee Wood.

1960   Can-Can, Shirley MacLaine, chor. Hermes Pan.

1961   West Side Story, Rita Moreno, Russ Tamblyn, chor. Jerome Robbins.

       Gypsy, chor. Jerome Robbins.

1963   Bye Bye Birdie, Dick van Dyke, chor. Onna White.

1964   The Unsinkable Molly Brown, Debbie Reynolds, chor. Peter Gennaro.

       Mary Poppins, Dick Van Dyke, Julie Andrews, chor. Dee Dee Wood and Marc Breaux.

       Wonderful Life, chor. Gillian Lynne.

1967   Half a Sixpence, chor. Gillian Lynne.

1968   Sweet Charity, Shirley Maclaine, Chita Rivera, Paula Kelly, chor. Bob Fosse.

       Finian's Rainbow, Fred Astaire.

       Oliver, chor. Onna White (winner of a special Academy Award for choreography).

1971   Fidder on the Roof, chor. Jerome Robbins.

1972   Cabaret, Liza Minnelli, chor. Bob Fosse.

1978   The Wiz, Michael Jackson, chor. Louis Johnson.

       Hair, chor. Twyla Tharp.

       Saturday Night Fever, John Travolta.

1979   All That Jazz, dir. and chor. Bob Fosse.

1980   Fame, chor. Louis Falco.

1981   Pennies from Heaven, chor. Danny Daniels.

1982   Grease, John Travolta, chor. Patricia Birch.

1983   Flashdance, Irene Jarrad, chor. Jeffrey Hornaday.

Staying Alive, John Travolta, chor. Albertina Rasch.

The Cotton Club, chor. Gregory Hines.

1984   Footloose, dir. Herbert Ross.

1985   A Chorus Line, chor. Jeffrey Hornaday.

1986   White Nights, Gregory Hines, Mikhail Baryshnikov, chor. Twyla Tharp.

1988   Salsa, chor. Kenny Ortega.

Dirty Dancing, Patrick Swayze, chor. Kenny Ortega.

1989   Tap, Sammy Davis, Jr., Gregory Hines, Savion Glover.

1990   Grease 2, chor. Patricia Birch.

1997   Cats (the Broadway musical, available on DVD). chor. Gillian Lynne.

1998   Les Miserables (the Broadway musical, available on DVD).

Dance with Me, Vanessa Williams, chor. Liz Curtis.

2000   Billy Elliot, chor. Peter Darling

Center Stage, chor. Susan Stroman.

2001   Save the Last Dance, Julia Stiles.

Moulin Rouge, Nicole Kidman, dir. Baz Luhrmann, chor. John O'Connell.

2002   Chicago, chor. Rob Marshall.

2004   Dirty Dancing: Havana Nights, dir. Guy Ferland.

2005   Rent, Taye Diggs, Rosario Dawson, dir. Chris Columbus.

2005   The Producers, chor. Susan Stroman.

2006   Happy Feet, chor. Savion Glover.

2006   Dreamgirls, chor. Fatima Robinson based on orig. chor. Michael Bennett.

2007   High School Musical 2.

2007   Hairspray, chor. Adam Shankman.

2008   High School Musical 3: Senior Year.

CHAPTER SEVEN

CAREERS IN DANCE

May I propose a toast. To dancers: for whatever personal hell you may go
through. For whatever professional calumny may be heaped upon you . . .
you ARE the profession. Without you there is no dance.
—*Murray Louis, modern dancer/choreographer*

Art changes because changes in science give the artist
a different understanding of nature.
—*John Cage, composer*

The critic who is satisfied is damned.
—*Alastair MacCaulay, dance critic, The New York Times*

I always need a reason to work. For me, it is not just turning out another dance,
like a machine . . . An artist should not only mirror his time, but reflect upon it.
—*Pauline Koner, modern dancer/choreographer*

As in the past, the performing arts will continue to be one of America's most important exports. Even the strongest holdouts against "westernization" are capitulating: China, for example, now has a professional modern dance company, formed in 1992 in Guangdong; American artists often find secure positions at state-supported theaters in foreign countries. At home, however, dance jobs in the 1990s became fewer and more difficult to maintain because of rising costs and cutbacks in funding from the National Endowment for the Arts and other sources. This has forced independent dance artists to scatter around the nation, rather than collect in a few large urban centers as did the previous generation. (This trend is a plus for audiences outside large urban centers.) Whether legislators will reverse this trend by providing more funding for the arts, or whether the private and corporate sectors will take up the slack, remains to be seen.

While technology continues to produce ever more sophisticated forms of "virtual" entertainment, it is unlikely that they will replace the immediacy and excitement of a live performance. Thanks to the technology that will bring new dance forms to new audiences, the interest in being part of the live performance experience may actually increase. Those who, today, create the dance world as we know it—the professional dancer, choreographer, and dance educator—will still be in demand in the future.

THE PROFESSIONAL DANCER

Choosing dance as a career is a decision that is often made at a very young age. The advantage to this is that the young person can start training early. The disadvantage is that he or she often sees this career as glamorous without understanding the amount of hard work and dedication needed to succeed. The life of a professional dancer in the United States is highly demanding and often not financially rewarding, so much so that only those who truly love what they are doing remain in the profession very long.

JODY OBERFELDER DANCE PROJECTS in *Re:Sound.* The influences of Pilobolus and contact improvisation meet the common hub cap.

Deanna McBrearty, a member of the corps de ballet of the New York City Ballet, describes her experiences as a professional dancer:

> *The hardest thing about being a dancer is what it asks of you mentally, physically, and spiritually. That is a lot you have to give at a young age. It isn't just an art form, it's a lifestyle . . . It is not something you can just go cold turkey and walk away from.*[1]

Even dancers who, like McBrearty, succeed in acquiring professional positions after years of training and numerous auditions, may face an uncertain future. Funding for dance companies fluctuates from season to season and is a constant issue for company managers. The dancer in a modern dance or ballet company may find the season cut short or the tour canceled for lack of funds, while the Broadway dancer may rehearse a show that closes before it even reaches Broadway.

The emphasis on youth, especially in the ballet world, puts an extra time crunch on prospective dancers. If a young woman is not accepted into a professional ballet company by the time she is nineteen, her chances for acceptance begin to diminish. There have been some notable exceptions to this pattern, however. Male ballet dancers, in shorter supply than females, have more leeway in terms of age. Modern dancers, in contrast, improve their chances for professional work by first attending a college or university with a good dance program.

Another stumbling block in a professional dance career is the preference among company directors for specific body types. Both ballet dancers and precision line dancers may be required to be a certain height: the former because it is considered ungainly for the woman on pointe to be taller than her male partner, the latter because the line must look homogeneous. For the Broadway or nightclub dancer, whether male or female, looking sexy is often a requirement. Some shows have much more specific requirements for hair color, height, weight, race and so forth. In recent years, a few dance companies have broken away from the stereotyped dancer's look. For example, choreographers Mark Morris and Bill T. Jones like individuality in the look of their dancers: tall, short, graying, bald, heavy or thin.

Unquestionably, the more dance styles the young dancer has mastered, the better the chances of professional work. Related skills may also make a big difference in employability. These skills include everything from tumbling and juggling to singing and acting. The result of having these skills may mean employment in related areas, such as in mime troupes and aerial teams (people in overhead harnesses allowing them to soar and dip to music), where dance training is a huge advantage.

Attending auditions, learning the protocols involved and presenting oneself in the best possible way are skills in themselves. Perhaps the most useful information the dancer can have before an audition is what the choreographer or director is looking for. This involves keeping one's finger on the pulse of the profession by reading the trade magazines and the newspaper dance critics, attending concerts and understanding the work of as many companies and the styles of as many choreographers as possible.

Once the dancer finds professional employment, she or he will be protected by one of several unions for performers. The American Guild of Musical Artists (AGMA) and the American Guild of Variety Artists (AGVA) have improved pay and working conditions for dancers and ensure that rehearsal time and the weekly number of performances will be within reason. Even so, performance schedules are usually rigorous, with only one day off a week during the season and even more difficult schedules when touring. Therefore, it is important for dancers to learn to pace themselves, conserve energy and maintain a healthy lifestyle: those who do not quickly suffer from burnout.

DANCERS' HEALTH CONCERNS

Physical Pressures on the Body

The ballet world is particularly hard-hit by injuries that can curtail a dance career. Clearly the professional dancer puts stresses on the body that are similar to that of a professional athlete. This makes the dancer subject to many overuse injuries. A small imbalance such as unequal leg length, misalignment or tightness in one muscle group, which might cause minimal problems in ordinary life, could result in an injury when a regimen of daily classes, rehearsals and performances is imposed. For ballet and jazz dancers, the constant stretching of ligaments required for high leg extensions can result in joint problems after a period of time. Turnout of the legs, if forced or improperly taught from the lower leg instead of the hip, can cause injuries to the knees. Pointe shoes for women have their own set of damaging injuries to the toes, arches and ankle joints. For all dancers, knees, feet and lower backs are subject to stress fractures from the constant impact of jumps and leaps. Dancers' footwear is generally lighter and not as protective as that of runners, basketball players and other sports participants; as a result, there is a high incidence of stress fractures of the lower leg and foot, which is further aggravated if the studio or rehearsal space has a poor floor.

Ethan Steifel, a principal dancer at American Ballet Theater who made his film debut in "Center Stage" (2000), was by 2006 suffering from knee problems. Steiffel was known for high-leaping virtuosity, the type of dancer most prone to injuries. Those who emphasize lyrical adagio work generally age more gracefully.

Dancers who injure themselves often return to dancing too soon for the injury to heal fully. As highly active individuals, dancers become impatient with slow rehabilitation; financial considerations and a fear of losing coveted performance opportunities are also factors. Since dancers like to take an active role in their own recovery, many seek out body therapies that retrain damaged muscles and joints, including Pilates Method®, Alexander Technique®, hatha yoga, tai chi, pool exercises and weight training. Chiropractic, acupuncture and massage therapies are also popular among dancers.

The Need to be Thin

Another health consideration, especially for female dancers, is the emphasis on extreme slenderness as a desirable aesthetic. Unfortunately, Balanchine's emphasis on model-style thinness for his ballerinas has reinforced this problem in America, while European dancers do not seem to go to the same extremes of dieting. Ballet dancers are most at risk of developing eating disorders such as bulimia and anorexia nervosa in an attempt to conform to company policies on weight. Perfectionist personalities who are highly self-critical and self-demanding—a type often found in ballet companies—are most prone to develop anorexia nervosa, a disease related to issues of self-esteem and a need for control. Because female ballet dancers are often still teenagers when they become members of companies, those who develop this disorder risk permanent stunting of bone development and a higher incidence of bone fractures because of delayed onset of menstruation. Women who do not have periods do not produce estrogen, which results in osteoporotic bones. Studies have found that such women in their thirties may have bones that, when scanned, resemble the bone density of women in their seventies. Extremely low body fat, averaging ten to fifteen percent below normal in female ballet dancers[2] also makes them more susceptible to disease and exhaustion.

Some dancers also smoke cigarettes in an effort to keep their weight down, a practice that causes a variety of health problems and can shorten their careers. Smoking for a dancer makes about as much sense as smoking for a long-distance runner. In 1997 the sudden death from heart failure of *Heidi Guenther*, a twenty-two-year-old Boston Ballet dancer with an eating disorder, publicized the issue of extreme standards for young dancers, underscoring the need for careful nutritional and lifestyle counseling for dancers rather than simply demands to lose weight. Today, many companies hold workshops on healthy eating habits for their dancers, and provide access to nutritionists and counselors for their dancers working through problems with eating disorders.

The AIDS Epidemic

During the 1980s and 1990s, the dance community was particularly hard-hit by the AIDS epidemic. Many artists with irreplaceable talents were lost to this disease, and many choreographic works were created expressing the sense of loss and devastation engendered by it. In the new century the dance community continues to be active in fundraising for AIDS research, and in improving understanding of the disease.

Dance medicine has become the specialty of a small group of doctors and researchers dedicated to the identification, treatment and prevention of illnesses and injuries in dancers. In recent years, much clinical and experimental research has been conducted on dancers. Many books have now been written on the topic of dancers' health. The International Association for Dance Medicine and Science was formed in 1990 by an international group of dance medicine practitioners and dance educators. It holds annual conferences and publishes the *Journal of Dance Medicine & Science*. It also published second editions of *Dance Medicine & Science Bibliography* and *Dance Medicine Resource Guide*.

CAREER TRANSITIONS FOR DANCERS

One of the most difficult parts of a dancer's life is the transition from performing to another career. Dancers who have poured their hearts and souls into performing for a large part of their lives often feel unprepared for any other career when age or failing health forces them to stop dancing. Some come to their performing careers directly from high school; they are used to socializing with other dancers almost exclusively and feel lacking in skills needed in the larger world. They are unaware that their experiences as dancers prepare them in many ways for other careers. The physical and mental self-discipline, ability to work as part of a group, memorization skills and self-reliance demanded of dancers make them reliable and desirable workers in other professions.

Some dancers find their skills are best used in fields closely related to dance. They may have expertise in the work of a particular choreographer and be in demand for setting his or her works on other companies.

If they have administrative abilities (a degree in arts administration is also helpful) they may become company managers, professional fundraisers or public relations advisers for dance companies or other arts organizations.

Others who acquire specialized training in massage therapy, Pilates, yoga or other body therapies have become particularly valuable in their work with performers. Those who have well-developed language skills and an educational background may parlay their understanding of the dance world into careers as dance critics, historians and biographers.

Many former dancers continue to be active in the dance world as teachers and choreographers. Organizations exist around the world to help dancers make the transition out of dancing, for example the Dancer Transition Resource Centre (DTRC-Canada), Career Transition for Dancers (New York and Los Angeles) and Swiss Association for the Career Re-orientation of Professional Dancers. The New York-based Career Transition for Dancers has counselors who were former dancers, including two Broadway dancers, a Rockette, a modern dancer and an ex-ballet dancer. The organization was formed in the 1980s with a grant from the National Endowment for the Arts, offering counseling to dancers as they moved from a period of mourning the loss of their ability to dance and transitioning into another field. Since then the New York City Ballet, The Alvin Ailey School, American Ballet Theatre, and Radio City Music Hall have all designated funding for their dancers to pursue other vocational training.

An example of a noted dancer who made the transition from performer to other ways of being active in related fields is Mikhail Baryshnikov. The famed classical dancer switched to modern dance by forming the White Oak Dance Project with Mark Morris, also dabbling in acting with roles in films ("White Nights," "Dancers,") and the television series "Sex and the City." In 2002, White Oak was disbanded and he began making plans for the Baryshnikov Arts Center, which opened in 2005. A large rehearsal and performance space located in New York's flower district, the Center has been a boon to choreographers, playwrights and multimedia creators, students and stars. Barishnikov and his assistant, Stanford Makishi, are responsible for selecting artists and companies qualified for residencies, providing them with stipends, housing, performing expenses and travel money. Because of his fame, connections and financial success, Baryshnikov is now able to devote himself to charitable projects of his choice in his adopted country.[3]

THE CHOREOGRAPHER/COMPANY DIRECTOR

Choreography is a learned skill as well as an art requiring years of practice to develop natural gifts. Success is not a steady progression for most choreographers; some achieve early recognition and then struggle to maintain it, while others work for years before their work gains acceptance. Even for a master choreographer, a Graham or a Balanchine, every work is by no means a masterpiece; often, it is difficult to tell how well a piece "works" until it has been performed many times.

Every choreographer has a unique method of creating a piece and working with dancers. The initial idea for a piece may come from any source: observing people on the street, listening to a concert, attending an art show, reading the newspaper or a personal life experience. Once the choreographer has an initial idea, she or he may work alone for a long period of time or immediately begin setting movement on dancers. Selection of music may start the choreographic process, or there may be an ongoing collaboration with a composer during rehearsals, or the music may be added very late in the process.

Improvisation is one tool the choreographer may use for developing an idea and expanding movement vocabulary. Some choreographers improvise on their own before bringing movement to their dancers, while others guide the dancers through improvisation and select movement from it. In this case, the dancers are actively contributing movement ideas to the piece, and the choice of dancers for the work becomes critical to the creative process.

While the choreographic process may seem both mysterious and highly personal, there are many manuals written about choreography and courses designed to develop these skills. Most of the courses are found in college dance-majors programs, where students can practice basic choreographic skills with the advantage of working with other students, instead of having to pay professional dancers for their time. Students can also mount their works without the usual stage production costs, hopefully benefiting from the critiques of teachers and peers in an environment conducive to learning. Sometimes new professional performing companies result from the experiences and contacts individuals developed in these programs. For example, the dance company Pilobolus grew out of a college (Dartmouth College) improvisation class.

In 1999 Merce Cunningham moved choreography into the digital age with his production of *Biped*, which uses "motion capture" images and computerized animation. The program he manipulated, known as Life Forms™, gives the user the capability of choreographing on computer models. Cunningham describes the process as looking at some things on the screen and saying to oneself, "'That's impossible for a dancer to do.' But if one looks at it long enough, a way could be thought of for it to be done . . . it can prompt the eye to see something never thought of before." Other choreographers, for example *Yacov Sharir* in Austin, Texas, have combined computer images with images of live dancers to produce a new art form, whose potential can only increase with new technology. Sharir cautions that the computer cannot turn a poor choreographer into a good one. Nevertheless, it can supply a whole new inventory of choreographic choices while keeping the interaction with live dancers.

Technological advances have resulted in a new study of interactive environments known as performance telematics. Many collaborative choreographed works have been the result; for example, the camera can become a component of the performance, which dramatically alters the viewers' experience. Experiments with on-stage motion sensing systems have enabled dancers to control the sound, lighting effects and video camerawork through their movements. Other experiments have involved dancers performing in two separate environments, linked together through the interactive use of video, sound and data. The Ohio State University in Columbus and Arizona State University in Tempe have been in the forefront of integrating dance and technology, offering workshops on this subject to prospective interactive choreographers.

In fact, there are so many opportunities for "dance and technology" that a simple Internet search provides pages of possible Web sites.

Contemporary dance companies, which often must build audiences slowly by introducing them to new dance forms, find it especially useful to affiliate with colleges or universities. The company director, or even the entire company, may be in residence for a period of time, teaching classes at the university and performing on campus. Or the university may simply make rehearsal space available to the company to provide enrichment and performance opportunities for talented dance majors. While contemporary dance company residencies may last a semester, a year or more, ballet companies, which tend to be larger and more expensive, do shorter residencies. Examples are the New York City Ballet's summer residencies at Saratoga Performing Arts Center in Saratoga Springs, NY, and the Joffrey Ballet's summer residencies at the University of Iowa.

For the choreographer on his or her own, marketing new choreography becomes a responsibility. Many choreographers develop a mailing and e-mail list of potential backers. They often have Web pages and some offer sample choreography to view online. If they choose to produce their own concerts, the problems of funding, booking a space, publicizing the concert, must be addressed. In order to assemble a group of dancers and mount a concert, choreographers must wear two hats—choreographer and company director—and must possess both good management skills and creativity. Some choreographers prefer to be free agents, setting pieces for other directors' companies on a commission basis. Freelance choreographers have additional opportunities in related areas, which some find challenging and financially satisfying. Gymnasts, bodybuilders, dance fitness competitors and ice skaters often seek out choreographers as consultants to help present themselves in the best possible way with a well-structured routine. The choreographer must understand the rules and requirements of each of these sports to be valuable to the competitor.

Solo singers, bands and swing choirs also need choreographic expertise. These jobs can lead into work in film and music video.

FUNDING

Since business and fundraising considerations are extremely time-consuming, many choreographers are happy to turn financial concerns over to a company director or business manager and serve their company as artistic director, making only artistic decisions like casting and the selection of pieces. Small-company choreographers often form alliances or "umbrella organizations," which produce concerts featuring several choreographers, in order to share the costs. Larger companies also have a board of directors from the community in which they are located, which may have final say in both business and artistic decision-making, including hiring and firing

In recent years, soaring production costs have created financial difficulties even for larger, well-established companies. Seasons with poor advance sales may be canceled, and touring expenses have been radically pared down. For example, companies that once toured with their own orchestras now tour with taped music. One solution being attempted is the sharing of expenses for new productions between two or more large companies. This was done by the Houston Ballet for two full-length works choreographed by its artistic director, Ben Stevenson. Pittsburgh Ballet Theater shared the costs of *Dracula* (1997) and American Ballet Theatre in New York co-produced *The Snow Maiden* (1998).

The lingering problem of what audiences for dance are actually going to see depends not just on audience preferences, but on funding issues. In America, government funding for dance companies and the salaries of dancers and choreographers, have not been a top priority at either the state or national level. In 2004, Dance Theatre of Harlem, directed by Arthur Mitchell, was forced for the second time to furlough its dancers, and was rescued by donors from closing its school for financial reasons. Commenting on this situation, Anna Kisselgoff (dance critic for *The New York Times*) stated: "American dance depends mainly on philanthropy, not state subsidy. Companies in the United States often disband and regroup; is this any way to run an art form?"[4]

Here is an example of an American best-case scenario for funding. The Cedar Lake Contemporary Ballet, a company located in the Chelsea area of Manhattan, has a single private donor who has provided sufficient funds for the following: year-round contracts for sixteen dancers and an artistic director, at a wage sufficient enough so that second jobs are not needed; health and retirement benefits; a theater and rehearsal space for their use; sufficient funds for costumes and their maintenance; and funding for guest choreographers and collaborating composers. The job security for such dancers is found more frequently in Europe, in countries that have sufficient state subsidies for their arts. It also allows them to charge ticket prices that are reasonable for the general public (see "Other Companies," this chapter). Indeed, private donors have filled a desperate need among all artists, due to continuous cuts in national and state funding starting around 2007. Private citizens, like Irene Diamond, who funds the New York City Ballet Diamond Project, have allowed up-and-coming choreographers to present their works and established choreographers to present more experimental works.

On the national level, the entity that makes decisions on funding the arts is called the National Endowment for the Arts. Its decisions for funding must be approved by Congress; therefore, such decisions tend to become political. In the 1980s, Senator Jesse Helms was outspoken in voicing objections to any artistic endeavor that promoted an "alternative lifestyle." To avoid controversy, NEA grants tend to be reluctant to fund new and unusual works; in dance this translates into more funding for ballet companies and a few long-established modern companies than for young contemporary choreographers.

REGIONAL DANCE COMPANIES

A welcome change in the American dance scene is that good quality ballet, modern dance, jazz and tap companies are now situated in smaller cities as well as in major population centers. Dancers no longer have to live in either New York or San Francisco to have a satisfying professional career, and American audiences have much more live dance accessible to them.

In addition to the professional companies in secondary cities, regional dance companies have proliferated across America. These companies are semiprofessional, in that some performers and guest choreographers are paid, while most of the company is made up of unpaid dancers who are often still in school or working in other fields. Regional dance companies are usually sponsored by a local dance studio but may include training for dancers at several studios. These companies serve as preparation for those intent on professional careers and as an outlet for those who wish to continue performing without leaving their hometowns. They may have very high performing standards and be the proving ground for rising young choreographers.

Regional Dance America, an organization that was the outgrowth of the National Association of Regional Ballet (begun in the mid-1950s), provides performing and competitive opportunities for regional companies. Reputable dance professionals judge the performances, giving the young dance student a taste of the process of constructive criticism. While most of the performances are ballet-oriented, some quality modern dance pieces also appear in these festivals. Since 1960 this organization has been sponsoring an annual Craft of Choreography Conference, a training program to encourage young choreographers, open to all who apply. In June 1997 Regional Dance America held its first National Festival in Houston, bringing together eighteen hundred (mostly teenaged) dancers to perform, take master classes and be adjudicated. It now has more than 92 member companies.

DANCE NOTATION, COMPUTER CHOREOGRAPHY AND COPYRIGHT ISSUES

Once a choreographer has created a work, there is the question of preserving it. Dance notation is a way of preserving, analyzing and copyrighting choreography. Notation systems have been around since the 15th century, but early systems lacked detail, relying on the reader's previous knowledge of both terminology and style of the dance. In the first half of the 20th century, two notation systems became widely used: the *Benesh* system is popular in England, while Rudolf Von Laban's *Labanotation* is the primary system used in America. Over the years, Laban original system has been refined and expanded by many scholars, notably *Ann Hutchinson Guest* (b. 1918) who was instrumental in founding the Dance Notation Bureau in New York in 1940. This organization teaches and certifies notaters, and is a repository for the notated scores of many choreographers. More recently, in an effort to make notation a more integrated part of dance education, Guest created the "Language of Dance." LOD is a simplified version of Labanotation called "motif notation." Dancers of all ages can now have a better intellectual understanding of their dance experiences. Through the Language of Dance Centre in London, students of this innovative approach can now receive Specialist Certification.

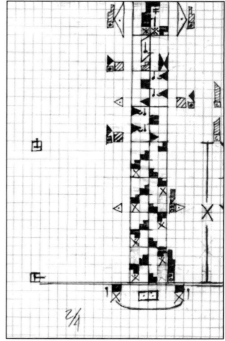

With new notation software programs, the painstaking process of hand-drawing notation on graph paper is disappearing. Labanwriter © software, designed for Macintosh computers only, copies, edits and stores more than 700 Labanotation symbols directly on the computer. Even so, becoming facile at notating still requires many years of study. Most choreographers, unable to devote this much time to the process, leave the job of preserving their work to professional notaters. The works are then registered at the Dance Notation Bureau. These written records make applying for copyrights less complicated. When combined with good-quality videotaping, the choreographer has an accurate record which allows for reconstruction of a piece for many years to come.

The Dance Notation Bureau began experimenting with video recording in 1970, in conjunction with notated blueprints to determine camera angles and other stage direction before taping. These tapes were far superior to the

AN EXAMPLE OF LABANOTATION, or "writing dance," drawn by the author.

usual videotapes of the period in terms of recording chorographic detail and overall coverage accurately. However, with the great improvements today in filming, using several camera angles to catch detailed movement, some college programs have decided that Labanotation is no longer as important as it was in the past, and are eliminating it from their dance majors programs or substituting Laban Movement Analysis.

In recent years, many young choreographers have raised the issue of authorship and originality in their work, which challenges the whole process of copyrighting movement through notation or other means. These choreographers are not creating their own unique movement language as did Doris Humphrey or Merce Cunningham, but are borrowing movements from a variety of sources, including YouTube and other internet sources. Usually the "collaborating" artist is not given the opportunity to approve the outcome of the collaboration before it is made available to the public. This challenges the very meaning of what choreography is and can be. New rules about the ownership of dance movement as intellectual property, and ways of requesting the rights through proper channels, need to be developed.

THE DANCE EDUCATOR

Many options are open to the individual who feels called to teach dance. The type of dance and the targeted age group are of premier importance when making career decisions. For some, dance's recreational aspects are the emphasis; these teachers are happiest at private studios that do not emphasize performance—city recreation departments, YW and YMCAs and (if they hold the required college degrees) in physical education-based college and university programs.

However, if the theatrical aspects of dance and opportunities to choreograph are the teacher's true bent, then an affiliation with a private dance school with an emphasis on performance, a regional or professional dance company, a conservatory or a college program located in a performing arts milieu would prove more satisfying. There is a world of difference, for example, in teaching in a conservatory such as Juilliard, which prepares its students for professional jobs as performers and choreographers, and in teaching at a college where the dance program is part of physical education. Occasionally, a gifted performer makes the transition to teaching and coaching young professionals and pre-professionals, helping to raise the standards of the smaller regional companies. Examples of this are *Fernando Bujones* (see Other Notables, chapter 8) and *Suzanne Farrell* (see chapter 8). These people are the exception, not the rule, because an outstanding dancer does not necessarily have the patience and personality to be an outstanding teacher/coach.

Additional teaching opportunities are available for dance educators at summer arts camps for children and adults. Top dance camps, such as Perry-Mansfield (Steamboat Springs, Colorado) and

Interlochen (Michigan) have prestigious long-standing reputations and are very selective in their choices of both faculty and students.

Teaching Dance in the Public Schools

Teacher certification programs for dance teachers exist in colleges in many American states, enabling the graduate to teach dance in the public schools at the elementary or secondary level. Those states without certification may still offer dance as part of physical education, theatre or in the classroom at the elementary level. Dance may also be offered as an elective student activity during or after school. In some parts of the country, dance/drill teams are an important part of athletic events.

Dance positions usually require a second teaching field for full-time employment on the secondary level, unless the school is an arts magnet school. Arts magnet high schools and middle schools, a concept that started in the New York public schools, are now found in many of America's cities. Magnet schools offer in-depth, affordable training in the performing and visual arts to talented young people, usually selected by audition. They also offer full-time dance teaching employment to qualified teachers, often requiring a performance background from their faculty as well as teaching experience.

Perhaps the most exciting development in public school teaching, however, is the growth of creative movement classes in both elementary and secondary schools. The goal of these classes is not to produce professional dancers, as in the training at magnet schools or private studios, but truly to educate the youngster about movement in all its aspects. The natural physicality of children makes them open to this training, and many values that are basic to human life can be taught through creative movement experiences.

The importance of dance as an educational tool in the public schools was reinforced in 1994 by the U.S. Senate when it passed *Goals 2000: Educate America Act*. This bill adds the arts to the nation's educational goals and sets standards for proficiency in four arts areas, including dance. Educational studies have found that teaching creative movement on the elementary level stimulates conceptual thought, cooperative interpersonal effort, acceptance of other cultures and self-esteem. At-risk students, including hyperactive children and those with limited language skills, benefit from dance sessions to an exceptional degree. With the excitement and pleasure of the act of moving assisting them, children are enabled to face the sometimes frustrating tasks of developing linguistic and mathematical intelligence. Experienced creative movement teachers can link their sessions directly to the classroom curriculum by teaching vocabulary, spatial concepts, fractions, geometric shapes and social/cultural studies through movement. Best of all, unlike many physical education activities, creative movement is noncompetitive. Every child who participates is a winner.

While some dance is now being taught during the school day, after-school programs held on school premises are also making their mark. A model for such a program is the National Dance Institute, formed in 1976 by the former New York City Ballet principal dancer *Jacques d'Amboise* (b. 1934). NDI strives to reach public school children of diverse ethnic, social and economic backgrounds, including the physically and emotionally challenged. The emphasis is not on technique-building or developing professional dancers, but on introducing many forms of dance to the children. Through dance, they are taught self-discipline, teamwork and respect for other cultures and are given opportunities for self-expression. In 1997 the program reached 1,800 children in schools in New York and New Jersey. Performing groups selected from the classes have danced at the United Nations, the White House and annually in a New York theater. There are now several NDI centers throughout the United States.

In 1975 Lincoln Center for the Performing Arts in New York City created a new kind of artist-in-residence program in conjunction with Harvard University's Project Zero, the Lincoln Center Institute (LCI). In the LCI model, now duplicated in cities around the country, units of study are developed that are taught by an LCI-trained Teaching Artist in conjunction with the classroom teacher in preparation for a trip to a concert or exhibition. In this way, students and teachers experience the creative process in addition to viewing the work.

Private Studio Teaching

The dancer who wishes to open her or his own dance studio after graduation will find that knowledge of small-business management, public relations and accounting are extremely useful to the studio owner. Working as an assistant to an experienced and able studio manager is one way of acquiring needed skills. The ability to relate to a variety of age groups, from preschoolers to senior citizens, is an advantage for the private studio operator. The ability to network with musicians, lighting designers, community theater directors and others involved in the arts as participants and patrons is also invaluable.

Private studio management, as in most small businesses, is highly competitive. If the product, outstanding dance instruction, is superior, one has an advantage but not a guarantee of success. Proper scheduling of classes, effective advertising and good interaction with students and parents are vital. Many studios produce annual recitals, which are very popular with students but may involve considerable expense for parents. Recitals may dominate the classroom time, limiting the amount spent on developing proper technique and good movement habits for the students. Again, good management of time and money can affect the quality of the recital experience for everyone concerned.

The private studio teacher must also have the determination not to give in to parental pressure when it interferes with quality teaching. For example, preschoolers are not ready for a full class of ballet technique, doing much better with creative movement that stimulates their imaginations and works the whole body. Parents observing these classes sometimes feel that the children are simply running or crawling around and would rather see them standing in neat lines in first position. The teacher needs to convince these parents that the students are being supervised, engaging in problem-solving activities and ones that stimulate their creativity, as well as learning how to work with other children to develop their ideas as a non-competitive group. This is not an easy task for the teachers when they are approached by a parent who just wants to see their child in a tutu onstage!

It is important for the dance studio owner to realize that he or she is an integral part of the artistic life of the community. As such, the studio owner may have a strong say on the quality of community arts and become involved in many collaborative projects. Dance teachers often make a deep impression on young people, providing ongoing influence over a number of years, while classroom teachers change every year. Many studio teachers are remembered as role models and inspirations for a lifetime. A poor teacher, however, may turn students away from dance and even cause physical damage by not correcting placement problems, giving improper warm-ups or putting children in pointe shoes too soon.

CONVENTIONS AND COMPETITIONS

Another addition to the dance scene, touring dance conventions—Dance Masters of America, Dance Educators of America, Tremaine Conventions—offer classes in a variety of dance forms to students and sometimes certification programs for teachers. Offering updated choreography and teaching methods to the local dance studio, these conventions have served to improve the quality of teaching in smaller cities and towns. The conventions also offer competitions for titles and prizes for dance studio groups and soloists in a variety of age and dance-style categories. The prestige that goes with a "Mr. Dance" or a "Junior Miss Dance" title also reflects on a teacher; as a result, many studios place great emphasis on these competitions, which have been increasing in popularity in the new millennium. In the August 2008 issue of "Dance Teacher," eleven competition organization tours were listed for fall 2008 and spring 2009. With as few as six and as many as fifty-four American towns and cities listed on the tour (one also went to London) there is no question that young dancers across the US are getting more and more opportunities to "get inspired, get educated, get opportunities, GET DISCOVERED!"

As a response to the needs of university dancers to see and experience a variety of dance choreography and teaching styles, the American College Dance Festival Association was formed in 1974. The association now produces nine regional festivals on college campuses each year and a national festival held every other year at the Kennedy Center in Washington, D.C. Students, college faculty and guest artists present choreography at these festivals, and teachers donate their talents to offer classes.

Another college-level competitive outlet for dancers is stepping competitions. Stepping is a hard-driving and disciplined group dance form that was first introduced on campuses in the 1940s. African-American fraternities originally used it as a ritual; in the 1970s, African-American sororities adopted it as well. Today, shows express the competitive spirit among various fraternities and sororities and are also useful for recruitment and fundraising purposes.

Competitions designed for spirit teams (drill teams), which perform jazz-style group dance routines, abound. These teams are usually connected with high school or college athletic programs but sometimes represent private studios. Competitions are considered a way of improving performance skills and expanding choreographic ideas. Groups such as American Dance Drill and United Spirit Association offer competitions, conventions and training camps for these teams.

In the professional dance world, competitions also exist. Ballet boasts the International Ballet Competition held in Varna, Bulgaria, the USA International Ballet Competition in Jackson, Mississippi, and the biannual New York International Ballet Competition. Choreography competitions in the modern dance world include cash grants and scholarship prizes. One that has helped launch many careers is the Young Choreographers and Composers Project at the American Dance Festival, held in Durham, North Carolina. Attracting students from all parts of the world, the annual festival offers a full summer of master classes and performance opportunities in a variety of dance genres. In recent years the festival has grown to four hundred participants and fifty teachers each summer.

Another award for the concert community are the Lester Horton Awards, originating from Los Angeles, that acknowledge achievement in choreography, education, production and performance. Contemporary choreographers also vie for a "Bessie" Award, named after Bessie Schönberg (1906–1997) who taught choreography classes at Jacob's Pillow Dance Festival and elsewhere for many decades. For musical theater dancers, there are the Gypsy Awards, which in 1998 honored Tommy Tune and Sandy Duncan. The Bob Fosse Awards, established in 1994, recognize choreographic achievement in motion pictures, television, music videos and commercials. The Gene Kelly Award from the National Alliance for Excellence, an advocacy group for gifted and talented young adults, annually selects an outstanding performer in dance.

Competitions for ballroom dancers have been organized for many years by the US Amateur Ballroom Dancers Association, with a recent addition of college-age competitions. The first international ballroom competition was held in 1934; today, these competitions have a worldwide following and are televised annually. They feature elegantly dressed couples competing in the waltz, foxtrot, quickstep and a melange of Latin dances. Winning medals at these competitions is very advantageous for couples wishing to establish themselves as ballroom dance instructors.

With the decision of the Olympic Committee to make ballroom dance a "sport"—Dance Sport—future Olympic competition in ballroom dance is a possibility.

Newest of all dance competitions are the Sport Aerobics championships. In these events, solo, duo and team competitors of both sexes perform routines built from exercise movements and dance combinations that demonstrate high levels of strength and flexibility. Not all of these movements are normally found in aerobics classes; some are taken from gymnastics, ballet and other dance forms. These competitions follow strict guidelines set up by the AAU (Amateur Athletic Union) and demonstrate the coordination, muscular strength and style of the competitors. However, since the routines last only between one-and-a-half to four minutes, they do not demonstrate cardiovascular endurance, the most important fitness component of aerobics.

FITNESS DANCE

In the early 1980s, a boom in aerobic dance classes evolved from the work of Kenneth Cooper, originator of the term "aerobic exercise." Cooper affirmed that cardiovascular fitness depends on doing continuous, repetitive movements on a regular basis—at least three times a week—and suggested a number of activities to achieve this end. Before long, gyms and health clubs realized that people maintain exercise programs longer if they move to music and use the variety of movements found in dance, instead of constantly repeating the same exercises. Individuals with strong dance backgrounds began developing fitness programs with diverse dance components taken from jazz, ballet and social dance forms. For example, Jazzercize®, created by Jackie Sorensen, is now franchised at gyms and studios nationwide. Step aerobics, slide aerobics and other variations have followed, as have many teacher-training organizations that offer certification courses and exams.

Aerobic dance has helped countless Americans increase and maintain fitness in an enjoyable way. Fitness dance classes for senior citizens and children, and specialty classes like country line aerobics and hip-hop aerobics, appeal to various demographic groups. New forms of fitness dance are constantly evolving: duo-step, a form of interactive step aerobics done with a partner; Rhythm Workout is mixed-impact dance form based on African-style movement performed to African drumming. Slowarobics is a non-impact version done at a slower pace for older dancers.

The fitness industry has provided a boon for the professional dancer in terms of improving long-term ability to survive the grueling effects of a dance career. Strength training, kickboxing, water aerobics, yoga and other offerings at gyms offer the dancer fitness alternatives when they have injuries, and useful supplements to their dance training. Aerobic dance has also become a second source of income for many dance educators, who already have the advantage of a large vocabulary of dance movements. However, dance teachers must learn to structure the aerobics class differently from the "regular" dance class, where more complex combinations are taught and the class is divided into groups, resulting in more starting and stopping and less cardiovascular benefit. Aerobic movements must be nonstop; the teacher must learn to give instructions and corrections while moving.

A recent trend, bringing actual dance classes such as ballet, modern dance and jazz into the gym, is resulting in "the ultimate in cross-training, all under one roof." Many adults who find private dance studios threatening or who simply do not want to take dance classes with teenagers find the gym environment more supportive of their needs. Teaching at a gym involves finding new ways of approaching these dance forms, while emphasizing fitness and fun.

DANCE THERAPY AND MOVEMENT STUDIES

In recent years the field of dance therapy has grown, owing to the acknowledgment by health professionals that dance can provide a healing outlet for people with a variety of mental disorders, emotional disturbances and physical disabilities. It has also become clear that many dancers and dance educators have fine-tuned their powers of observation of the human body as a window to the human personality. This understanding, coupled with scientific knowledge, can produce very effective therapists.

The American Dance Therapy Association lists five basic functions for dance therapy: body awareness, catharsis (letting go of suppressed emotions), interpersonal communication, restructuring (postural changes) and communicating with the unconscious. Trained professionals with graduate degrees in dance therapy are now working as a part of clinical teams in a variety of settings: preschool and elementary schools, institutions for the disabled, mental health clinics, homes for the elderly and rehabilitation hospitals. Universities like Antioch New England offer graduate studies in this field; Antioch's degree is an M.A. in dance/movement therapy with a minor in counseling psychology.

The postmodernist *Anna Halprin* has worked since 1980 with people suffering from AIDS, cancer and other life-threatening diseases. Describing her use of dance therapy, she states, "To heal is to operate on many dimensions simultaneously, by aiming at attaining a state of emotional, mental, spiritual and physical health." Her approach involves four components: sensation, movement, feelings/emotions and imagery.

Other systems of movement study have become prominent as both choreographic tools and instruments for therapy. For example, Bartenieff Fundamentals is a system of body reeducation based on developmental movement, which focuses on finding ease and efficiency in movement patterning. Bartenieff Fundamentals is sometimes studied in conjunction with Laban's Movement Analysis work, and certification is offered at several universities. Hatha yoga and t'ai chi practitioners with dance and choreography backgrounds have used these movement vocabularies to supplement and strengthen their choreographic material. Yoga practice, with its emphasis on proper breathing techniques and gentle stretching, the cultivation of body awareness and the acknowledgment of spirituality, can provide a welcome relief from the competitive focus of dance training.

At the School for Body-Mind Centering® in Amherst, Massachusetts, students explore an integrated approach to movement that includes experiential anatomy, touch and repatterning, developmental principles and yoga. These studies help the student to overcome movement limitations and explore new possibilities for personal and professional development. Also in Amherst, located in Hampshire College's Dance Department, a program known as Authentic Movement explores movement as spiritual practice, artistic resource and psychological narrative.

Many of the movement studies rely on one-on-one hands-on supervision of a certified teacher. In Alexander Technique®, developed by *Frederick Matthias Alexander* (1869–1955), a method originally designed to improve vocal performance, simple movements such as sitting into a chair, walking and lifting the arm are practiced with a teacher's hands guiding the movement. Students learn to move using the least amount of tension, especially in the neck. Similarly, the Awareness Through Movement technique developed by *Moshe Feldenkrais* (1904–1984) uses early childhood coordination, breathing patterns and attention to individual movements to reeducate his students. With many movements performed lying on the floor, Feldenkrais work is a useful tool for healing injuries.

The Pilates Method®, invented by *Joseph Pilates* (1880–1967) in the 1920s, emphasizes flexibility and coordination, and uses breathing techniques to help increase abdominal strength and lengthen muscles. Specially designed apparatus is used to assist with the repetitive exercises. Many well-known dancers have added Pilates work to their training with remarkable results.

Some individuals who have been involved with contact improvisation as a choreographic and performing tool have also become involved in therapeutic work. Contact improvisation is promoted by an international group of adherents from many walks of life who explore in depth the power of touch. Work in contact improvisation raises psychological issues, such as interpersonal trust and boundaries. Properly approached, contact improvisation develops sensitivity toward oneself and others. Consequently, it has great therapeutic value, providing both a physical and emotional outlet. Contact improvisation can become a way of life.

THE CENSORSHIP ISSUE

The issue of censorship, which also is linked to issues of funding is complicated by the fact that in the new millennium our culture is more open to images that would have once been off-limits to minors. Live dance considered lewd or suggestive, found only in burlesque houses a generation ago, are now accessible online to computer-savvy children. When it comes to contemporary concert dance, nudity is on the increase, making some people unwitting and uncomfortable voyeurs. Gia Kourlas, a writer for *The New York Times*, comments on this:

> *Contemporary dance and nudity are hardly strangers, but in many recent performances skin has practically taken the place of costume. At the moment, the surge isn't rooted in sexual liberation, as it was when nude bodies appeared onstage in the 1960s, or in political defiance, as when they re-emerged in the 1980s. Instead, choreographers are baring it all as a way to reveal something essential about human experience. The nudity on few occasions is tough and raw yet unmistakably vulnerable.* [5]

That being said, is censorship the answer? If so, who is qualified to decide what should and should not be censored? A look at dance history reveals that some works that created outrage at their inception for religious or political reasons are now considered important milestones, for example, Vaslav Nijinsky's *Rite of Spring* and Kurt Jooss' *The Green Table* (see chapters 4 and 5). Perhaps a better solution would be a rating system for dance concert pieces, so one knows which ones not to bring one's five-year-old niece to, or even to go to themselves.

PROFILE: KRISTINE RICHMOND
Ballet Dancer and Theater Performer

Harriet Lihs   Krissy, tell me about your early history in dance, and how you got to where you are today.

Kristine Richmond   I started with Marsha Woody in Beaumont, Texas, and then went to the Washington Ballet School, where I met Ben Stevenson, ended up coming back with him to Houston when he became director of Houston Ballet in the late 1970s. I went through the ranks of corps de ballet, soloist and principal dancer. Along the way I had met Gwen Verdon. She came and taught us Fosse technique and also performed with us.

This really stirred my interest in theater, and I was always really close to her. When Houston Ballet went to L.A. to perform, I met an agent who offered to represent me for theater. It seemed like the right time, so I left the ballet in 1993. I immediately went on the road with "Phantom of the Opera," that was my first show. But I wanted to sing and act more than I did in that show. I did a lot of regional theater, and then I got the tour of "Chicago," then appeared in Matthew Bourne's "Swan Lake" on Broadway as the Queen.

KRISTINE RICHMOND

Then I went back on the road with "Chicago," ended up as dance captain, did the show in Paris for five months, and was on Broadway with the show for three years. During this time I got to know Ann Reinking well, and got in on the ground floor of the developing "Fosse," the Broadway show: she coached me and the other principals. Then I went to the West Coast and got interested in new projects, because Broadway has changed in the last five years.

HL In what ways has Broadway changed?

KR It is much more corporate, much more commercial, and uses television stars without a Broadway background for principal roles because the producers feel that they will draw audiences. When "A Chorus Line" was created, (dancers) were in the studio for a year, and nobody was paid. The stories they told were real stories. Its unfortunate that doesn't seem to be the norm any more; I'm not sure why.

HL Do you feel that the ballet world has also changed and become more corporate?

KR Ballet is different because so much technique is demanded—not everyone can do it. The producing end of it may have become more corporate, we've lost the original leaders, Mr. B (Balanchine) at NYCB (New York City Ballet), and at ABT (American Ballet Theatre). I love Kevin (McKenzie) but his direction is not the same as Misha's (Baryshnikov) or Lucia's (Lucia Chase).

HL Are you doing some of your own choreography now?

KR Even when I was at Houston Ballet, I choreographed for the Houston Grand Opera and for the Houston Ballet Academy, and I also staged a lot of plays in the Houston area.

HL If you had to put a name on your choreographic style, what would you call it?

KR I would probably have to call it contemporary ballet. That's what I've done most, even though I've just started choreographing musicals. The Fosse influence is big, he was kind of my hero. I think he was a brilliant man, a genius. Over the last five or six years I've done more musicals that ballets. I'm still evolving—my eye has changed and my likes have changed. I noticed that when I began reviving some older ballets for my first teacher, Marsha Woody, at Beaumont Civic Ballet.

HL   If you are working with a civic ballet company, would the dancers need additional classes, for example Fosse-style jazz classes, to do your choreography?

KR   Dancers in civic ballet companies should be encouraged to take all forms of dance, including jazz, tap, even acrobatics. More than ever, dancers now are expected to be very versatile. Hip-hop, which everyone can see on TV, is finding its way into concert choreography.

HL   Do you think the audiences for dance have changed in recent years? Are they more knowledgeable about dance?

KR   I'd like to say yes, but I don't think so, especially in the smaller cities. There needs to be more education about various dance styles and where they came from. There is a point where the support for the arts has to come along with education and outreach. If I were asked what activity I would really like to do, I would ask for funding to go and speak in my own words to various audiences about my experiences as a professional dancer, not necessarily in a classroom but as part of a workshop about dance.

HL   What advice would you give the young dancers of today on how to develop their careers?

KR   Be able to do it all, because you will be asked to do it all. You might even be asked to do an improvisation or a monologue. If you are involved in ballet, getting affiliated with a company is important to do early. New York City Ballet takes on apprentices at age 16. Regional ballet companies allow you more time, even time to finish four years of college. Now there are so many other opportunities outside of New York. I think that is very healthy.

HL   What about health issues for dancers? Do you think things have gotten better?

KR   Yes and no. Because of the high stress levels, I think there will always be a high incidence of anorexia and bulimia among female ballet dancers. New York City Ballet dancers look like skin and bones up close; Houston Ballet is much better in this area.

PROFILE: NANCY FITZPATRICK
Modern Dancer and Pilates Educator

Harriet Lihs   Does modern-dance training provide a good preparation for Pilates training?

Nancy Fitzpatrick   Anatomy and human movement potential were essentials in my undergraduate and graduate dance training, but at the time I was a dance major, the Pilates method was not offered in my dance curricula. Also, at that time in my life, the creative path and performing were more appealing. As I matured and

NANCY FITZPATRICK

followed a dance/teaching career, I began seriously studying anatomy and kinesiology to have a greater understanding and a more in-depth knowledge of efficient movement as it applied to dancers. My goal was to train the dancers to use the right muscles for movement, and use the core correctly to keep their alignment. Since the Pilates method demands knowledge of anatomy my final career change from a modern dance performer, choreographer and assistant professor of dance to a certified Pilates instructor was a natural transition.

HL How did you train for your new career?

NF The ongoing study of the Pilates method has been an enriching experience. I have been able to explore my interest in the movement principles and pertinent anatomical facts by learning and teaching the exercises created by Joseph Pilates. The Pilates exercises are a whole body experience. Focus on balanced muscle development, breathing, abdominal strength, muscular flexibility, coordination and control is like putting pieces of a puzzle together. It is the coordination of body, mind and spirit.

HL Tell me about the certification process for Pilates.

NF Certification is extensive and intense. There are a number of Pilates certification programs and each organization has its own certification goals and guidelines. A student of the Pilates method traditionally begins instruction with Mat, which is the most popular form. Mat exercises are performed on the floor, usually on a supportive Pilates or yoga mat. Other instruction is offered on fitness equipment developed by Joseph Pilates. The equipment includes the Reformer, Barrels, Chair and Cadillac.

HL How long did your certification training take you and what was the final exam like?

NL My certification course began with the essential Mat training, which was four consecutive eight-hour days for five weekends. Some organizations combine exercises on equipment with the Mat instruction. The certification course I took consisted of theory, observation and practice with the instructor.

The final examination was divided into two parts. First, a practical, which included a postural analysis of my subject, then taking my subject through an appropriate Pilates workout. Following the practical exam was a written exam consisting of multiple choice and essay questions on anatomy, postural alignment and the exercises for the Mat and equipment. Two hundred to six hundred hours of observation, personal practice, and personal teaching is an approximate number of hours required for certification.

HL What do you find particularly satisfying about being a Pilates educator?

NF Seeing the understanding and progress of students who commit to the study of the Pilates method is what keeps me continuing as an instructor and also as a student myself.

A SAMPLING OF DANCE ORGANIZATIONS

American Dance Therapy Association
2000 Century Plaza, Suite 108, 10632
Little Patuxent Pkwy. Columbia, MD 21044 (brochure available).
Career Transition for Dancers: counseling and workshops for retiring dancers.
1-800-581-CTFD.

Congress on Research in Dance
an international organization that encourages research in all aspects of dance and related fields.
annual convention and publication.
CORD, Dept. of Dance, SUNY College at Brockport, Brockport, NY 14420-2939.
www.cordance.org

Corps de Ballet International
ballet teachers in higher education.
http://www.ballet.utah.edu/cdbhome.html

Dance and the Child International
promotes creative models for teaching dance, especially in public schools. Conferences and workshops.
Chair: Anne Green Gilbert, 7327 46th Avenue NE, Seattle, WA 98115

Dance Educators of America
teacher training workshops. 1-800-229-3868,
e-mail: DanceDEA@aol.com
www.deadance.com

Dance Masters of America
an organization for dance teachers and their students. Teacher training and conventions with competitions.
Email: dmamann@aol.com
www.dma–national.org.

Dance Notation Bureau
repository of Labanotated scores, classes and workshops.
111 John Street, Suite704, New York, NY 10038.
e-mail:notation@mindspring.com
www.dancenotation.org

International Association of Blacks in Dance
information and networking for dancers of African descent.
9 North Philadanco Way, Philadelphia, PA 19104-8203. (215) 387-4009

Pilates Method Alliance
P.O.Box 370906, Miami, FL 33137-0906 email: info@pilatesmethodalliance.org

Laban/Bartenieff Institute of Movement Studies, Inc.
31 West 27th St., New York, NY 10001

National Dance Association
information on educational issues, conferences and job listings.
1900 Association Drive, Reston, VA 22090. (703) 476-3436.

National Dance Education Organization
advances dance education in legislatures, dance studios and public schools, and in higher education.
Workshops for professional development and alliances with other arts organizations.
Publication, *Journal of Dance Education*.
NDEO, 609 Second Avenue Ave., Suite 2038, Silver Spring, MD 20910. (301) 585-2880

Society of Dance History Scholars
an organization dedicated to western and non-western dance history, with working groups in early dance and reconstruction; a series of publications on historical dance topics and an annual conference.
www.sdhs.org

SUGGESTED READING

Magazine Articles and Periodicals

Aguirre, Abby, "Tentative Steps Into a Life After Dance" *The New York Times*, p. 24, Oct. 21, 2007

"Ballet and the Alexander Technique," *Dance Gazette*, June 1993, pp. 46–47.

"Beyond Performance: Next Steps," *Dance Magazine* supplement, Sept. 2006.

Choreography and Dance: An International Journal (ballet and modern dance choreography, video supplement). Harwood Academic, 48 Sentinel Hill Rd., Milford, CT 06460.

Contact Quarterly: A Vehicle for Moving Ideas (contact improvisation). P.O. Box 603, Northampton, MA 01061.

Dance and Fitness West (film, television, nightclub dance). 627 N. Palm Dr., Beverly Hills, CA 90210.

Dance Gazette (ballet). Royal Academy of Dancing, 36 Battersea Square, London SWll 3RA, UK.

Dancing USA (ballroom dance). 10600 University Avenue NW, Minneapolis, MN 55448–6166.

Dance Magazine (all dance forms). 110 William Street, 23rd Floor, New York, NY 10038.

Dance Medicine and Science J. Michael Ryan Publishing, Inc. 24 Crescent Drive North, Andover, NJ 07821–4000

Jones, Todd D., "Dances with Yogis," *Yoga Journal*, March/April 1995.

Journal of Dance Education, official publication of National Dance Education Organization, vol. 1, 1/2001.

Journal of Physical Education, Recreation and Dance (dance in education). AAHPERD, 1900 Association Drive, Reston, VA 22090.

La Rocca, Claudia, "Say, Just Whose Choreography is This?" *The New York Times*, Aug, 24, 2008, p. 25.

Rockwell, John, "In Ballet, Old Age Comes Early" *The New York Times*, May 21, 2006.

Webster, Margaret, "Dance: Stepping in the Schools," *Mothering*, summer 1995.

Books

Adair, Christy. *Women and Dance: Sylphs and Sirens*. New York: New York University Press, 1992.

Bishop, Jan Galen. *Fitness Through Aerobic Dance*: 3rd ed. Scottsdale, AZ: Gorsuch Scarisbrick, 1995.

Chmelar, Robin and Sally Fitt. *Diet for Dancers*. 1984. Pennington, NJ: Princeton Book Company, Publishers, 1995.

Cohen, Selma Jeanne, Founding Editor. *International Encyclopedia Of Dance,* 6 vols. New York: Oxford University Press, 1998.

Feder, Bernard and Elaine Feder. *The Expressive Arts Therapies*. Englewood Cliffs, NJ: Prentice-Hall, 1981.

Halprin, Anna. *Dance as a Healing Art: Returning to Health with Movement and Imagery*. Mendocino, CA: Liferhythm, 2000.

————. *Dance as a Healing Art: A Teacher's Guide & Support Manual for People with Cancer*. Kentfield, CA: Tamalpa Institute, 1997.

Hamilton, Linda H. *Advice for Dancers: Emotional Counsel and Practical Strategies*. San Francisco: Jossey-Bass Publishers, 1998.

Hanna, Judith Lynne. *Partnering Dance and Education: Intelligent Moves for Changing Times.* Champaign, IL: Human Kinetics, 1999.

Hawkins, Alma. *Creating Through Dance*. Princeton, NJ: Dance Horizons, 1988.

Louis, Murray. *Inside Dance*. New York: St. Martins Press, 1980.

Metz, Mark, editor. *Conscious Dancer: Movement for a Better World*. Collector's Issue, fall 2007.

Murray, Jan. *Dance Now*. Hammondsworth, England: Penguin Books, 1979.

Penrod, James and Janice Gudde Plastino. *The Dancer Prepares*, 4th ed. Mountain View, CA: Mayfield Publishing, 1998.

Pryor, Esther and Minda Kraines. *Keep Moving; It's Aerobic Dance*, 3rd ed. Mountain View, CA: Mayfield Publishing, 1996.

Roseman, Janet Lynn. *Dance Masters: Interviews with Legends of Dance*. New York: Routledge, 2001.

Solomon, Ruth and John Solomon. *Dance Medicine and Science Bibliography*. Andover, NJ: J. Michael Ryan Publishers, 1996.

Sorrell, Walter. *Looking Back in Wonder: Diary of a Dance Critic*. New York: Columbia University Press, 1986.

Watkins, Andrea and Priscilla Clarkson. *Dancing Longer, Dancing Stronger*. Pennington, NJ: Princeton Book Company, Publishers, 1990.

VIDEOGRAPHY

AM & PM Yoga with Rodney Yee and Patricia Walden. Gaiam, Inc., 2007

Ballet Class: Intermediate and Advanced. With David Howard. Kultur, 1984.

Ballet with Style. Kathryn Sullivan, Insight Media, 2007

Pointe to Pointe: Ballet Barre Exercises. Dance Horizons, 1994.

Ballet Floor Barre (Zena Rommett's). Dance Horizons, 1995.

Dance and Grow: Developmental Activities for 3—8 Year Olds. Dance Horizons, 1994.

Dancing, Volumes I and VIII. Kultur, 1993.

The Dancer. A film by Donya Feuer about Katja Bjorner and the Royal Swedish Ballet School. www.firstrunfeatures.com, 1994.

Discovering Your Expressive Body. Peggy Hackney. Dance Horizons, 1989.

Fit and Flexible: The Balanced Body Mat Program. Elizabeth Larkam. Balanced Body, 1996.

Paul Taylor: Dancemaker. Matthew Diamond. Medium, 1999.

Standing Pilates. Physicalmind Institute, 2009.

Suzanne Farrell: Elusive Muse. Fox Centre Stage, 2001.

Yoga Mind and Body with Ali MacGraw. Warner Home Video, 1994.

INTERNET SOURCES

adfvideo.com – modern dance choreographers

artslynx.org – dance, dance therapy, health issues

artsmed.org – Performing Arts Medicine Association

contemplativedance.org – Authentic Movement theraphy

dancecritics.org – site of the Dance Critics Association (DCA)

danceheritage.org – site of the Dance Heritage Coalition, a consortium of major dance libraries

dancehorizons.com – Princeton Book Company, Publishers; books, DVDs, links

dancemagazine.com – *Dance Magazine* and annual college guide

dtrc.ca – Dancer Transition Resource Center (for Canada)

IADMS.org – International Association for Dance Medicine and Science

Insight-media.com – Produces and distributes academic visual media to supplement university, secondary and vocational instruction

laban.org – (Laban Centre in London), events and performance reviews

sdhs.org – (Society of Dance History Scholars), reviews and resources

societyartshealthcare.org – Society for the Arts in Healthcare

voiceofdance.com – advice from dancers and choreographers, auditions, dance directory

OTHER RESOURCES

CD Rom: complete listing of the material in the New York Public Library for the Performing Arts, Jerome Robbins Dance Division, Lincoln Center. Available from Simon & Schuster, P.O. Box 70660, Chicago, IL 60673

CHAPTER EIGHT
DANCING IN THE NEW MILLENIUM

A dance can make you shift what you are thinking, or feeling.
—*Jody Oberfelder*[1]

Is art a haven, an escape from everyday life,
or is it part of the messy social reality we live in?
—*Wendy Perron*[2]

I say: Make something beautiful . . .
Make something that comes honestly from you. Dare to fail.
—*Bill T. Jones*[3]

Sometimes I've just been in the right place at the right time
—*Benjamin Millepied*[4]

As the 21st century gathers momentum, many people are speculating on the future of dance and the other performing arts. The performing arts reflect a culture's needs and values, change as the culture changes and sometimes are in the forefront of new social directions. Obviously, in our rapidly-changing global culture, there will be many changes and adaptations in store for dance.

The new millennium has seen dance expand in all directions: forward, with new explorations, back with the revitalizing of old classics, and sideways with new interminglings of what were originally separate dance forms, as well as new multicultural exchanges. Using the year 2004 as an example, the centennial

QUARRY, CHOREOGRAPHY BY MEREDITH MONK

137

birthdays of two preeminent ballet choreographers, George Balanchine and Frederick Ashton (both discussed in chapter 4) were celebrated with festivals and retrospectives of their work. Balanchine's one-hundredth birthday was celebrated by festivals of performances both in the US and in the country of Georgia, where he was born, while Englishman Frederick Ashton's Lincoln Center Festival featured four companies—two British, one American, and one Japanese. In the ballet world, companies have continued the trend to dispense with the star system, which created superstars like Baryshnikov, Nureyev, Fonteyn and Alicia Alonso in the mid-20th century: now it is the ensemble in the spotlight.

Also in 2004, postmodern choreographers Karole Armitage (American), Jiří Kylián (Czech), Bill T. Jones and Ralph Lemon (African-American) were pushing outward from dance by fusing several idioms and creating dramatic story-pieces. Finnish choreographers Tero Saarinen in France and Jorma Elo in Boston were rising new talents. The year 2006 saw the 75th anniversary of the Jacob's Pillow Dance Festival, still going strong, and the Joffrey Ballet's 50th anniversary. 2007 saw the 20th anniversary of the International Ballet Festival (held in Havana for the first time) with companies from all over the world, except the US, participating. In New York that year, the 30th anniversary of the DanceAfrica Festival was organized by Chuck Davis. In 2008 more than 150 dance conventions and competitions for young dancers occurred in the US alone.

Two Butoh festivals were also held in the US, with *Kazuo Ohno*, a founder of the form, performing live at the age of 101. That year also saw the Royal Ballet of England tour the US, under the direction of former premiere danseur Anthony Dowell in his farewell appearance. The year 2009 saw festivals all over the world honoring the centennial of the formation of Diaghilev's Ballets Russes. At the same time, old problems have continued to plague American dance, including the lack of government funding.

What follows examines trends in theatrical and concert dance as well as others that are changing dance:

Beginning in the late 1960s, the early postmoderns have continued to grow in the new millennium. They (1) blend theatrical forms such as ballet, jazz, tap and modern dance; (2) blend theatrical with social and ethnic forms, sports and even circus movements; and (3) blend dance with other media such as film, computer graphics and the spoken word—a result of the increased number of collaborations among choreographers and writers, filmmakers, visual artists and lighting designers. When dance is only one element of many, the total theatrical event is called "performance art," "physical theater" or "dance theater."

Choreographers of the current generation also continue to experiment with both minimalism and extreme athleticism. The underlying philosophy for these artists is that it is valid and acceptable to experiment with dance in any way one desires. As a result, many new forms have evolved. These trends have been reinforced by increased opportunities to view dance from other parts of the world via satellite and cable and by the concurrent development of "world beat" and other blended musical forms.

POSTMODERNISTS AND NEXT WAVE

During the 1960s, many experimental dance forms began to appear, expressing the spirit of experiment prevalent throughout American culture at the time. The works of this period were such a radical departure from the more technique-oriented works of earlier periods that this movement was named postmodern. However, many of the second-generation artists, especially Merce Cunningham, Erick Hawkins and Alwin Nikolais, laid the groundwork for this movement. For example, Nikolais was at the forefront of experiments in performance art, or "total theater." Following are some of the interests of the postmoderns:

1. The use of improvisation, or spontaneous movement, as a choreographic tool. While in some cases these works developed into rehearsed and repeatable finished products, in other cases they were left in their spontaneous state, so that they were different every time they were performed. Often the pieces were the result of collaborative improvisation, known as contact improvisation, which today has become a separate branch of the contemporary dance scene.

2. Some also seek to break down the dependence on dance technique in choreography and often use untrained performers in their pieces. In some works, known as "happenings," it was virtually impossible to tell the performers from the audience.

3. Some increase the level of physical difficulty of movement, adding high-powered strength and endurance movements requiring heightened levels of fitness.

4. Some experiment with new environments, taking their works off the proscenium stage and putting their dancers in urban streets, on rooftops, hilltops and in deserts, museums and parking lots. These works are known as site-specific pieces.

5. To experiment with accompaniment, using music collages, spoken word and sounds such as street noises as accompaniment for their works. Some even worked in silence, as Doris Humphrey did in her early work *Water Study*. A great many are now using live musicians in full view of the audience, taking a cue from Erick Hawkins. In Jody Oberfelder's *Dido and Aeneas* (2007), for example, the orchestra and a large women's choir are in full view, and sometimes mingle with the dancers.

6. Exploring new choices of subject matter, such as subjective works built on their own histories and serious social issues (also explored by early modern dance choreographers: an example is Charles Weidman's *Lynchtown*).

7. Many postmoderns are exploring the use of varied body types, proportions and sizes. With this comes the use of more personalized costuming that emphasizes individuality rather than conformity. Each costume, for example, may be shaped differently, with only the use of a color or a similar accessory to link the dancers together as a unit. Facial hair for the men shaved heads, and unusual hairdos and colors for the women are now acceptable.

8. Many postmoderns choreograph in a unisex style, so there is no longer a "masculine" and a "feminine" movement vocabulary. This demands strength from the women in partnering and lifting men, and more attention to lyricism for the men. In pieces of this kind, cross-dressing is often used to make the audience aware of how non-traditional costuming can help dissolve gender-movement clichés. For example, in Mats Ek's full-length piece *Appartement* (2000), one man is costumed in a skirt, and one woman appears wearing a man's hat. Choreographers Mark Morris and Matthew Bourne have put men on pointe in tutus as snowflakes and enchanted swans.

9. Some have become fascinated with the possibilities of new technologies meshing with choreography. An example is the use of LED (light-emitting diode) surfaces as dance stages or backdrops. LED panels are made of tempered glass with light emitting from beneath the panel; optics can be added to the internal chip to create patterns and shapes, and colors can be varied depending on the composition of the semiconducting material. The largest LED used as a dance surface appeared in the opening ceremonies of the 2008 Olympic Games in Beijing, China. Modern dancers used their bodies on the surface as "brushes," creating designs resembling the ancient Chinese art of pen and ink design. Another technology becoming popular is the use of computer-generated "choruses" of dancers behind the live dancers as used in Radio City Music Hall's Christmas Spectacular to create a chorus of hundreds of dancing santas. As these technologies become more accessible and affordable, the postmodern experimental spirit will put dance companies on the bandwagon.

The postmodern movement was galvanized by a collective of New York choreographers known as the Judson Dance Theatre, sometimes called Judson Church, because they performed in a desanctified church. These experimental choreographers developed a following in the early 1960s, despite being virtually ignored by the press. The choreographers *Yvonne Rainer* (b. 1934), *Trisha Brown* (b. 1936), *Deborah Hay* (b. 1941) and *Lucinda Childs* (see "Others" this chapter) gave many free concerts, often in collaboration with artists, poets, and composers. Toward the end of the 1960s, new members were added and the group re-formed under the name *Grand Union*.

While Trisha Brown's early work was minimalist, taking dance out of the theater onto rooftops, walls or rafts on a lake, her more recent work uses repetitive patterns to build a rich texture of structured yet fluid movement. Her dancers seldom move in unison, forcing the audience to concentrate in an effort similar to listening to polyphonic music. She continues to explore creative uses of stage sets and alternative ways of moving, such as horizontal walking in harnesses. She has performed regularly in France since her debut there in 1973. *Set and Reset*, an exploration of the choreographic process, debuted in 1983 and has become a postmodern classic. In 2001 she premiered *El Trilogy* in New York, her first exploration into postmodern/jazz fusion movement and jazz music. Today, although Ms. Brown herself retired from performing in 2008 but her company continues to tour and she continues to create exhilarating movement experiments.

In San Francisco, choreographer *Anna Halprin* (b. 1920) experimented with semi-improvisational but intense works. For many of these works she collaborated with her husband, an architect, to create kinetic indoor and outdoor environments. Much later, in the 1980s and 1990s, Halprin became involved in workshops and choreography for people seriously ill with AIDS and other illnesses (see Dance Therapy, this chapter). In an effort to reconnect dancers Halprin designed a film project called *Embracing Earth* (1995). *Finding Home* (2002) documents her explorations of nature, working with the elements of earth, wind, water and fire, and reminding us that we come from and return to nature with nature's shapes and rhythms. As of this writing, Halprin, in her late eighties, continues to teach, concentrating on awakening the creative energy in her students that has informed her nearly seventy-year career in dance.

Other postmoderns such as *Steve Paxton* (b. 1939), *Nancy Stark Smith* (b. 1952) and *Simone Forti* (b. 1935) continued to make contact improvisation their major interest. This dance form, based on an exchange of energy, weight and momentum between two or more people, was influenced by Asian martial arts like tai chi, and was perfectly suited to the egalitarian spirit of the 1970s. Paxton, who is considered the founder of this genre, worked with many other artists, and today contact improvisation is a branch of contemporary dance with its own journal (*Contact Quarterly*) and a loyal community with a network of teachers and active groups worldwide. Ms. Smith is the publisher of *Contact Quarterly* and continues to teach and perform improvisational dance.

Pilobolus, a company formed in a 1971 in a Dartmouth College dance improvisation class, continues to be one of the foremost proponents of this movement genre. The group is committed to collective creativity and produces work that gives the impression of solving mathematical body-puzzles. The results are intriguing. Dance writer Mindy Aloff states, "Pilobolus specializes in picture-making that fools the eye into seeing two or more things at once." The six-member group has seen many new

PILOBOLUS DANCE THEATRE in *Bonsai*.

dancers since its inception. Early works were all in slow motion, but some newer works, such as as *Apoplexy* (1998) and *Davenen* (2000) have a high level of athleticism, frenetically fast sections and many solo explorations. Pilobolus now has work that involves no contact improvisation at all. In 2004, friction among its four artistic directors (Jonathan Wolken, Michael Tracy, Robby Barnett and Alison Chase) nearly caused the demise of the company. The situation was saved by the hiring of an outsider, Itamar Kubovy, to serve as executive director.

Moses Pendleton (b. 1949), a "graduate" of Pilobolus, became director of his own company, Momix, in 1981. Pendleton produced the site-specific film piece *Pictures at an Exhibition* (1991) for Momix, in which he converted a Connecticut farmhouse into a site for a series of mysterious dreamlike episodes. His recent works, full-length pieces, include *Opus Cactus, Passion, Baseball* and *Lunar Sea*. In 2007, a year after the company's silver anniversary, Pendleton produced the "Best of Momix" at New York's Joyce Theater.

Many American choreographers continue to devote themselves to themes of social investigation. An example is *Bill T. Jones* (b. 1952), who combines energetic, forceful movement with film and dialogue to produce his own style of performance art. *Still /Here* (1994), a powerful full-length work, explored the feelings of those confronted with terminal illnesses. It uses filmed interviews with patients as background to the dance. (Jones's partner, dancer/choreographer *Arnie Zane*, died of AIDS in 1988 at forty years old). Other Jones works that are based on his personal experiences and those of his dancers have dealt with the themes of racism and injustice in America. Many of his works are thought-provoking full-evening pieces, while others are simply movement-driven, exploring his hard-driving style to a variety of musical choices.

Another innovative contemporary choreographer, *Mark Morris* (b. 1956), uses his background in Eastern-European folk dance, his love of classical music and his flair for storytelling in his choreography. In 1988 Morris replaced Maurice Béjart as resident choreographer for the Théâtre de la Monnaie in Brussels, where he produced many works, some considered masterpieces, others not well received by critics. *L'Allegro, il Penseroso, ed il Moderato* (1988), a work exploring the three moods of joy, sadness and equanimity to the music of Handel, is considered by some critics to be his finest creation In *Dido and Aeneas* (1989), a remake of Purcell's opera, he cast himself as both the tragic heroine and the malicious sorceress.

Returning to the United States from Brussels in 1991, Morris became involved in a contemporary dance touring company known as the White Oak Dance Project, a collaboration with Mikhail Baryshnikov. Some of his works during this period convey his penchant for gender jokes. An illustration of this humor *is The Hard Nut* (1991), a retelling of the *Nutcracker* story set in the 1970s, in which Morris puts both men and women on pointe. *The Waltz of the Snowflakes*, featuring both men and women in white tutus, is especially entertaining.

By late 2001, the Mark Morris Dance Group's school had opened, with a roster of classes ranging from ballet to West African and full of people of all ages and at all levels of dance experience. Gradually during this new-century period, he began cutting back on his own stage appearances. A revival and update of an earlier work, *Four Saints in Three Acts*, the opera by Gertrude Stein and Virgil Thompson that Morris first choreographed in 2000, was well received. In 2007 he performed a riveting solo in *Italian Concerto*. One of his best works in this period was *All Fours*, a lively dance for four couples to Bartok's *Fourth String Quartet*, masterfully linked to the musical score. In 2008 he also choreographed a new *Romeo and Juliet* to a recently discovered alternative score by Prokofiev, which diverged in important ways from the Shakespeare play, including a different ending. He continues to enjoy choreographing for ballet companies, premiering his *Drink to Me Only With Thine Eyes* for American Ballet Theatre in July of 2007. His version of the semi-opera *King Arthur*, presented in London, Berkeley, and New York in 2008, is a joyful romp that highlights his innovative sense of humor.

Experiments with site-specific pieces continue in the works of several choreographers, including *Stephan Koplowitz*, whose dance-theater productions are designed to transform spaces into spectacles of light, sound, and movement. New York's Grand Central Station was the site of such a work, *Fenestrations*, in 1998, and in 2000 he created a work for the dedication of a new humanities building at Rice University in Houston, in which the audience walked through classrooms, offices, courtyards and stairwells to view the action. In October 2001 Koplowitz's dancers "danced" the newly renovated New York Public Library's Library for the Performing Arts at its reopening celebrations.

A significant breakthrough that began in the late 20th century was the establishment of contemporary dance companies that serve local communities, including smaller towns and inner-city communities. Some of these companies rely solely on local support and remain connected with community issues and values.

In Tacoma Park, Maryland, *Liz Lerman* (b. 1947), who founded the Liz Lerman Dance Exchange in 1976, explores the interaction of senior adults and younger dancers in a dance-theater format. Her interest is the choreographic ramifications of putting people of diverse ages onstage together. Her company, located with her school in this small city, continues to tour the country offering performances

JUICE, CHOREOGRAPHY BY MEREDITH MONK, 1969, performed at the Guggenheim Museum, New York.

and workshops. In 2002 Lerman was involved in *Hallelujah*, a series of dances *In Praise Of* . . . that encompassed singing, movement, storytelling and the music of a variety of American composers and collaborators as well as community participation. As a teacher at New York's Hebrew Union College, she continues exploring crossing cultural barriers with her choreography for Dance Exchange, as in her 2006 work *Prayer as a Radical Act/Radical Action as Prayer*.

Rennie Harris Puremovement, a hip-hop company based in Philadelphia, broke new ground by turning hip-hop into a concert dance form. Harris, whose only dance training is hip-hop, seeks to break down the barriers between all dance forms. In addition to setting his hip-hop to a wide range of music, he also has set hip-hop movement on ballet and modern-trained dancers. *Rome and Jewels*, for example, is a concert hip-hop version of *Romeo and Juliet*. Puremovement has performed in traditional dance venues such as the American Dance Festival and the Joyce Theater in New York. For "Alive and Kicking," a video documentary series showcasing contemporary dance and performance artists, Harris recorded *Endangered Species*, which includes *March of the Antmen*, a fascinating slow-motion section recorded to violin music which simulates gang warfare, then concludes with an upbeat high-energy challenge dance travelling through the whole stage space with vocals that assure "Everything is all right!." Performed in 1998 in New York's Performance Space 122, it celebrates hip-hop as the ultimate vehicle for self-expression.

Ballet /Modern/ Jazz Blends

In the mid-20th century, ballet, essentially an import from Europe; modern dance, originally a revolt against the mechanism and lack of serious content in ballet; and tap and jazz dance, both deeply rooted in ethnic American culture, were quite separate and appealed to very separate audiences. More recently there have been many individuals who have sought to intertwine these diverse threads, so today it is often difficult to define the difference between contemporary modern dance, jazz and ballet. While different types of dancers trained in very different ways during the early 20th century, serious dance students today study many dance styles, producing technically strong and versatile dancers. Dancers who train this way may not be so easily inclined to categorize themselves, but may explore a variety of performance interests. Jazz classes have always incorporated ballet movement, and today jazz music and movement occasionally find their way into ballet classes. The old enemy of ballet, modern dance, now uses ballet in classes and ballet-trained dancers in companies.

These exchanges began during the time of the second generation of modern dancers, and since then a great deal of cross-pollination has been happening. For example, in 1959 Martha Graham and George Balanchine collaborated to produce *Episodes*, which was performed by both their companies together (Graham's section, which included a solo for Paul Taylor, was only performed for two seasons). In her later years Graham choreographed works for Rudolf Nureyev and Margot

Fonteyn. In 1976 Alvin Ailey choreographed the jazz ballet *Pas de Duke* for Mikhail Baryshnikov and Judith Jamison to music of Duke Ellington. Merce Cunningham set two works on the New York City Ballet, *The Seasons* in 1947 and *Summerspace* (1958) in 1966, and choreographed *Duets* (1949), a blend of classical technique and modern movement, for American Ballet Theatre dancers.

In 2000, a Ballet Russes Reunion and gala performance, featuring the survivors of all the Ballet Russes companies, was held in New Orleans. Meanwhile, in Monte Carlo, a new company under the aegis of Caroline, Princess of Hanover, was formed in 1985, called simply Les Ballets de Monte Carlo. The company is now directed by the French choreographer Jean-Christophe Maillot and performs outstanding 18th to 20th century choreography, from Bournonville to William Forsythe. The forty-eight dancers include a wide range of nationalities, not only of Europe but from America and Japan. Although the company is no longer Russian, the bust of Diaghilev remains in the courtyard of the small but elegant Monte Carlo Opera House, celebrating the company's history.

The postmodern generation saw an increase in the intertwining of dance styles. Unlike their predecessors, many are very open to the use of popular music and street-dance moves, giving them a stronger link to jazz dance. In addition, the anti-ballet sentiment of the early modern dancers has been replaced by a more tolerant approach; ballet is used as an enrichment tool in the same way that ethnic or social dance or gymnastics is a means of increasing the possibilities of human movement. Some contemporary ballet companies are almost indistinguishable from modern companies, except that the women perform on pointe.

But even being on pointe no longer always defines movement as ballet. For example, the innovative circus *Cirque du Soleil* has an acrobatic team that balances on each other with the anchoring dancer poised on one immobile pointe shoe. Fascinating as this is to watch, it would be stretching the point to classify it as ballet! Most recently, a great deal of jazz movement is now being performed on pointe; these jazz ballets, so popular with audiences and the dancers themselves, have given a whole new look to ballet—a chic, sexy and very modern look. Joffrey Ballet's *Billboards* (1993) and the final ballet in the film "Center Stage" (2000) are examples of this genre.

The cross-influence between modern dance and ballet actually began quite early in the 20th century. The American modern dance innovator Isadora Duncan performed in Russia during the winter of 1905, greatly influencing the Russian choreographer Michel Fokine as well as the ballerina Anna Pavlova, who began dancing in a more open, expressive style. At this time, ballet in Russia was beginning to break out of its predictable formula of tragic love stories and choreographic clichés (see chapter 4). Serge Diaghilev, during his entire career as impresario of the Ballets Russes, continued to promote choreographic works that were essentially new and exploratory—especially those of Vaslav Nijinsky. In *Rite of Spring* (1913) Nijinsky used sharp, angular movements and crouched body positions with turned-in legs to establish a primitive style (see chapter 4).

THE BALANCHINE LEGACY

George Balanchine, Diaghilev's last principal choreographer, displayed an interest in broadening and modernizing the vocabulary of ballet and inculcating musicality as the basis of movement, even in his early works, such as *Apollo* (1928) and *The Prodigal Son* (1929) (see chapter 4 for his early history). He had a strong sense of artistic design, the ability to weave bodies in new patterns and a penchant for new music. An accomplished musician himself, he formed an association with the modernist composer Igor Stravinsky that was to last a lifetime. Balanchine's career in America as a choreographer and director of the New York City Ballet has resulted in a new style for ballet: less courtly, more athletic, full of glamour and high-speed bravura, which he felt suited the American personality. Both modern dance and jazz influenced Balanchine's style, and he often experimented with syncopated movement and turned-in, sharply angular positions not usually associated with ballet. The variety and extent of his output as a choreographer between 1934 and his death in 1983 is staggering. When *Agon* was first performed, more than fifty years ago, it was considered the acme of modernism in ballet. Balanchine, who was already famous for the ease with which choreographic ideas poured from him, was especially careful crafting the *pas de deux* from *Agon*, spending days to get it exactly right; it is often performed today as an excerpt from the whole ballet.

In addition to his work with his own company, Balanchine also choreographed more than twenty Broadway shows, including "On Your Toes" (1936), "Babes in Arms" (1937), "The Boys from Syracuse" (1938), "Song of Norway" (1944), "Where's Charley?" (1948) and "House of Flowers" (1954). He also made dances for four movies, one circus dance —the *Ballet of the Elephants* (1942) for Ringling Brothers—and a number of revues in Paris and London before he came to the United States.

Although Balanchine redesigned some full-evening classics such as *The Nutcracker* (1954), he preferred programming an evening of several short ballets for his new American audiences in an effort to appeal to a variety of tastes. To meet his developing neoclassical aesthetic, costumes and sets were simplified, focusing the audience on the lines and shapes of the movement itself.

From the outset of his company's development, Balanchine

GEORGE BALANCHINE rehearsing Patricia McBride and Mikhail Baryshnikov.

encouraged the talents of young choreographers in both ballet and modern veins from within the company and from the outside. Lew Christensen, Lar Lubovitch, Paul Taylor and Mark Morris produced ballets for his company as guest choreographers.

Since Balanchine's death in 1983, the New York City Ballet has been directed by a former principal dancer, the Danish-born (1946) *Peter Martins.* Before becoming ballet master in chief (artistic director), Martins set an interesting contemporary ballet, *Calcium Night Light* (1977). His subsequent ballets were more closely aligned to the Balanchine style, sometimes indistinguishable from it. In 1992, Martins proposed the guidelines for the Diamond Project, to encourage new works focused on the classical technique, by offering the use of NYCB's first-class dancers, as well as a showcase for performing the new works. The Project was named for philanthropist Irene Diamond, who supported the NYCB's new projects for many years. By the time this project celebrated its 10th anniversary, the clear success of it became evident. Established choreographers like Angelino Precaj from France, William Forsythe, director of the Frankfurt Ballet, Helgi Tomasson, artistic director of San Francisco Ballet, and Martins himself, have done some of their best work under the aegis of the Diamond Project.

Jerome Robbins joined NYCB as assistant artistic director in 1948. Robbins was a charter member of Ballet Theatre, for which he created the popular one-act *Fancy Free*, a dance-story about sailors on leave in New York (1944). He moved back and forth between Broadway and ballet throughout the 1940s to the 1960s, choreographing a succession of neoclassical, plotless, but emotion-filled ballets like *Afternoon of a Faun* (1953). Dismissing Nijinsky's scenario, Robbins made the nymph and faun a pair of self-absorbed contemporary dancers who meet briefly for a duet in a studio. In 1969 Robbins returned to classical ballet, becoming co-director of NYCB, first with Balanchine and then with Peter Martins, until retiring from that position in 1990. The creative period in ballet continued until Robbins' death; during that time he choreographed some sixty-six ballets for the company, beginning with *Dances at a Gathering* (1969), the ultimate "piano ballet"—a piano is onstage and the dancers interact with the pianist—and culminating with his third ballet to the music of Bach, *Brandenburg* (1997). (See chapter 6 for Robbins' contributions to Broadway dance.)

Arthur Mitchell (b. 1934), a protégé of Balanchine and the first African-American to dance and star in a major ballet company, used his education at NYCB to provide unique opportunities for young black dancers. Mitchell is remembered for his electrifying performances in *Agon* (1957) and *A Midsummer Night's Dream* (1962). Mitchell left the NYCB at the age of 35, not long after the assassination of Martin Luther King, Jr., to form a school and company in Harlem, the center of New York's African-American community. His goal was to channel the restless energy he saw there into a physical art. In order to encourage the participation of local boys in the school, the ballet classes were at first taught to drum accompaniment. The result of his effort was the Dance Theatre of Harlem, which debuted in 1971 and today performs around the world. Mitchell was given permission to use Balanchine repertory, as well as producing his own works and those of his ballet master Karel Shook and many American choreographers. Geoffrey Holder's *Dougla* (1974), for example, depicts the movements of the Hindu-African group of that name. The company today has a wide range of contemporary works by choreographers such as Holder, Dwight Rhoden and Alonzo King, as well as some reworked classics, such as *Creole Giselle* (1984) and an African *Firebird*. It has retained the Balanchine style and training methods in its school. There is no question that Mr. Mitchell's mission to bring minority children ages three to seventeen to the school for a fully-rounded education in music, theater, dance and art has had a far-reaching effect.

Balanchine's visits to his native Russia in the 1960s resulted in several defections to the West of Soviet dancers who were looking for wider artistic opportunities. Notable among these defectors were Rudolf Nureyev, Natalia Makarova and Mikhail Baryshnikov (b. 1948), who have had outstanding careers as freelance performers, also setting Russian repertory in the West. Baryshnikov, who had a strong interest in having the opportunity to work with Balanchine, danced with the New York City Ballet before becoming artistic director of American Ballet Theatre. During his directorship he brought several works by Twyla Tharp into the ABT repertory. After his retirement as a dancer, Baryshnikov became involved with other contemporary choreographers, exemplifying a very successful crossover career. He founded the White Oak Dance Project with Mark Morris, performing in ensemble pieces choreographed by a variety of postmodern choreographers until the company was disbanded in 2002.

In the new millennium, NYCB continues to produce retrospectives of Balanchine's work, as well as those of the company's second most-important choreographer, Jerome Robbins. In 2008, a Robbins festival reconstructed thirty-three Robbins ballets, making his legacy larger than any other choreographer except Balanchine. Not wanting to become a museum company, the 2008 season also featured daring new works such as *Concerto DSCH* by *Alexei Ratmansky*, which one reviewer called "A major event . . . a vivid, novel-like account . . . a breakthrough in choreography."[5]

While Russian choreographers and imported dancers continued to strongly influence American ballet, American-born artists were also making important contributions.

The intertwining of ballet, modern and other concert dance forms is beautifully embodied in the work of *Twyla Tharp*. Born in 1941, Tharp trained in ballet, tap and jazz, then danced with both Cunningham and Taylor before forming her own company. At first wildly iconoclastic, her choreography has become, over time, more mainstream. In addition to Tharp's personal loose "squiggly" style, combined with ballet technique, her work includes elements of tap, folk and social dance. She has choreographed the films "Hair" (1978), "Ragtime" (1980), and "Amadeus" (1984). Encouraged by collaborations with Baryshnikov, Tharp has choreographed for jazz and ballet companies, notably American Ballet Theatre, where she served as associate director from 1988 to 1990. She is particularly well-known for her long-term collaboration with Baryshnikov. The popular satirical ballet *Push Comes to Shove* (1976), with an extraordinarily funny modern/ballet solo for Baryshnikov, was the result of their collaboration.

Tharp was the featured choreographer for the inaugural episode, *Sue's Leg, Remembering the Thirties*, of the public television "Dance in America" series. This PBS series continues to bring both new and innovative as well as established choreographers to the attention of the American people—which is especially important for those who do not live in major dance centers. The television special "Baryshnikov by Tharp" won two Emmy awards. Today, Tharp makes dances for many of the companies she has worked with in the past—American Ballet Theater among them, as well as overseeing and creating work for an ongoing troupe that tours worldwide.

Robert Joffrey (1930–1988), a gifted American dancer from the Pacific Northwest, came to New York and established first a school, then his own company in 1954—originally made up of only six dancers. The company repertory featured works by Joffrey and his principal choreographer, *Gerald Arpino* (1923–2008), but included reconstructions of 19th century ballets, especially from the Bournonville repertory. In 1967, Joffrey choreographed a duet, *Astarte*, the first "psychedelic" ballet. As the company grew, Joffrey also developed a mission to reconstruct works from the Diaghilev era by Nijinsky and Massine. He also reconstructed Kurt Jooss' masterpiece *The Green Table* with Jooss in his seventies assisting the project. In 1989, *A Wedding Bouquet*, a 1937 collaborative comic work by Frederick Ashton and Gertrude Stein, was performed by the Joffrey company. Arpino, who assumed artistic directorship of the company upon Joffrey's death, had a wide range of choreographic interests and styles, giving the company its identity as "the voice of young America in dance."[6]

In the early 1990s, the Joffrey Ballet relocated to Los Angeles. There, the full-evening contemporary ballet *Billboards* (1993), created to the music of Prince in four sections by four choreographers, attracted a new, young audience to ballet. In 1995 the company was once again reorganized and moved by Arpino to become The Joffrey Ballet of Chicago. Today it has a remarkable repertory of more than 225 ballets. Joffrey Ballet of Chicago has been exploring works once considered modern dance territory only, such as reviving Alwin Nikolais's *Masks, Props and Mobiles*. Many notable American contemporary choreographers, including Laura Dean, Mark Morris, Glen Tetley and Twyla Tharp are also represented. Lively reconstructions of Balanchine's 1957 work, *Square Dance*, Jerome Robbins' *NY Export: Opus Jazz*, and Anthony Tudor's *Dark Elegies* (1937) have been well received. As the millennium progresses, dance DVDs are carving a niche of their own, with ballet classics leading the way. The classics, especially those with well-known stars dancing, have an appeal to mainstream America.

WORLD CONTEMPORARY DANCE

Throughout Europe, choreographers and performing groups have made significant contributions to contemporary dance. France has become a center for innovative work, as has Germany. The French penchant for "modernism" was launched by *Roland Petit* (b. 1924) a Paris Opera Ballet dancer whose popular version of *Carmen* appeared in 1949. He created the role of Carmen for his wife Renée "Zizi" Jeanmaire, later he created nightclub acts for her. From 1973 to 1997 he continued his contemporary forays as artistic director of the Ballet de Marseille.

Reinforced by young American choreographers in the 1970s, contemporary French ballet choreographers soon began to emerge. Notable is *Maguy Marin* (b. 1951), a dancer from Maurice Béjart's company, who has set works on the Lyons Opera Ballet, the Paris Opera Ballet and Strasbourg Opera Ballet. Many are updated versions of classics, like *Cinderella* (1985) and *Coppélia* (1993), in urban present-day settings. Her movement vocabulary, which combines the classical dance and contemporary techniques is interlaced with gestures and combined with mixed-media techniques. The result is a highly theatrical presentation that is most aptly described as performance art.

The Frenchman *Maurice Béjart* (1927–2007) produced strikingly dramatic contemporary ballet choreography for his company, the Ballet of the Twentieth Century, which he formed in 1960 in Belgium. His works such as *Le Sacre du Printemps* (1959) and *Notre Faust* (1975) scandalized some audiences with their powerful emotional content and sexuality; however, he also garnered an enthusiastic group of followers in Europe who felt he added new vigor to classical dance. Mudra, Béjart's school in Brussels, trained and influenced many European ballet and modern dancers and choreographers. After leaving the Théâtre Royale de la Monnaie of Brussels in 1987, he relocated his company to Lausanne, Switzerland, renaming it Béjart Ballet Lausanne.

The German interest in modern dance thrives in a movement known as Tanztheatre (dance theater), considered a new form of expressionist and dramatic dance. Many of the works of this movement have a darkly violent cast, arising out of a generation contemplating the causes and effects of two world wars begun in Germany. *Pina Bausch* (1940–2009), one of the chief proponents of Tanztheatre, was influenced by Kurt Jooss and José Limón, but also trained in ballet at the Juilliard School in New York. She became director of the Wuppertal (Germany) Dance Theater in 1973, where she has continued to explore the themes that preoccupy her: sexual warfare, loneliness and power struggles. Dance historian Martha Bremser calls her the choreographer who "rediscovered body language . . . the movement of a leg, a hip, a shoulder . . . the whole repertoire of everyday gestures, unconsciously learned, in which dangerous clichés manifest themselves."[7]

Jiří Kylián (b. 1947), the artistic adviser and choreographer of the Nederlands Dans Theater, who trained at both London's Royal Ballet and the Martha Graham School, creates contemporary works that are a combination of ballet and modern dance. Kylián frequently uses music by his Czech countryman Leos Janácek, but he diverged from this pattern in several works, such as *Road to the Stamping Ground* (1983), inspired by Australian aboriginal dance. Nederlands Dans Theater now has two other companies: with dancers ages seventeen to twenty-two, NDT II provides young choreographers with ample opportunity to experiment; in 1991 NDT III was established by Kylián to provide a platform for very experienced dancers who are forty or older. The five-member group performs personal and theatrical works specially created for it by such leading choreographers as Kylián, Hans van Manen, Ohad Naharin, Shusaku Takeuchi, Paul Lightfoot and Johan Inger.

In the former Soviet Union, *Boris Eifman* (b. 1946) is being hailed as one of the major figures in modern ballet. He has earned the title of "The People's Artist of Russia"—the highest level of distinction for a performing artist in the former Soviet Union. The Eifman Ballet of St. Petersburg, founded by him in 1977, received international acclaim in 1988 with its first performance abroad at the Champs-Élysées Theatre in Paris, and has since appeared annually in New York. Seen as working in the traditions of Noverre and Fokine, Eifman blends modern dance and classical ballet into emotionally charged dances. Fond of depicting the personalities of other artists, he has created works about Molière and Tchaikovsky, and in 2004 choreographed a ballet about George Balanchine.

In Japan after World War II, a movement form known as Butoh was founded by *Tatsumi Hijikata* (1928–1986). Hijakata was interested in finding movement roots that transcended any particular culture. His dancers sought connection with nature and the earth, often moving with the torso parallel to the floor. Butoh is a slow-motion movement form that sometimes uses outdoor sites, nudity and body painting and powdering. Translated as "the dance of darkness" or "the dance of the dark soul," it has been seen by Westerners as a political statement about the devastation of Hiroshima and Nagasaki, cities obliterated by atomic bombs, ending World War II. It can also be seen as a form of catharsis for both the performers and audience, sometimes travelling from despair and the abandonment of self to a sense of peaceful acceptance. Practitioners, both Eastern and Western, assert that it is primarily a way of exploring imagery and gaining insight into one's own psyche.

Butoh did not become popular in Japan until the 1960s, because in the 1950s artists in Japan were imitating western arts, including dance. Even today many Japanese are unfamiliar with the term which was first used by Hijikata. Hijikata's works are extremely varied, including some done in silence, some set to rhythmic drumbeats, some very violent, some sexual, some nearly nude and others fully clothed in traditional Japanese layered costuming. Facial expressions are extremely important. Sometimes faces are twisted and anguished. Faces are painted white, and in some works the entire body is painted with grey clay. Kazuo Ohno, who became a collaborator in the movement early on, has a gentler, less athletic style in his choreography.

Performers who began bringing Butoh to the west in the 1980s include *Sankai Juka* and the husband-and-wife team *Eiko* (b. 1952) and *Koma* (b. 1948), whose mysterious duets have been described as "a highwire act unerringly poised between hopefulness and hopelessness."[8] They first began working with Hijikata in Tokyo in 1971. In a fine example of fusion of styles and traditions, Eiko (female) and Koma (male) collaborated with eighty-one-year-old Anna Halprin in a new work, *Be With*, in 2001. Their newest outdoor work had its New York premiere in May of 2008.

Notable contemporary companies have formed in Israel and Australia, with smaller companies in all countries of South America. In Guangdong (Canton) China, a training program in modern dance began in 1987 with American and British postmodern teachers. Renamed in 1990, the Guangdong Modern Dance Company was officially established in 1992 as the first full-time modern dance company in mainland China. It has already developed a unique identity and now tours internationally.

PROFILE: MEREDITH MONK, INTERDISCIPLINARY ARTIST
Performer, Choreographer, Composer, Musician,
*   New York*

Harriet Lihs   Meredith, who were the early influences on your work?

Meredith Monk   My mother was a professional singer. Her father was also a singer, her mother was a concert pianist and my great-grandfather was a cantor (a singer in a Jewish temple.) I was not very coordinated as a child, due to eye problems, so my mother enrolled me in Dalcroze Eurythmics classes. Dalcroze Eurythmics is a method of teaching the fundamentals of music through the body.

MEREDITH MONK

So the idea of integrating voice, music and space with movement was imprinted very early. Because of this background, the rhythms in my music are very complex, and the music and movement elements are carefully woven. Later, I studied modern dance with Ernestine Stodelle, and ballet with Olga Tarassova. In New York I studied Cunningham technique and at the Robert Joffrey School. I went to Sarah Lawrence College, where my major influences were Bessie Schönberg (dance) and Ruth Lloyd (music).

HL   I see on your website that your Vocal Ensemble is very busy, and both a CD and DVD have come out recently. Do you still prefer the description of your work as interdisciplinary?

MM   There is a CD of *impermanence*, which was nominated for a Grammy in 2008. My films "Ellis Island" and "Book of Days" both came out on DVD, and the "Meredith Monk Piano Album" was released as a book of my piano scores. In 2008 I also premiered *Songs of Ascension*, which I wrote for voices and string quartet. I still make many of my discoveries between the cracks of what are considered separate art forms. Each work is a balance of perceptual elements.

    All of my musical works (even music concerts) are staged and fully lit, with a lot of movement. The instrumentalists must have their parts memorized, no music stands in the way, so they can move. For example, in *Songs of Ascension*, they must be able to play their instruments lying on their backs: I have always worked with singers in this way. I think of my work as the dancing voice and the singing body.

HL   What kind of people do you like to work with?

MM   I like to work with people who have an affinity for my language of images, voice, and movement and are committed to it. Some are dancers who sing well, and others are singers or theater artists who move well. I'm privileged to have been working with my performers for a very long time, one since 1976. I appreciate continuity, because replacing one person in the group can change the whole chemistry of the group. We function more like a family or tribe than simply a professional unit. I also like to collaborate with visual artists from time to time as I did with Ann Hamilton in *Songs of Ascension* and *mercy*, presented at the American Dance Festival in 2001.

HL   Are there any downsides to having your own ensemble?

MM   I don't have enough work to keep the group together for forty weeks full-time, so I encourage my performers to pursue other interests. Sometimes a conflict in schedules arises, but we manage around it.

HL   Are you still doing site-specific pieces? I am remembering *Vessel* (1971), where the audience travelled to three different locations.

MM   Yes, I recently premiered a site-specific version of my new work, *Songs of Ascension* in Ann Hamilton's Tower in Northern California. The piece will also be presented at the Guggenheim Museum in New York in March (2009). It will contain a few echoes of *Juice: A Theater Cantata in Three Installments* which I originally presented at the Guggenheim in 1969. I was the first to use the Museum as a performance space.

HL   Has your own work gone in new directions in the past six to eight years?

MM   My work has gotten simpler and more transparent. In the years I have left, I want to do work that is life-affirming, that reveals the inner radiance of the people onstage. In the early years my choreographic viewpoint was rebellious, sometimes brash, but this newer viewpoint reflects my spiritual and philosophic beliefs, developed gradually through the study of Buddhism.

HL   Anything else you would like to add?

MM   It's been a fascinating and wonderful life. What I did I did for love.

PROFILE: JOE ISTRE ON CONTEMPORARY DANCE
Contemporary Choreographer/Teacher,
    New York

Harriet Lihs   Joe, tell me how you first got interested in dance and who your early influences were.

Joe Istre   My mother, who was exposed to a lot of culture. We were living in a small town in Texas, and when a dance studio opened up there she convinced me to try it. I was 15 at the time. I took one class (jazz) and knew I was a dancer. The teacher, Kathy Skinner, offered me free classes, and after a year, I started taking ballet. By the time I was 17, I was teaching jazz at Kathy's. I then started college as a dance major, and another Kathy, Kathy Treadway, became my greatest influence. She was a proponent of Bill Evans' modern technique.

JOE ISTRE teaching a class at Sherry Gold Summer Dance Camp.

HL   You've been working in New York as a freelance choreographer and teacher now for a number of years. What would you call your choreographic style?

JI   I just call it contemporary. "Jazz" is not so contemporary; a jazz class is more like Broadway work. When I teach, my warm-up is modern-based, with a lot of floor stretches and progressions across the floor. My center combinations may not be jazz, they are whatever the music inspires—lyrical, modern or even a fusion with another style such as hip-hop. I like to give my dancers a theme and an intent for a combination, and approach it in segments.

HL   What kind of dancers do you work with?

JI I do a lot of choreography for regional ballet companies and semi-professional companies who want contemporary works. This summer I am teaching daily contemporary classes at American Ballet Theater's Summer Intensive for college students. I like to work with dancers with good ballet training, but dance is not just about getting your leg up; focus and passion in dancers is equally important with technique.

HL What are some special events in your career?

JI In 2007 the Regional Dance Association had a national convention in Pittsburgh. I taught contemporary dance and choreographed *Blow by Blow* for six girls from the Twin City Ballet. This piece received the convention's award for choreography, and got me several new offers from companies in Detroit, Utah and Santa Barbara.

HL Do you think the audience for dance has changed in the past few years?

JI Yes, it has grown through word of mouth, there are more people interested in seeing contemporary dance and more spaces that are performing it. Dance on the whole is on the upswing, and the dance technique of young dancers is a whole different game in terms of elevated abilities. But popularity in the arts can be cyclical.

HL What advice would you give young people who, like yourself, seek to make a lifelong career in dance?

JI That would be based on the level they are at. I would tell them to study as many dance forms as they can, as companies are all demanding versatility. If they are advanced, I would tell them to start going to auditions of all kinds. If they aren't ready for that, I would tell them to go to a college with a good dance majors program. Whenever they are performing, auditioning, or taking class, I would tell them to "put dance back into dance!"

PROFILE: JODY OBERFELDER
Postmodern Choreographer and Company Director,
  New York

Harriet Lihs Jody, what and who were the early influences that led you into becoming a choreographer?

Jody Oberfelder Modern dance 101—Emery Hermann from the Alwin Nikolais Company came to teach improvisation at Michigan State University. Dixie Durr was the chair and often invited guest artists. I was smitten with the idea of creating out of idea and concept with my body.

After two years at SUNY (State University of New York) at Purchase, I made it to New York, studied at the Alwin Nikolais/Murray Louis School. There the concepts of space, time, shape, and motion to serve exploration struck me. I danced with Phyllis Lamhut and toured around the country for two years with her company before moving to California, where Nita Little was teaching improvisation, which totally shook up any "conservatory" ideas of what I thought a dancer should be. I tried to start a company in Santa Cruz, but everybody wanted to go to the beach. Finally I made it back to New York, sang in a rock band for three years, and then started my own company in 1988.

HL How would you define your choreographic style?

JO If I had to define my movement style I'd say "athletic postmodern." There is a blur now with 'contemporary' vs. modern. And now one could say there is classic modern, which has a gloss, commercial feel to me. I like to think of my technique always changing to suit a piece. Adding to the idea of choreographic style, I always start with ideas or concepts for each piece—something I'm going through, perception of the world, or in the case of recent commissions, for example, Stravinsky's "The Soldier's Tale" by the Brooklyn Philharmonic, spurred by music and a story.

HL Has your gymnastics background affected your choreography?

JO Gymnastics, diving, water ballet, cheerleading—all have influenced my choreography. I was not a ballet baby. I had always been a tomboy, played outside whenever I could. I gravitate toward the intensely physical that allows the human body to soar and be playful with possibilities. I almost danced with Elizabeth Streb. It was at her audition that I realized that I wanted to work with other dancers who enjoyed moving in wild ways.

HL What kind of dancers do you like to work with? Do you look for a particular personality, body type or training?

JO I look for dancers who are strong, smart, creative, articulate, intuitive, demi-daredevils who are great with partnering. I look for dancers who are real, quirky, human, show their emotions, embody what they do with what they feel about what they are doing and have willingness in rehearsal to go with a creative process. Bland dancers bore me.

Nobody is bland per se, but training makes them feel they have to be a certain way. My imagination has to be struck. I want to be inspired by their mystery and powers and amazing possible combinations of energies. I also look for women who are as strong as men, and try not to weed out divas. I want to be able to walk into a rehearsal and know that these dancers are up for anything. It has to be play as well as work.

HL   Do you think the audiences for contemporary dance have changed in the past six to eight years?

JO   It is changing. With YouTube, and all the competitive dance shows, people are more aware of dance. But I do question if they are more aware of art. I long for the day when people go to dance as they would to a movie. I'm afraid that people don't trust that they can respond kinetically to something before their eyes, that they can be moved by motion. Because media is making us sit at our desks more and look at screens, live action is more challenging and yet imperative, so we don't become automatons.

Also, I think the general audience is not used to looking at bodies except as sports competitors, objects for glamour, high kicks and sex objects. Dance is art. I do think that commercials and styling have always borrowed from the art of dance. Perhaps with a new culture of yoga, more people will internalize a physical connection to mind—or perhaps education from a young age will do it. Look at dance, see what you see, feel what you feel, not: who's the best? It is subjective.

HL   Has the subject matter for contemporary dance in general changed in the past six to eight years?

JO   I think post-9/11 there is (thankfully) less of a stigma about being emotional.

HL   What about your own work? Is it going in new directions?

JO   With time, age and experience I have a more sure hand. I think on a bigger scale, and yet keep it intimate. The last few years have brought new projects that have expanded my range. Choreographing *Dido and Aeneas* with the Orchestra of St. Luke's led to a new commission for BAM [Brooklyn Academy of Music]. Can't wait.

HL   What are some of the downsides and upsides to having you own company?

JO   Ohhhhhh . . . I'd like to pay everyone more, and tour more, and give all my dancers what they need to grow as artists. The best part is creating with my group and seeing the work performed. The hard part is keeping all the balls in the air, the administration, marketing, and infrastructure. How to survive? Just keep making art. The rest somehow falls in place.

OTHER CONTEMPORARY NOTABLES AND COMPANIES

Aeros, a company based on the aerial virtuosity of gymnastics, features athletes from the Romanian Gymnastics Federation and produces spectacular and exciting performances. It is co-choreographed by Daniel Ezralow, David Parsons and Moses Pendleton, in collaboration with the creators of

Stomp. This group of exuberant performers was first assembled in 1997 for a hairspray ad; in 2001 they toured the US extensively, sixty cities in all.

Nina Ananiashvili born in Tiblisi, Georgia, in 1962, became the first Russian ballerina to divide her time between the East and West, dancing both at New York's American Ballet Theatre and Moscow's Bolshoi Ballet. She made her American debut in 1987 with the Bolshoi tour. In 2008 she distinguished herself in the lead role of Kitri, in the ABT revival of Petipa's complete *Don Quixote*, and has for many years dazzled audiences as *Giselle.*

In 2004 she returned to her native country of Georgia to revitalize the State Ballet of Georgia, located in the capital city of Tiblisi. In its first two years under her directorship, she produced eighteen new ballets, including Russian classics, Balanchine, Bournonville and contemporary Americans including Stanton Welch and Trey McIntyre. In 2007 she brought her company to New York for its first American tour.

Karole Armitage (b. 1954), who left NYCB and joined Merce Cunningham's company in 1975, evolved a style that she describes as "precarious—high energy—virtuoso—off-balance—extreme."[9] Ballets like *Drastic Classicism* (1981) were set to rock music and mix pointe and classical technique with a gamut of other movements. Her "punk-rock" ballets became popular in Europe, where she has made a career as a freelance choreographer. Armitage is currently choreographer-in-residence for Ballet de Lorraine, based in Nancy, France. Using New York as a base, she continues to work as an independent choreographer, alternating projects for Armitage Gone! Dance (her own company), Ballet de Lorraine and work for other companies. After nearly two decades in Europe, Ms. Armitage returned to New York to premiere *Gamelan Gardens* in 2006, created for the Alvin Ailey American Dance Theater.

Ballet Hispanico, located in New York's upper east side, combines ballet with Spanish dance from a variety of nationalities. The school and company, founded by *Tina Ramirez* (b. ca. 1928) in 1970, now also include outreach programs all over the country. Ramirez studied ballet with Alexandra Danilova and Spanish dance from the legendary Lola Bravo. Her company includes members from Cuba, Puerto Rico, the US and several non-Hispanic countries. "Latino music and dance are so powerful," says Ramirez, that "in the end, few can resist."[10]

BalletMet, located in Columbus, Ohio, is directed by Gerard Charles, who trained at the Royal Ballet School in London In an effort to draw new audiences to ballet, Charles has employed very innovative choreographic ideas. In 2003, his 28 member troupe performed onstage with Ohio State University's marching band. He has also choreographed to club dance music—for example, Moby. Postmodern choreographers James Kudelka, Stanton Welch and Deanna Carter were commissioned to set works on the company. BalletMet made its New York debut in the spring of 2004.

Fernando Bujones (1955–2005) was born in Miami of Cuban parents and is considered to be the one of the finest male dancers of the 20th century, "dazzling." He trained at the School of American Ballet in New York and became the youngest principal dancer at American Ballet Theatre. In 1974 he won the gold medal at the Varna International Ballet Competition, the first American man to do so. After retiring as a performer, he became artist in residence at Texas Christian University Dance Department. He also formed his own company in Madrid, Spain, the Ballet Classico Mediterraneo. In 2000 he became artistic director of the Orlando Ballet, and was subsequently inducted into the Florida Hall of Fame.

Matthew Bourne (b. 1960), composed an altogether different interpretation of Tchaikovsky's classic ballet *Swan Lake* in 1995, which made history as the longest-running ballet ever in London's West End. With a full corps de ballet of male swans, this new version immediately captured the public imagination and was included in the final scenes of the movie "Billy Eliott." In 2002 Bourne formed a touring company called New Adventures, that toured the US and other countries performing his popular story-ballets. In 2006, his version of *Edward Scissorhands* was successfully added to the repertory.

Christopher Bruce (b. 1945). A principal dancer with Ballet Rambert, Bruce began choreographing for Rambert, becoming one of the first British choreographers to successfully combine ballet and modern dance. Strongly drawn to social and political themes, his dramatic ballets include *There Was a Time* (1972), that criticizes political power struggles, and *Cruel Garden* (1977). The haunting *Ghost Dances* (1981) condemned political repression in South America. Bruce was artistic director of Ballet Rambert from 1994 to 2002.

Cedar Lake Contemporary Ballet, a troupe located in the Chelsea area of New York City, is not afraid of showing unusual new works by international choreographers, including Jo Strongmen, Angelin Prelijocaj, Nicolo Fonte, Luca Veggeti and numerous others. Founded in 2003, it is funded by the Wal-Mart heiress Nancy Laurie; as a result its dancers receive 52-week contracts with paid vacations, health benefits, beautifully appointed studios and its own performing space. The company's current director is Benoit-Swan Pouffer, a French-born former member of the Alvin Ailey American Dance Theater.

H. T. Chen, born in Shanghai (birthdate unknown) and raised in Taiwan, came to New York in 1971. In 1980 he launched the Arts Gate Center as a year-round performing arts school, and in 1980 he established the Mulberry Street Theater, Chinatown's first performing arts space. He is choreographer for Chen and Dancers, also located in Chinatown, and considered the primary Asian-American contemporary choreographer in the US. The company is dedicated to contemporary works on subjects of interest to the Chinese community, such as acculturation and ancestry.

Lucinda Childs (b. 1940) studied with Merce Cunningham at Sarah Lawrence until she graduated in 1962, then took Robert Dunn's workshop in the summer. She joined the Judson Church Group, appearing in works by Yvonne Rainer, Steve Paxton and Robert Morris, as well as her own. She choreographed twelve works while at Judson; her solo *Carnation* was performed at the Brooklyn Academy of Music and in Boston in 2001.

John Cranko (1927–1973). The first South African choreographer to earn an international reputation, Cranko began creating ballets for the Sadler's Wells Ballet in the 1940s. He also choreographed for Ballet Rambert and the Paris Opera. His early works include *Sea Change* (1949), *Pineapple Poll* (1951) and (1957). His great era of creativity followed his appointment in 1961 as artistic director of the Stuttgart Ballet, for which he made the still-performed ballets *Romeo and Juliet* (1962), *Onegin* (1965), *The Taming of the Shrew* (1969) and *Initials R.B.M.E.* (1972) before his untimely death.

Laura Dean (b. 1945). Dean studied with Merce Cunningham and performed with Paul Taylor. Considered one of the most controversial of the postmodernists, she launched her first company in 1972, today called Laura Dean Musicians and Dancers. She has also choreographed extensively for ballet companies, including five commissions for the Joffrey Ballet. She has a fascination for spinning and repetitive movement patterns, and since 1986 she has composed her own scores.

Anne Teresa de Keersmaeker, the avant-garde Belgian choreographer, created early works with strictly minimalist movement. She developed an all-women company called Rosas, in Brussels. For her ground-breaking piece *Achterland* (Outback), which premiered in 1990, she expanded the company by adding male dancers. She filmed this work in 1993, restaging it for the camera. This piece uses a miked section of the floor to very interesting effect, and has the two musicians, a violinist and a pianist, integrated into the dancer's movement. She has been a strong proponent of the avant-garde music of Steve Reich throughout her choreographic career; his score was the background for part of her 2003 film, *Counterphrases*, and in 2008 she presented *A Steve Reich Evening* at the Brooklyn Academy of Music.

Mark Dendy (b. 1961). After two years in the Martha Graham Company, Dendy formed his own company in 1983. His work is a combination of high-powered dance, theater and site-specific art. Many themes reflect his North Carolina roots. Works include *Garden* (1986), *Busride to Heaven* (1993), *Fauns* (1996) (based on the life of Nijinsky) and *Ritual* (1996), set on fifty American Dance Festival students.

Dialogue Dance Company is part of Russia's rapidly-growing contemporary modern dance scene. Dialogue made its New York debut in 2008, after a residency at the American Dance Festival in Durham, NC. The company specializes in duets that explore human interaction.

David Dorfman (b. 1956). A choreographer who won the "Bessie" (Schönberg) Award in 1996, Dorfman's works have been commissioned by companies in the United States and Europe, his a blend of movement, music and text with strong emotional overtones. He continues to run his own company based in New York, David Dorfman Dance, while also serving as Chair of the Department of Dance at Connecticut College.

Ulysses Dove (1947–1996). Dove danced with Merce Cunningham's company, then taught and choreographed at the Paris Opera. In 1979 he began choreographing for the Alvin Ailey American Dance Theater. Episodes, choreographed for the company in 1989 was awarded a "Bessie." He also made important works for ballet companies: *Red Angels* (1984) for the New York City Ballet; *Dancing on the Front Porch of Heaven* (1992) for the Royal Swedish Ballet; and his last work, *Twilight* (1996), for NYCB.

Robert Ellis Dunn (1928–1996), a musician, taught choreography to the Judson Church group in the 1960s, encouraging the decomposition of music and experimentation with time structures. A disciple of John Cage, Dunn encouraged the creation of dances following the avant-garde methods Cage had used in his music-making.

Mats Ek (b. 1945) is the son of Swedish choreographer Birgit Cullberg, Mats studied ballet as a child and drama as a college student in Sweden. He joined the Culberg Ballet in 1973, dancing in works by Jiří Kylián and Maurice Béjart. During this period he choreographed several works for the Cullberg Ballet, including a completely revised postmodern *Giselle* in 1982. In 1985 he became the director of the company, resigning in 1993. He has also choreographed for other companies as well, including the Hamburg Ballet, Paris Opera, Nederlands Dans Theater and Les Grands Ballets Canadien de Montreal.

Doug Elkins (b. 1950) began his career as a b-boy, touring the world with breakdancing groups. Elkins's fast-paced choreography is a blend of modern, ballet and hip-hop. He formed the Doug Elkins Dance Company in 1988. Although each of the members of his troupe has highly individual style, the emphasis is on ensemble work. The popular postmodernist has offered works like *Narcoleptic Lovers* (1995) at the Edinburgh Fringe Festival, and performed at the Altogether Different Festival in New York and the Next Wave Festival at Brooklyn Academy of Music. In 2006 he choreographed *Fraulein Maria* which lovingly deconstructs "The Sound of Music." Other millennial works include *I Hear Mermaids Singing, The House Project* and *The Look of Love*.

Garth Fagan (b. 1940). A native of Jamaica, Fagan studied with Martha Graham, Pearl Primus and Alvin Ailey. His company, Garth Fagan Dance, located in Rochester, NY, blends modern dance, jazz and ethnic forms and tours internationally. In 1991 he collaborated with trumpeter Wynton Marsalis to create the acclaimed evening-length *Griot New York*. His choreography for the Broadway musical "The Lion King" (1997) earned a Tony award. In spite of the draw to join the more renowned Alvin Ailey company in New York City, Fagan's dancers stay with him for unusually long stretches, continuing to dance into their 40s and 50s.

Louis Falco (1943–1993), a New Yorker who attended the High School of Performing Arts, Falco became a principal dancer with the José Limón Dance Company, often appearing in roles Limón had created for himself. In 1967 he presented his first formal program of his own dances performed by his own company, the Louis Falco Dance Company, and was hailed as a choreographer of exceptional promise.

Suzanne Farrell (b. 1945 in Cincinnati) became a member of New York City Ballet at the age of sixteen, an extraordinary ballerina for whom Balanchine created many roles including Diamonds in *Jewels* and Dulcinea in *Don Quixote*. After years as Balanchine's muse, Farrell turned down his offer of marriage and left the company. She and her then-husband Paul Mejia, also from NYCB, danced for Maurice Béjart in Brussels and co-directed the Fort Worth Ballet for several years. Subsequently she has become a noted teacher and the foremost reconstructor of Balanchine repertory.

Eliot Feld (b. 1942), a New Yorker who made his debut with American Ballet Theatre, leaving them with two outstanding ballets, *Harbinger* (1967) and *At Midnight*. He then danced in several Broadway shows. He formed his first ballet company, the American Ballet Company, in 1969, but by 1971 it had became a financial, though not an artistic, disaster. In 1974 he returned with a new company called the Eliot Feld Ballet, renamed Feld Ballet and Feld Ballets/NY, and finally Ballet Tech Company and School. Since 1967 Feld has choreographed 133 ballets, many for European, Canadian and American companies. Since 2003 Ballet Tech is no longer a full-time company, but produces an annual season of three or four weeks in New York. Feld's choreography is contemporary and brisk, sometimes difficult and convoluted, taking witty and daring chances with balance, and showing a strong link to his variety of musical choices.

Molissa Fenley (b. 1954). A choreographer interested in athletics, Fenley trained in running and weightlifting as well as dance. Her works are physically grueling, especially the solos for herself. In one of these, *State of Darkness* (1988), Fenley depicts herself as a female warrior. *Cosmic Variations 1–4*, with music by John Cage, appeared in 2004 at the White Wave Festival in Brooklyn and the American Academy in Rome. Fenley is in residence at Mills College, her alma mater, every spring semester.

William Forsythe (b. 1949), an American choreographer strongly influenced by Balanchine's revolutionary spirit, developed an explosive style that explored the destabilization of the body overlaid on classical technique. He made his name as director of the Frankfurt Ballet in Germany and now stages pieces for such companies as the New York City Ballet, San Francisco Ballet, the National Ballet of Canada, the Royal Ballet, Covent Garden, the Royal Swedish Ballet and others. In 2006, he choreographed a stunning multimedia piece, *Kammer/Kammer*, mixing film, theater and dance, which had its US debut at the Brooklyn Academy of Music. At the Barishnikov Art Center in New York, Forsythe presented *You Made Me a Monster*—a work with audience participation—in 2007, as part of a four-day multidisciplinary festival. His fiercely modern *In the Middle, Somewhat Elevated*, originally choreographed for the Paris Opera in 1987, was revived by that company in 2008. He has also worked on a project to teach contemporary dance to children from the slums of Rio de Janeiro, Brazil.

Simone Forti (b. 1935) Born in Italy, Forti danced with Martha Graham, Merce Cunningham and Anna Halprin. She was interested in natural and pedestrian movements and is a careful observer of children and animals. She frequently used improvisation and themes of chance as choreographic tools. With her husband Robert Whitman, she became involved in "happenings" given in a Lower East Side studio in New York. Choreographing from 1960 to 1991, she has 35 works to her credit, plus a book on the choreographic process, *Handbook in Motion*.

Judith Jamison (b. 1944) was the most exciting star dancer during Alvin Ailey's American Dance Theater in its early years, making the dances *Revelations* and *Cry* her own. She then became executive director of the company and school upon Ailey's death in 1989. She tends to place a stronger premium on individuality in the performer than did her mentor. The school, which began with 169 children, now trains more that 3,000 annually, and she instigated a shared BFA program with Fordham University. In 2008, the 50th anniversary of AAADT, *Dance Teacher* magazine named Ms. Jamison as their Lifetime Achievement Award winner.

Alonzo King is the founder/director of Lines, a contemporary ballet company located in San Francisco. King received scholarships to study ballet in New York at the Harkness School, American Ballet Theater and the Alvin Ailey School. He danced professionally with Donald McKayle, Lucas Hoving and the Harkness Youth Company, then returned to San Francisco to form Lines Ballet in 1982. In addition to classical music, he uses multicultural sources—for example, in *Koto* (2002) he uses and original score played live on the Japanese instrument an electric koto, by the composer, Miya Maoka. Altogether he has created 165 ballets for Lines and other companies.

Lar Lubovitch (b. 1943). A painter who was a latecomer to dance, Lubovitch trained in both ballet and modern dance, studying with Graham, Limón, Anna Sokolow and Antony Tudor while a student at Juilliard. He formed a company in New York which celebrated its thirtieth anniversary in 1998. His choreography is rhythmic, sensuous, forceful and full of large body changes. The critic Marcia B. Siegel terms his style "spectacular chic."[11] His musical tastes range from Bach and Mendelssohn to 20th century composers. He has choreographed several Broadway shows including "Into the Woods" (1987) as well as for the New York City Ballet, Alvin Ailey American Dance Theater and the White Oak Dance Project. *Pentimento*, created in 2004, honors his own history as a native of Chicago, and the aesthetics absorbed from his Juilliard teachers.

Ralph Lemon (b. 1952) trained at the University of Minnesota and co-founded Mixed Blood Theater in 1976 in Minneapolis. He then came to New York and danced with Meredith Monk and Company. In 1985 he founded the Ralph Lemon Dance Company and choreographed for other companies including Alvin Ailey, Boston Ballet, Lyons Opera Ballet and Batsheva Dance Co. Stylistically he is known for his ability to express dramatic and emotional content. His company disbanded in 1995. More recently he has been working on a multicultural trilogy; *Geography*, formulated on Africa (1997), *Tree*, formulated on Asia (2000), and *Come Home Charley Patton*, reflecting American culture (2004).

Bebe Miller (b. 1950) A native New Yorker, Miller began making dances in 1978 and formed her own company in 1984. Her thought-provoking works, ranging from solos to full-evening collaborations, reflect her interest in finding a physical language for the human condition. She and her company have toured extensively in the United States, South America, Europe and Africa. *Necessary Beauty*, a 2008 piece about memories and fleeting impressions and swift changes of mind, used images going in and out of focus projected on two large screens behind the dancers.

National Ballet of China is making a unique contribution to dance this millennium, by combining Western ballet with Chinese culture and folk traditions. *Raise the Red Lantern,* a full-length ballet that toured four US cities in 2005, tells the story of a daughter sold into marriage in feudal China, requiring strong ballet technique, acting ability and knowledge of traditional movement from the Peking Opera. The company's director, Zhao Ruheng, was trained by Russian teachers at the Beijing Dance School, and has survived many political changes in China that have affected the content of ballets. She now speaks sufficient English to negotiate many cultural exchanges with the west. In 1986, NBC toured the US for the first time and was coached by choreographers Paul Taylor and Alvin Ailey. In addition to Chinese choreographers, the company also has ballets by Balanchine and Bournonville in its repertory.

John Neumeier (b. 1942), artistic director of Hamburg Ballet since 1973, is an American making his mark on German ballet. He has received particular acclaim for his works set to symphonies by Gustav Mahler and choreographic arrangements to Bach's *Saint Matthew's Passion* (1981), Mozart's *Requiem* (1991) and Handel's *Messiah* (1999). Other important works are *Nijinsky* (2000) and his 2001 ballet *Winterreise*. In 2006, a DVD of his ballet *Sylvia*, to music by Leo Delibes, was released. In 2007, he choreographed *Die Kleine Meerjungfrau* (The Little Mermaid); 2007 was also the year that Hamburg Senate appointed him Hamburg's cultural ambassador.

David Parsons (b. 1959) exemplifies the increased athleticism among some of the postmodernists. He has danced with both Paul Taylor and Merce Cunningham. The Parsons Dance Company, formed in 1987, continues to tour in the new century and has become internationally known for its dynamic, youthful style. In 2004 Parsons returned to New York to perform a 12-minute solo titled *The Last Breath*, in which he emerges from the fog onstage and climbs off the stage into the audience. "I'm a populist choreographer," he states. "I like to touch people, and this time I literally will."[12]

Philadanco, a company formed in 1970 by Joan Myers Brown, features a repertory of modern, jazz, ethnic and ballet. The company does forty to fifty concerts annually and forty-five residencies in various states. Those who have choreographed for the company include Lynne Taylor-Corbett, Rennie Harris, Milton Myers, Bebe Miller, Jawole Willa Jo Zollar, Ronald K. Brown and Trey McIntyre. In 2000, the company gained permanent residency at Philadelphia's major stage, the Kimmel Center for the Performing Arts. By 2002, her fortunate dancers were on a 52-week contract. A large percentage of her teaching staff is made up of former Philadanco dancers.

Alexei Ratmansky (b. 1986) studied at the Moscow Academic College of Choreography. He performed as a soloist with the National Opera of the Ukraine and the Royal Winnipeg Ballet. In 2004 he was appointed Bolshoi Theatre's Director of Ballet. Since then he has choreographed more than twenty ballets, and received many awards for his choreography, including the 2007 Critics Circle prize for *The Bright Stream*, to music of Shostakovich. *Middle Duet*, which was choreographed for the Kirov Ballet, has been performed by NYCB since 2006. He is considered by some dance writers to be the most promising Russian-born choreographer since Balanchine.

Cleo Parker Robinson (b. ca.1948) directs and choreographs for her company Cleo Parker Dance Ensemble in Denver's Five Points district—an example of a company dedicated to community empowerment through dance. Robinson has focused her repertory on themes such as social injustice and the celebration of life through spiritual connection. A student of Merce Cunningham and Alvin Ailey, she has preserved the works of Donald McKayle, Eleo Pomare, Talley Beatty and Katherine Dunham. In 1999 she was named to the National Council of the Arts by President Bill Clinton.

Elizabeth Streb (b. 1950). Streb's work defies gravity and catapults dancers through space with a circuslike agility. For her concert company, appropriately named Ringside, Streb uses props and set pieces to further enhance her unique movement explorations. She is also fond of site-specific pieces, such as *Grand Central Station* and *Central Park*. In 2002, her production of *Streb Go! Action Heroes!* had a three-week run at the Joyce Theater in Manhattan. In it, the eight dancers hung from, jumped over, piled into and crashed through the industrial-strength equipment designed by Ms. Streb.

Michael Smuin (b. 1938). After a career as a soloist and freelance work with his wife and partner Paula Tracy, Smuin became director of the San Francisco Ballet in the early 1980s. In 1991 he formed his own company, Smuin Ballets/SF, for which he has choreographed many works including *Fly Me to the Moon* (2005) for his company, a nostalgic and lyrical tribute to Frank Sinatra.

Helgi Tomasson (b. 1942). A native of Iceland, Tomasson began his American career as a dancer in the Joffrey Ballet. After thirteen years with the Harkness Ballet, he had a distinguished career as a principal dancer in the New York City Ballet. In 1985 he became artistic director of the San Francisco Ballet, replacing Michael Smuin. He has broadened the company's repertoire by including works by Mark Morris and Balanchine, and by mentoring young neo-classical choreographers.

DOUG VARONE

Doug Varone (b. 1956). Varone is director of a small New York–based company, Doug Varone and Dancers, formed in 1987, that critic Jennifer Dunning describes as "a company of daredevils, profoundly human superhumans who dance on a dime—wheeling, darting and slicing the air at lethal–looking speeds." The company has performed throughout the United States, including at Jacob's Pillow and the Kennedy Center, and has been in residence at more than fifty universities. Varone has also choreographed for film, Broadway, opera, television and couture.

Edward Villella (b. 1936), a New Yorker, began studying ballet reluctantly as a child, developed a love for it, and continued studying in secret as a teenager because his parents opposed it as a career. He continued his secret ballet studies in college, winding up with the curious combination of a Batchelor's degree in Marine Transportation and a professional dance career. For many years a principal dancer at New York City Ballet, Villella distinguished himself in roles such as the Son in *The Prodigal Son* and Puck in *A Midsummer Night's Dream*. He retired from performing to become director of the Miami Ballet Company. In 1997 he was named a Kennedy Center Honors recipient for artistic achievement, popularizing the role of the male in dance and awarded the National Medal of Arts by President Clinton. He continues to reconstruct Balanchine works and to choreograph.

Dominic Walsh is artistic director of the Dominic Walsh Dance Theater in Houston, which made its debut in 2003. Walsh created a Mozart trilogy for this company, which has also presented works of Jiří Kylián and Mauro Bignozetti. He has also choreographed a full-length version of *Orfeo and Euridice* for Tokyo's New National Theatre. In 2006 he produced *E_Merging*, an evening featuring his and other new wave choreographers. *E_Merging II* appeared in 2008, with choreography by Walsh and Gustavo Ramirez Sansaro of Spain.

Jawole Willa Jo Zollar (b. 1950) danced for three years in Dianne McIntyre's Sounds in Motion company before forming Urban Bush Women in 1984. In her choreography for the all-female company, Zollar intensely explores the inner and outer experiences of African-American women. Signature works include *Walking with Pearl* (a celebration of the life of dancer/choreographer Pearl Primus), *Girlfriends* and *Give Your Hands to Struggle*. Zollar received a "Bessie" award in 1992 and the

Capezio Award in 1994. Since 1997 she has been a professor and artist-in-residence at Florida State University in Tallahassee. The 20ᵗʰ anniversary of her company was celebrated by a season at the Joyce Theater in New York in 2005.

SUGGESTED READING

Anderson, Jack. *Art Without Boundaries: The World of Modern Dance.* Iowa City, Iowa: University of Iowa Press, 1997.

Backland, Ralph. "From a Garage on West 152ⁿᵈ St. a Ballet Company Soars to Moscow," *Smithsonian*, July 1998, p. 28.

Banes, Sally. *Democracy's Body: Judson Dance Theater 1962–1964.* Ann Arbor, MI: UMI Research Press, 1983.

———. *Terpsichore in Sneakers: Post-Modern Dance.* Middletown, CT: Wesleyan University Press, 1987.

———. *Writing Dance in the Age of Postmodernism.* Middletown, CT: Wesleyan University Press, 1994.

Blom, Lynne Anne and L. Tarin Chaplin. *The Moment of Movement: Dance Improvisation.* Pittsburgh, PA: University of Pittsburgh Press, 1988.

Bremser, Martha. *Fifty Contemporary Choreographers.* London: Routledge, 1999.

Cano, Nan Dean, *Acts of Light: Martha Graham in the 21ˢᵗ Century.* Gainesville, FL: University Press of Florida, 2006.

Cohen, Selma Jeanne. *Dance as a Theatre Art*, 2ⁿᵈ ed. Pennington, NJ: Princeton Book Co., 1988.

———, ed. *International Encyclopedia of Dance.* New York: Oxford University Press, 1998.

Dance Magazine: Dance and Technology Issue, pp. 32–56, December 2007

Crump, Juliette T. "One Who Hears Their Cries: The Buddhist Ethic of Compassion in Japanese Butoh" *Dance Research Journal*, Summer/Winter 2006.

De Mille, Agnes. *The Book of the Dance.* New York: Golden Press, 1963.

Dunning, Jennifer. "Rough, and Proud of It: Jawole Willa Jo Zollar" *The New York Times*, June 19, 2005, p. 8.

Forti, Simone. "Handbook in Motion," *Contact* Editions.

Goodwin, Joy. "No Rest for a Russian Renegade." *The New York Times*, April 15, 2007, p 12.

Gottschild, Brenda Dixon. *The Black Dancing Body: A Geography from Coon to Cool.* Macmillan, 2003.

Emery, Lynn Fauley. *Black Dance, From 1619 to Today*, 2ⁿᵈ Edition. Hightstown, NJ: Princeton Book Company, 1988.

Halprin, Anna. *Moving Toward Life: Five Decades of Transformational Dance.* Middletown, CT: Wesleyan University Press, 1995.

Hay, Deborah. *Lamb at the Altar: The Story of a Dance.* Durham, NC: Duke University Press, 1994.

———. *My Body, the Buddhist.* Hanover, NH: University Press of New England/Wesleyan University Press, 2000.

Jonas, Gerald. *Dancing: The Pleasure and Power of Movement.* New York: Harry N. Abrams, 1992.

Kisselgoff, Anna. "All That's New, Creative and Loyal to the Classical." *The New York Times*, May 5, 2002.

Kraus, Richard, Sarah Hilsendager and Brenda Dixon. *History of Dance in Art and Education*, 3rd ed. Englewood Cliffs, NJ: Prentice Hall, 1991.

Montague, Sarah. *The Ballerina*. New York: Universe Books, 1980.

Novack, Cynthia J. *Sharing the Dance: Contact Improvisation and American Culture*. Madison, WI: University of Wisconsin Press, 1990.

Ramsey, Christopher. *Tributes: Celebrating Fifty Years of New York City Ballet*. New York: William Morrow, 1998.

Reardon, Christopher. "In Step with Marching Bands." *The New York Times,* May 23, 2004, p. 16.

Rowell, Bonnie. *Dance Umbrella: The First 21 Years.* London: Dance Books Ltd., 2000.

Sims, Caitlin. "China Ascendant." *Pointe* Magazine, Dec. 2005, pp. 44–49.

Sorell, Walter. *The Dancer's Image: Points and Counterpoints*. London: Hamish Hamilton, 1987.

Tracy, Robert. *Balanchine's Ballerinas: Conversations with the Muses*. New York: Linden Press, 1983.

Traiger, Lisa, "Liz Lerman Dance Exchange: Still Questioning After 30 Years." *Dance* Magazine, Nov. 2006, p. 20.

VIDEOGRAPHY

Achterland. Anne Teresa De Keersmaeker, 1993.

Alive & Kicking, #47. Rennie Harris Puremovement. 1999.

Antony Tudor (excerpts from his choreography). Dance Horizons, 1992.

Appartement. chor. Mats Ek, Ballet de l'Opera de Paris, TDK, 2004

Bill T. Jones: *Dancing to the Promised Land*. Music Video, 1994.

Bill T. Jones: *Still/Here*. WNET, 1995.

The Book of Days. Meredith Monk. The Stutz Company, 1988.

Botoh: Piercing the Mask. Insight Media/AKA Productions, 1991.

Catherine Wheel. Twyla Tharp. Viewfinders, 1982.

Baryshnikov by Tharp. Twyla Tharp. American Ballet Theatre, 1982.

Baryshnikov Dances Sinatra. Twyla Tharp. Kultur, 1985.

Black Tights. Roland Petit. VAI, 1962.

Bold Steps: A Portrait of the National Ballet of Canada. CBC Entertainment.

Bujones: In His Image. chor. Béjart, Petipa, and Fokine. Kultur, 1986.

Dance of Darkness (Japanese butoh troupes). Electronic Arts Intermix, 1989.

Dance Theatre of Harlem chor. Agnes De Mille, Robert North, Lester Horton, and Arthur Mitchell. Kultur, 1988.

Dance of the Century. Sonia Schooerans. La Sept/Pathé (British), 1992.

Dancing, Volume VII: The Individual and Tradition. Kultur, 1993.

Dancing for Mr. B: Six Balanchine Ballerinas. Music Video, 1989.

Dead Dreams of Monochrome Men. DV8 Physical Theater, Art Haus Musik, 1996.

Dido and Aeneas. Jody Oberfelder Dance Projects, 2008.

Ellis Island. Meredith Monk. The Stutz Company, 1982.

Embracing Earth: Dances with Nature. Anna Halprin, 1995.

Daphnis and Chloe. chor. Graeme Murphy, Sydney Dance Co. Viewfinders, 1982.

An Evening with Ballet Rambert. chor. Christopher Bruce and Robert North. Kultur, 1986.

An Evening with Jiří Kylián and the Nederlands Dans Theater chor. Jiří Kylián. Kultur, 1987.

An Evening with the Royal Ballet. chor. Fokine, Ashton and Petit. Kultur, 1963.

Falling Down Stairs. Mark Morris with Yo-Yo Ma. Rhomis Media, 1995.

Frederick Ashton: A Real Choreographer. BBC, 1979.

Ghost Dances. chor. Christopher Bruce, Ballet Rambert. Viewfinders, 1989.

Hans van Manen. Nederlands Dans Theater and HET National Ballet, 2007.

Heavey/Light and *The Title Comes Last*. Jody Oberfelder Dance Projects, 2007.

The Margot Fonteyn Story. dir. Patricia Foy. Viewfinders, 1989.

New York City Ballet's Diamond Project: 10 Years of New Choreography. PBS, May 30, 2002.

Stravinsky Violin Concerto and *Jewels Selections*. chor. George Balanchine. Music Video, 1996.

Tzigane, Divertimento No. 15 and *Four Temperaments* (George Balanchine). Music Video, 1995.

INTERNET SOURCES

Karole Armitage: www.visionintoart.org/fourth.html

Matthew Bourne's Swan Lake: http www.kdmanagement.co.uk/

Eifman Ballet: ardani.com/Ballet.html and http://ardani.com/Eifman.html

www.cyberdance.org (ballet and modern dance)

Daniel Ezralow: www.danielezralow.com/

William Forsythe: www.frankfurt-ballett.de/frame.html

Jiří Kylián: www.ndt.nl/index3.html

Liz Lerman: www. danceexchange.org/lizhome.html&code

Meredith Monk: www.meredithmonk.org/music/index.html

Mark Morris: www.mmdg.org

Sambasia: www.Sambasia.com

Twyla Tharp: www.twylatharp.org/bio/bio_page.htm

Discussion Questions

CHAPTER ONE

1. Which of the definitions of dance included in this chapter do you feel is the most complete? How and why would your own definition differ from it?

2. What are the four "raw materials of dance" as expressed in Laban's effort/shape theory?

3. Why is it important to know the role of a particular dance within its original culture?

4. How is dance used today in our own culture?

5. What characteristics of dance make it more difficult to study and reconstruct than other arts?

6. What is the value in learning about dance forms that you don't particularly enjoy watching?

7. What is *your* personal aesthetic—your likes and dislikes—when it comes to dance? From what sources do you think you acquired this aesthetic?

CHAPTER TWO

1. What are the four categories of religious dance, based on purpose?

2. What types of evidence exist for dance among ancient peoples?

3. What ancient cultures incorporated dances of imitation into their religious observances?

4. What dance form depicts the bliss of union between man and God in terms of union with a lover?

5. What religious group uses repetitive whirling as a means of reaching a state of religious ecstasy?

6. What was the basis for objections to dancing among Christian leaders of the early middle ages?

7. What 19th century group of American Christians incorporated a great deal of dance into their religious services?

8. How did dance become such an important part of Christian worship in Brazil and the Caribbean?

9. What is the connection between the modern dance movement and religious dance?

CHAPTER THREE

1. Describe the social dances of your parents' generation. How do they differ from those of your generation?

2. Give an example of a current American dance you have observed. In which of the four categories of social dance does it belong? Of today's social dances, which ones most suit your own attitudes and social needs?

3. What social dances from other cultures have you observed live or on film? How do they differ from our own?

4. As an example of a blended dance form, describe the progression of gypsy dance into Spanish flamenco, and then into new-world Latin dance.

5. What might a culture's attitudes toward marriage be if there are no couple dances? Name a culture with this attitude.

6. Name a dance that was once a religious dance and is now primarily social. In what culture did it originate?

CHAPTER FOUR

1. Describe the ritual observances found in performances of Japanese bugaku.

2. Describe the stylistic similarities and differences between ballet and bugaku.

3. What are the important contributions to dance made by Louis XIV? Why is ballet terminology in French used throughout the world today?

4. What reforms to 18th century ballet were suggested by Noverre? What changes were made by Marie Camargo and Marie Sallé?

5. What important advances in ballet technique were made in the 19th century during the Romantic Period? During the Classical Period?

6. How did the loss of court patronage change the story content of ballets during the Romantic Period? Why did it change again during the classical period in Russia?

7. Describe the particular genius of Serge Diaghilev.

8. Pick three of Diaghilev's choreographers and describe their contributions to ballet.

9. Select two countries and describe the development of ballet in these countries since the death of Diaghilev.

10. Describe the status of court or state patronage of ballet in western Europe today.

CHAPTER FIVE

1. What were the reasons for the emergence of a new form of dance very early in the 20th century?

2. What three Americans of the pioneer generation can be credited with important developments in modern dance?

3. Describe the work of the first-generation choreographer that you feel contributed the most to the growth of modern dance.

4. What changes in subject matter and approach to dance technique were the second-generation choreographers exploring? Be specific in your answer for the following artists: Hawkins, Taylor, Cunningham and Horton.

5. In what way do you think the advent of modern dance changed the development of other theatrical dance forms—for example, ballet?

CHAPTER SIX

1. What ethnic dance forms contributed to the early development of tap dancing?

2. What were the differences between the touring minstrel shows of the 19th century and the vaudeville shows of the 20th century?

3. How did the growth of the film industry in the 1930s and 1940s affect the dance world?

4. What three choreographers had exceptionally long careers in both Broadway and film, strongly influencing subsequent generations?

5. What are the special contributions of the following dancers: Bill "Bojangles" Robinson, Gene Kelly, Katherine Dunham, Gregory Hines and Paula Abdul?

6. Give some examples of popular social dance trends that have affected musical theater and film dance.

7. How did the advent of music videos change dance?

8. What new directions do you see opening up for jazz and tap dance?

CHAPTER SEVEN

1. What changes in our culture have brought about changes in dance in the past two decades?

2. What mental and physical qualities do you see as essential for the professional dancer to maintain a successful career?

3. What are some of the health issues that particularly affect dancers?

4. What are the demands on time, energy and expertise faced by the professional choreographer?

5. What are the advantages of "umbrella" organizations for small dance companies?

6. What are the considerations for a dance educator when choosing between private studio, public school and college teaching?

7. What are the benefits of competitions for dance students? Do you see any drawbacks?

8. What are some of the applications of dance therapy in our society?

9. What is your personal opinion on the issue of censorship for concert, film, and televised dance?

10. Do you think that dance and the other performing arts should receive more or less public (state and federal) funding than it does currently in the US?

Chapter Eight

1. What three trends are likely to continue changing concert dance in the 21st century?

2. What are some of the choreographic interests of the postmodernists?

3. Describe the work of a Russian-born choreographer you feel was influential in the development of American ballet.

4. Describe the work of an American-born choreographer you feel was/is influential in the development of American ballet.

5. Describe the work of a contemporary European choreographer you find interesting.

6. Describe the work of a postmodern American choreographer you find interesting.

7. What stylistic changes are particularly noticeable in ballet in the past twenty-five years?

8. Describe innovations in technology that you see may be combined with choreography in the future. What other possible directions do you see for new choreographers?

9. What controversial issues do you see continuing in the world of dance?

Endnotes

CHAPTER ONE

1. Selma Jeanne Cohen, *Dance as a Theatre Art*. New York: Harper and Row, 1974, p. 149.

2. Twyla Tharp, *Push Comes to Shove*. New York: Bantam Books, 1992, p. 148.

3. Walter Sorell, *The Dancer's Image*. New York: Columbia University Press, 1971, p. 11.

4. Jean Morrison Brown, Naomi Mindlin and Charles H Woodford, *The Vision of Modern Dance*, 2nd Edition. Hightstown, NJ: Princeton Book Co., 1998, p. 104.

5. Ibid., p. 33.

6. Ibid., p. 10.

7. Joseph Mazo, *Prime Movers*. New York: William Morrow, 1977, p. 243.

8. "News" from *DACI USA*, vol. 1, no. 4 (Fall/Winter 1999), n.p.

9. Cohen, p. 190.

10. Brown, p. 67.

11. Curt Sachs, *World History of Dance*. New York: W.W. Norton, 1937, p. 3.

12. Betty Redfern, *Dance, Art and Aesthetics*. London: Dance Books, 1983, p. 17.

13. Barbara Erinrich, *Dancing in the Streets: A History of Collective Joy*. New York: Metropolitan Press, 2006, p. 246.

CHAPTER TWO

1. A. Barucq and F. Dumas, *Hymnes et Prières de l' Égypte Ancienne*.

2. Jean Morrison Brown, Naomi Mindlin and Charles H. Woodford, *The Vision of Modern Dance*, 2nd Edition. Hightstown, NJ: Princeton Book Co., 1998, p. 32.

3. Lincoln Kirstein, *Dance: A Short History of Classic Theatrical Dancing* New York: Dance Horizons, 1969, pp.13–14

4. Gerald Jonas, *Dancing: The Pleasure, Power and Art of Movement* New York: Harry N. Abrams, Inc., 1992, p. 53.

5. An example of Haitian possession ritual can be seen in Katherine Dunham's *Shango,* which can be viewed on *Dance Black America* (see Videography, end of chapter 5). Also, Lynne Fauley Emery, *Black Dance in the United States From 1619 to 1970,* New York: Dance Horizons, 1980, pp. 49–51.

6. Denise Lardner Carmody and John Tully, *Original Visions: The Religions of Oral Peoples*. New York: Macmillan Publishing Co., 1993, p. 83.

7. Jonas, p. 40.

8. George Kliger, ed., *Bharata Natyam in Cultural Perspective.* New Delhi: American Institute of Indian Studies, 1993, p. 1.

9. Jonas, p. 36.

10. Marilyn Daniels, *The Dance in Christianity.* New York: Paulist Press, 1981, p. 11.

11. Rabbi David A. Cooper, *God is a Verb.* New York: Riverhead Books, 1997, pp. 6, 12.

12. Carmody, p. 22.

13. Virgilius Ferm, ed., *Ancient Religions.* New York: The Citadel Press, 1965, p. 295.

14. Nora Ambrosio, *Learning About Dance*, 2nd ed. rev. Dubuque: Kendall/Hunt, 1999, p. 6.

15. Joan Chatfield-Taylor, *Dance of Life to Honor Death. The New York Times*, Feb. 22, 2004, p. 8.

16. Jersted, Luther, *Mani-Rimdu: Sherpa Dance Drama.* Seattle: University of Washington Press, 1969, pp. 64, 100.

17. Rev. Joseph B. Gross, *The Parson on Dancing, As it was Taught in the Bible and Practiced by the Ancient Greeks and Romans* (1879, reprint), Brooklyn, NY: Dance Horizons, 1995, p. 14.

18. Joseph E. Marks, *The Mathers on Dancing.* New York: Dance Horizons, 1995, p. 38.

19. Sister Adelaide Ortegel, *A Dancing People.* West Lafayette, IN: Center for Contemporary Celebration, 1976, p. 11.

20. "Dance," in *Oxford Dictionary of Byzantium.* New York: Oxford University Press, 1991, vol. 1, p. 582.

21. Ortegel, p. 13.

22. Jonas, p. 45.

23. Lynn Matluck Brooks, "Los Seises in the Golden Age of Seville," *Dance Chronicle*, vol. 5, no. 2, 1982, pp. 132–135.

24. Barbara Erenreich, *Dancing in the Streets: A History of Collective Joy.* New York: Metropolitan Press, 2006, p. 248.

25. Erenreich, p. 249.

26. Ibid. p. 260.

CHAPTER THREE

1. Agnes DeMille, *The Book of the Dance.* New York: Golden Press, 1959, p. 47.

2. *Millennium*, video pt. 1, Wodaaba Dance. narr. Adrian Malone, Biniman Productions, 1992.

3. György Martin, *Hungarian Folk Dances.* Budapest: Corina Press, 1974, p. 18.

4. Lincoln Kirstein, *Dance: A Short History of Classic Theatrical Dancing.* 1935; reprint, New York: Dance Horizons, 1969, p. 119.

5. Another theory of the origins of the Morris Dance places it in pre-Christian times, when it may have been a fertility dance. In Peter Buckman, *Let's Dance.* New York: Paddington Press, 1978.

CHAPTER FOUR

1. Maureen Needham, "Louis XIV and the Académie Royale de Danse, 1661, A Commentary and Translation." *Dance Chronicle*, vol. 20, no. 2, 1997 p. 180.

2. Gerald Jonas, *Dancing*. New York: Harry N. Abrams, 1992, p. 107.

3. Walter Sorell, *The Dancer's Image*. New York: Columbia University Press, 1971, p. 133.

4. Alexander Bland, *A History of Ballet and Dance in the Western World* New York: Praeger Publishers, 1976, p. 14.

5. Richard Kraus, Sarah Hilsendager, and Brenda Dixon, *History of Dance in Art and Education*, 3rd ed. Englewood Cliffs, NJ: Prentice Hall, 1991, p. 47.

6. Noel Singer, *Burmese Dance and Theater*. Kuala Lumpur: Oxford University Press, 1995, p. 11.

7. "Chinese Opera," brochure. Taipei Economic and Cultural Office, pp. 7–8.

8. "Shintō" translates into "continuity." Gerald Jonas, *Dancing: The Pleasure, Power, and Art of Movement*. New York: Harry N. Abrams, 1992, p. 99.

9. Kraus, Hilsendager, and Dixon, p. 258.

10. Jonas, pp. 86–87.

11. Jack Anderson, *Dance*. New York: Newsweek Books, 1974, pp. 21–22.

12. Kraus, Hilsendager, and Dixon, p. 78.

13. Sorell, p. 386.

14. Ibid., p. 417.

15. Bournonville saw the *La Sylphide* created by Filippo Taglioni for his daughter Marie Taglioni in Paris, which predates his own 1836 version.

16. In 1987 this ballet was reconstructed for the Joffrey Ballet by Millicent Hodson and her husband, Kenneth Archer, who used the original score, designs, notes and personal interviews with surviving cast members to recreate the original.

17. Sarah Montague, *The Ballerina*. New York: Universe Books, 1980, p. 39.

18. Ibid. pp. 26–27.

CHAPTER FIVE

1. Ted Shawn in *The Vision of Modern Dance*, Jean Morrison Brown, Naomi Mindlin and Charles H. Woodford, eds. Princeton, NJ: Princeton Book Co., 1979, p. 32.

2. James Penrod and Janice Gudde Plastino *The Dancer Prepares*, 4th ed. Mountain View, CA: Mayfield Publishing, 1998, p. 64.

3. Dennis Sporre, *Perceiving the Arts*. Englewood Cliffs, NJ: Prentice Hall, 2000, p. 146.

4. Isadora Duncan, *My Life*. New York: Liveright Publishing Corp., 1927, p.12.

5. Walter Sorell, *The Dancer's Image: Points and Counterpoints*. New York: Columbia University Press, 1971, p. 199.

6. Anna Kisselgoff, "Paul Taylor, Ballet's Beloved Enemy." *The New York Times*, March 4, 2001, pp. 1 and 11.

CHAPTER SIX

1. Twyla Tharp, *Push Comes to Shove*. New York: Bantam Books, 1992, p. 1.

2. Syncopation is the accentuation of a normally weak beat (off-beat). Polyrhythm is the combination of a number of individual rhythms in one musical composition.

3. The nickname "Bojangles" was given to many musicians. It derives from "bone jangler;" the bones were a homemade percussion instrument.

4. Astaire's other partners included Cyd Charisse, Barrie Chase, Vera-Ellen, Eleanor Powell and Leslie Caron.

5. Margaret Lloyd, *The Borzoi Book Of Modern Dance*. New York: Alfred A. Knopf, 1949, pp. 266–267.

6. Glenn Loney, *Unsung Genius: The Passion Of Dancer-Choreographer Jack Cole*. New York: Franklin Watts, 1984, p. 22.

7. "Dancing" PBS Video Series, 1993, Vol. VII. Martin Scorcese.

8. Julie Bloom, "Street Moves, in the TV Room" *The New York Times*, June 8, 2008, p. 8.

CHAPTER SEVEN

1. "Life in the Corps," *Dance Spirit*, January 2001, p. 4.

2. Female modern dancers average six percent below normal body fat, while male dancers average a few pounds below normal. Linda H. Hamilton, "The Dancer's Dilemma: How to be Healthy and Thin," *Dance Magazine*, August 1995, pp. 48–49.

3. Roslyn Sulcas, "Barishnikov Takes his Building for a Test Run." *The New York Times*, Sept. 25, 2005, p. 30; and Sulcas, "A Giant's New Right Hand." *The New York Times*, Oct 5, 2008, p. 7.

4. Anna Kisselgoff, *The New York Times*, December 26, 2004, p. 24.

5. Gia Kourlas, "The Bare Essentials of Dance." *The New York Times*, 2006.

CHAPTER EIGHT

1. Jody Oberfelder, in an email to author, July 20, 2008.

2. Wendy Perron, "Bill T. Jones Searches for Beauty," *The New York Times*, January 27, 2002, "Art & Leisure," p. 6.

3. Perron, ibid, p.6

4. Roslyn Sulcas, "Choreographer Studies His Nonchalance," *The New York Times*, Dec. 7, 2008, p. 8. The French-born Millepied is a principal dancer at NYCB and a free-lance choreographer.

5. Anna Kisselgoff. *The New York Times*, December 26, 2004, p. 24.

6. John Gruen, *The World's Greatest Ballets*, New York: Harry N. Abrams, 1981, p. 205.

7. Martha Bremser, *Fifty Contemporary Choreographers*, London: Routledge, 1999, p. 66.

8. Bremser, ibid.

9. Karole Armitage, "Dance of the Century: European Post-Modern to the Present," Video, La Sept Pathe, 1992.

10. Valerie Gladstone, "Proselytizers for a Culture that Sells Itself," *The New York Times*, Nov. 21, 1999, p. 40.

11. Marcia B. Siegel, *At the Vanishing Point: A Critic Looks at Dances*, New York: Saturday Review Press, 1972, p. 125.

12. Valerie Gladstone, "Working His Way Back to New York," *The New York Times*, June 6, 2004, p. 32.

Illustration Credits

Preface
Mikhail Baryshnikov.

Chapter One
Dancing Boys, from a relief by Luca della Robbia. In *A History of Dancing* by Gaston Vuillier. New York: Appleton and Company, 1898.

Martha Graham. Collection of Charles H. Woodford.

Physically Inclined, Jody Oberfelder Dance Projects. Pictured are Daniel Giel, Kerry Chookaszian and Jody Oberfelder. Photo by Dieter Blum.

Chapter Two
Egyptian figure dance. Tomb carving.

Dragon dance, performed at Lamar University, Texas. Photo by Mark Smith.

May Day in California, The Pageant of America Collection. New York Public Library of the Performing Arts, Miriam and Ira D. Wallach Division of Art, Prints and Photographs. Astor, Lenox and Tilden Foundations.

Jyoti Dugar, a young Bharatya Natyam dancer. Photo by Dugar.

Men's Fancy Dance, Alabama-Coushatta Reservation, Texas. Photo by Harriet Lihs.

Praise Dancer D'Syre Joseph. Photo by Michelle Ozmun.

Charles Moore in *Awassa Astrige* at the Black Dance: Tradition and Transformation Festival, Brooklyn, NY, 1983.

Chapter Three
Fred Astaire and Ginger Rogers in "Flying Down to Rio," 1933. Photofest, New York.

A nineteenth century waltz. Lithograph by Jacques-Louis David in Vuillier, op. cit.

Fishermen's dance, Taiwan. Government Information Office, Republic of China.

Cinco de Mayo celebration in Texas. Photo by Harriet Lihs.

Ukrainian Hopak. The Tamburitzans of Duquesne University, Pittsburgh, PA. Photo by Michael Haritan.

Bretonne gavotte, from a picture by Theophile-Louis Deyrolle. Vuillier, op. cit.

Chapter Four
Drawing, Louis XIV in *Ballet de la Nuit*, 1653.

Peking Opera. Government Information Office, Republic of China.

Marie Sallé. Vuillier, op.cit.

Fanny Elssler in *La Chatte Metamorphosée* in Femme. Vuillier, op.cit.

Marie Taglioni and Signor Guerra. Lithograph by Bouvier, ca. 1940. The New York Public Library of the Performing Arts, Dance Collection, Astor, Lenox and Tilden Foundations.

Swan Lake pas de deux. Patricia McBride and Conrad Ludlow, New York City Ballet. Photofest.

Mikhail Fokine as the Golden Slave in Scheherezade. Courtesy Phyllis Fokine Archive.

Chapter Five

Doris Humphrey in *Passacaglia*. Collection of Charles H. Woodford.

Ruth St. Denis, Ted Shawn and the Denishawn Company. Courtesy Phillip Baribault.

Ted Shawn in Japanese Spear Dance, 1919. Jerome Robbins Dance Division, The New York Public Library of the Performing Arts, Astor, Lenox and Tilden Foundations. Photo by Arthur Kales.

Martha Graham in *Primitive Mysteries*. The New York Public Library of the Performing Arts, Astor, Lenox and Tilden Foundations. Photo by Edward Moeller.

Doris Humphrey and José Limón. Collection of Charles H. Woodford.

Paul Taylor in *Arden Court*.

The Moor's Pavane with Betty Jones and José Limón, choreography by Limón.

Alwin Nikolais Dance Theater in Nikolais' *Tensile Involvement*.

Anna Sokolow in *Slaughter of the Innocents*. © Barbara Morgan Archives, 1939.

Chapter Six

Bill "Bojangles" Robinson in *King for a Day*. Photofest.

Katherine Dunham.

Gene Kelly in "Singin' in the Rain." Photofest.

Bob Fosse as The Snake in "The Little Prince," 1974. Photofest. Copyright 1974 by Stanley Donen Films Inc. and Paramount Pictures Corp.

Agnes De Mille. Photo by Maurice Seymour.

Chapter 7

Jody Oberfelder Dance Projects in *Re:Sound*, choreography by Oberfelder. Courtesy of Jody Oberfelder.

An example of Labanotation, or "writing dance," drawn by the author.

Kristine Richmond. Photo by Jack Mitchell.

Nancy Fitzpatrick.

Chapter Eight

Quarry, choreography by Meredith Monk. Photo by Johan Elbers.

Pilobolus Dance Theatre in *Bonsai*. Photo by Clemens Kalischer ©.

Juice, choreography by Meredith Monk, 1969. Photo by Peter Moore. Used by permission of Meredith Monk/The House.

George Balanchine rehearsing Patricia McBride and Mikhail Baryshnikov. Photofest.

Meredith Monk. Photo by Bunko.

Joe Istre teaching at Sherry Gold Summer Dance Camp. Used by permission of Joe Istre.

Jody Oberfelder Dance Projects in *Stack Up*, choreography by Oberfelder. Courtesy of Jody Oberfelder.

Doug Varone. Photo by Lois Greenfield ©.

Index